The One Year®
DEVOTIONS FOR WOMEN

The ONE YEAR®
DEVOTIONS
FOR *women*

TYNDALE HOUSE PUBLISHERS, INC.
CAROL STREAM, ILLINOIS

Visit Tyndale's exciting Web site at www.tyndale.com

TYNDALE and Tyndale's quill logo are registered trademarks of Tyndale House Publishers, Inc.

The One Year is a registered trademark of Tyndale House Publishers, Inc.

The One Year Devotions for Women

Edited by S.A. Harrison and Linda K. Taylor.

Designed by Dean H. Renninger

Scripture quotations are taken from the *Holy Bible*, New Living Translation, copyright © 1996. Used by permission of Tyndale House Publishers, Inc., Carol Stream, Illinois 60188. All rights reserved.

Material in this book was previously published in *The One Year Book of Quiet Times with God* © 1997 by Jill Briscoe and *The Daily Study Bible for Women* © 1999 by Tyndale House Publishers.

ISBN-13: 978-0-8423-5233-8
ISBN-10: 0-8423-5233-3

Printed in the United States of America

13   12   11   10   09
14   13   12   11   10

Introduction

When David penned Psalm 23, he pictured a good shepherd leading his flock beside peaceful streams and resting them in green meadows. The Lord is our Shepherd, and we are his sheep. The nourishment he provides for us is found in the green meadows of Scripture. As we follow him and "graze" the passages of the Bible, we will discover our strength renewed all the days of our life! There will always be a fresh thought, a truth to be relearned, or an insight we have never had before.

Sometimes, however, it's hard to know how to follow the Shepherd, or to find the green pastures he longs to lead us to. That is why we have created *The One Year Devotions for Women*. It is designed to help women read the Scriptures regularly and see that what God said years ago to David and all the other biblical writers still speaks to women today.

As you turn to these green pastures for a word of comfort, direction, or instruction, you will find relevant biblical passages and helpful explanations, which will serve to make the truth of the Bible clear, its message understandable, and its points applicable.

May your cup overflow with God's blessings as you "graze" on the pages of God's word, grasp its meaning, and embrace its truth.

Jill Briscoe

JANUARY

TO READ: *Genesis 1:1-25*

ELOHIM

In the beginning God created the heavens and the earth.

GENESIS 1:1

U sed 2,500 times in the Old Testament, the name *Elohim* reveals the mighty strength of God. *El* is the Hebrew word for "strength," while *alah* or *oah* means "faithfulness." God's faithfulness begins afresh each day (Lamentations 3:23). God is always fresh, never stale. We can depend on it!

The Bible is not a scientific textbook, but a book about faith. It does not tell us how the heavens go, but how to go to heaven. It also tells us who makes the heavens go and who upholds them "by the mighty power of his command" (Hebrews 1:3).

Elohim meets us in Genesis. In the beginning of days and nights, flowers and trees, fish and mammals, he tells us by his name that he is the Creator of all. God is strong enough to make myriad universes and faithful enough to keep them all spinning safely at the right speed.

And what does this name mean to me? It gives me confidence. It tells me that if God made the world, he can make my world spin around with a little more order than I've managed to create in it! It gives me something— Someone—on whom I can depend. If God is perfect faithfulness, renewing his pledge to me morning by morning, I can go to sleep in peace evening by evening. Elohim can be known; Elohim can be trusted; Elohim is there!

TO READ: *Genesis 3:1-24*

DIABOLICAL FOOTSTEPS

Now the serpent was the shrewdest of all the creatures the LORD God had made. "Really?" he asked the woman. "Did God really say you must not eat any of the fruit in the garden?"

GENESIS 3:1

S atan is called the "serpent" both in Genesis and in Revelation (Revelation 12:9). In one frightening chapter of Genesis, we catch a glimpse of his powers. He is seen to be cunning, articulate, a liar, a deceiver and destroyer, and an enemy of the Lord Jesus Christ.

Eve's mistake was to take him on! She was no match for the serpent; neither are you and I. The second Adam, Jesus Christ, met Satan and withstood his temptations (Matthew 4:1-11). Jesus overcame and destroyed Satan at the Cross. Because of Christ's victory, true Christians have the same power to overcome.

We are promised discernment to match Satan's cunning, truth to counter his lies, and weapons to fight the unseen battles of the spirit (Ephesians 6:12-18). If we take on the old serpent in our own strength as Eve did, there is no contest. But that is more easily said than done! I like the story of the little boy who told his Sunday school teacher that when Satan knocked on the door of his heart, he sent Jesus to answer it! Very wise! The serpent is stronger than all our best intentions, but God is stronger than all the serpent's worst designs!

Do you not believe in Satan? Then you really have been deceived! The Bible plots his diabolical footsteps from Genesis 3 to Revelation 20. Jesus believed in him and showed us how to counter his subtlety with triumphant truth.

TO READ: *Genesis 5:18–32*

WALKING RIGHT ON HOME

[Enoch] enjoyed a close relationship with God throughout his life.
Then suddenly, he disappeared because God took him.

GENESIS 5:24

E noch was a faithful friend of God. He was in constant touch with him (Genesis 5:24). The King James Version renders this verse, "Enoch walked with God." Another word for that is "fellowship." His consistency in his fellowship with God gives us something to think about! In the end, after he had lived 365 years, he was favored by being taken to heaven in a supernatural way.

"He disappeared because God took him" (Genesis 5:24). The King James Version says, "He was not." One moment he "was"—the next he "was not." It was as if these two—God and Enoch—had taken so many walks together through life, talking and delighting in each other, that one day as they walked along, God said to Enoch, "It's late; why don't you come home to my house tonight?" And they walked right on home! To be fruitful, faithful, and favored in such a way shows us what true friendship with God is all about.

Do we enjoy such closeness with God? Walking with God speaks of a commonality, a communion, an easy, conversational "walk" with our Creator on the road of life. It involves being honest with our heavenly Companion. Hurt feelings must be discussed, misunderstandings laid on the table. Fellowship means warmth of understanding and an interest in the thoughts and feelings of another. When we walk together with God all our days, we'll find ourselves walking right on home.

TO READ: *Genesis 6:1–22*

STRIVING
WITH THE SPIRIT

Then the LORD *said, "My Spirit will not put up with humans for
such a long time, for they are only mortal flesh. In the future,
they will live no more than 120 years."*

GENESIS 6:3

G od gets upset with us. He wrestles with us, showing us how to live,
move, be, and worship him. He does this as he does anything big—
by his Spirit.

In Genesis days, "the Spirit of God was hovering over" the surface of
the earth (Genesis 1:2). The angel who announced the Incarnation told
Mary, "The Holy Spirit will come upon you" (Luke 1:35). The adult Jesus,
"full of the Holy Spirit . . . was led by the Spirit" into the wilderness to be
tempted by the devil for forty days (Luke 4:1). In his temptation, Jesus
resisted Satan in the power of the Spirit. Jesus, "by the power of the
eternal Spirit . . . offered himself to God as a perfect sacrifice for our sins"
(Hebrews 9:14). He was raised from the dead by the Spirit (Romans
8:11). He works with the Spirit in regeneration, bringing eternal life to
men and women.

But men and women do not always allow God's Spirit to have his
way in their lives. Whenever God does anything big, he does it by his
Spirit. One of the biggest things he does is change self-seeking people into
servants! In fact, that is just what the Bible says: "Christians become new
persons. They are not the same anymore, for the old life is gone. A new
life has begun!" (2 Corinthians 5:17).

It is the Holy Spirit's work to strive with us to bring about that
creative regeneration in our lives.

TO READ: *Genesis 6:1-22*

A PLEASURE OR A PAIN

But Noah found favor with the LORD.

GENESIS 6:8

N oah was a pleasure to the Lord. We are either a pleasure to the Lord, or a pain! What are the conditions of being a pleasure, of having such favored friendship with God?

First, we need to find out how we can bring pleasure to the Lord. Sometimes we really want to please the Lord, but we don't bother to find out *how* to do that. We're a lot more interested in how *he* can please *us*. The first thing that pleases God is our right behavior—our holy living even when no one around us is behaving properly.

Noah was the only truly righteous man living on the earth at that time (Genesis 6:9), for Noah knew and understood God. It wasn't easy. It's hard to be the only one pleasing God when no one else is bothering. What was the state of Noah's society? The crime rate was rising—there was "violence and depravity everywhere" (Genesis 6:12). God saw that the world was rotten to the core. Noah was God's friend when others chose the friendship of the devil. But Noah tried always to conduct his affairs according to God's will and commands (Genesis 6:9, 22).

Do we care more about pleasing God than pleasing others or ourselves? Do we see our world as "rotten to the core" as God sees it, and do we side with him? Then we can call ourselves God's friends! When God looks at us, are we a pleasure to him, or a pain?

TO READ: *Genesis 9:1–17*

NEVER AGAIN

*"I will remember my covenant with you and with everything that lives.
Never again will there be a flood that will destroy all life."*

GENESIS 9:15

W hen God says, "Never again," he means never again! No doubt
Noah believed God's word. One experience of the faithfulness of
God leads us to trust in him more. Life's experiences help us to look back
and see God's promises and judgments that have come true.

Noah began his new life in a brand-new world very wisely. He had a
worship and devotional time! It was a time to praise and thank God for
his faithfulness. And perhaps he needed God to assure him that things
would be better in the future. Noah and his family had just "ridden out"
the storm, and now it was time to move on with their lives.

After a cataclysmic event in your life, it helps to reestablish
your devotional life. It's more important than ever to listen for God's
"never again" and start looking for rainbows. Spend time reading the
promises of God in the Bible. Underline them if it helps.

But what exactly can we be sure about? God promises that sin need
never again control us (Romans 8:9-11). He promises that we need not be
afraid ever again (John 14:27). He promises that his peace will guard our
hearts and minds (Philippians 4:7). He promises that we need never be
ignorant of his will, for his word will be a "lamp" and "light" to our path
(Psalm 119:105). He promises that we need never again be defeated
Christians (Romans 8:37). As we read our Bibles, God's rainbows color
our perspective. Be encouraged! God's promises never fail.

TO READ: *Genesis 12:1-9*

WHAT'S A CHRISTIAN FAMILY FOR?

"I will cause you to become the father of a great nation. I will bless you and make you famous, and I will make you a blessing to others."

GENESIS 12:2

H ave you ever wondered why God blessed you by calling you to himself? Did you realize that when he gave this promise to Abraham he had all the families of the earth in mind—even those yet to come? God called Abraham and blessed him in order that he might become a blessing to others. God promised him, "All the families of the earth will be blessed through you" (Genesis 12:3). This is one of the most important verses in the whole of Scripture. Our families—whether Jew or Gentile—can be part of this blessing promised to Abraham. The blessing has to do with a spiritual inheritance— a promised Savior, forgiveness for our sins, and a home in heaven for people of all races, colors, and creeds.

If we belong to the Lord, we have not been blessed just to be blessed. We have been blessed to be a blessing to others. The same applies to our families. God wants us to have not only our families in mind but all the families of the world. This is what Christian families are for.

Everything that God gave Abraham—children, fame, honor, and status (Genesis 12:2-3)—was given to him in order that his descendants would continue what God had begun in his promise to Abraham. They were to pass on the blessing to future generations. We ordinary people in a family are saved to serve the extraordinary purposes of God. We must use whatever material, substance, social standing, influence, and honor that God has given us for the good of others.

TO READ: *Genesis 17:1–8*

EL SHADDAI

When Abram was ninety-nine years old, the LORD *appeared to him and said, "I am God Almighty; serve me faithfully and live a blameless life. I will make a covenant with you, by which I will guarantee to make you into a mighty nation."*

GENESIS 17:1-2

Whats's in a name? Comfort, instruction, and an invitation to trust what is revealed! "I am God Almighty," said *El Shaddai*, the God who is enough.

This was news to Abraham, but he needed some good news at that moment. He was well aware he was ninety-nine years of age, and well past the time to be able to have "millions of descendants" (Genesis 17:6); even one would be a miracle! Yet God was telling him that he would have a child! The fact that his wife was no spring chicken herself added to his confusion. Abraham knew he had a grand opportunity to find out if God was as big and as powerful as his name! And find out he did. Abraham believed El Shaddai, and Sarah conceived! God had said that he was the nourisher, the fruitful one, the supplier, the one who satisfies—and Abraham and Sarah found it to be so.

What impossible situation are you facing? Does it seem as "dead" as Sarah's womb, as unlikely as a ninety-nine-year-old man producing a child? El Shaddai would tell you he can make the impossible possible. "Abraham never wavered in believing God's promise. In fact, his faith grew stronger, and in this he brought glory to God. He was absolutely convinced that God was able to do anything he promised" (Romans 4:20-21).

God performs what he promises to perform!

TO READ: *Genesis 21:1-21*

A WELL OF WATER

*Then God heard the boy's cries, and the angel of God called to Hagar
from the sky, "Hagar, what's wrong? Do not be afraid! God has heard
the boy's cries from the place where you laid him."*

GENESIS 21:17

Have you ever been crying so hard that you've been blinded
to the help that is right under your nose? Hagar knew about that.
Rivalry between Sarah and Hagar had become so intense that Sarah
demanded that Hagar and Ishmael be sent away.

Abraham had sent Hagar and Ishmael into the wilderness. It was very
hot, and the water they had been given was soon gone. Hagar left her son
under a bush and, going a little distance away, waited for him to die. She
couldn't bear to watch him suffer: "She burst into tears. Then God heard
the boy's cries" (Genesis 21:16-17). It doesn't say that God heard Hagar's
voice; it says that God heard the boy's cries! Then God asked her, "Hagar,
what's wrong? Do not be afraid! God has heard the boy's cries from the
place where you laid him" (Genesis 21:17).

Have you ever been so busy crying that you couldn't pray? Maybe
you need to dry your tears and hush your voice to listen in expectancy.
Our cries can block out the voice of God, and our tears can blind us to the
well of water that is right under our nose. God is waiting to show us the
solution to our problem. There will always be a well of living water
available to help us cope with our distress. We just need to stop crying
long enough to see it.

TO READ: *Genesis 22:1-18*

JEHOVAH-JIREH

Abraham named the place "The LORD Will Provide." This name has now become a proverb: "On the mountain of the LORD it will be provided."

GENESIS 22:14

The name *Jehovah* speaks of God's involvement in people's lives. Many patriarchs recognized God's hand of mercy and blessing in their circumstances. There are eight compound names of Jehovah that explain God in a fuller sense. We come across the first here in Genesis 22; it is *Jehovah-Jireh*.

God tested Abraham's faith by asking him to sacrifice his only son, Isaac, as a burnt offering. Incredibly, Abraham set out to do so. Taking Isaac with him to Mount Moriah, he said to the young men who accompanied them, "Stay here with the donkey. . . . The boy and I will travel a little farther. We will worship there, and then we will come right back" (Genesis 22:5). Notice he said, "*we* will come back." He had faith to believe that even if he did kill his son, God would raise him from the dead. After all, God had told Abraham that Isaac was a very important part of his plan of redemption for the whole world.

As Abraham raised his knife to kill Isaac, the angel of the Lord called to him from heaven and stopped him. "Now I know that you truly fear God. You have not withheld even your beloved son from me" (Genesis 22:12). Abraham saw a ram caught in a thicket and sacrificed the animal instead of Isaac.

Because God had provided a sacrifice in place of Isaac, Abraham called that place *Jehovah-Jireh* meaning "The Lord Will Provide." Little did Abraham know that God would one day provide the ultimate sacrifice— his Son—to die in our place as punishment for our sins.

TO READ: *Genesis 28:10-22*

JEHOVAH-YAHWEH

*"What's more, I will be with you, and I will protect you wherever you go.
I will someday bring you safely back to this land. I will be with you
constantly until I have finished giving you everything I have promised."*

GENESIS 28:15

When God appeared to Jacob, he called himself *Jehovah*, the *Elohim* of Abraham (Genesis 28:13). The name *Jehovah* was first used in Genesis 2:4 when God made man. The title speaks of the special relationship between God and Israel.

When Moses talked with God and asked his name, God replied, "I Am" (Exodus 3:14). Jehovah told Moses he had heard the people of Israel crying because of their Egyptian taskmasters and had chosen to redeem them. "I am all that you will need as the occasion arises," he promised Moses. He is all that is needed as our occasions arise as well!

He cares when we are in bondage to some earthly taskmaster. Perhaps food or some other appetite has us whipped, and we long to be free. Yahweh has revealed himself as our Redeemer from all bondage.

It is exactly at this point that some reject Christianity. The idea of God's relating to them in a personal way is too much for them. Somehow the concept diminishes him in their thinking. People feel that if God can be known, this brings him down to their size; if he is their size, why do they need him? But knowing someone does not necessarily mean knowing all about that person. The pot knows the feel of the potter's hands, but because it is not the potter, it cannot fully fathom its Creator's mind. Jehovah-Yahweh wants us to know him. His name assures us that he made us capable of knowing enough to experience his salvation.

TO READ: *Genesis 34:1-31*

OFF TO SEE THE WORLD

He arrived just as Jacob's sons were coming in from the fields.
They were shocked and furious that their sister had been raped.
Shechem had done a disgraceful thing against Jacob's family,
a thing that should never have been done.

GENESIS 34:7

D inah was young and daring and wanted to see how the women in the rest of the world lived (Genesis 34:1). She went to the annual Canaanite festival of nature worship even though this was forbidden for an Israelite. Dinah, so young and naive, roamed around the festival awestruck, no doubt, by the town girls' oriental garments.

Then Prince Shechem "saw her." *Saw* means "lusted after," for the text says that immediately after seeing her, "he took her and raped her" (Genesis 34:2). After that, he "tried to win her affection" (Genesis 34:3), but his lust had already done the damage.

The sons of Jacob were furious and plotted their revenge (Genesis 34:24-29). Simeon and Levi, "two of a kind—men of violence," were the main culprits and earned Jacob's curse when he was dying (Genesis 49:5-7).

We are not told any more about Dinah. We do know that when Simeon and Levi came to do their dirty work, Dinah was rescued from Shechem's house while her brothers killed all the men in the town (Genesis 34:25-26). Dinah had let curiosity lead her into disaster, and the little escapade caused suffering and death to many.

There is a Dinah in all of us. Suspicious that God is withholding fun and happiness from us, we go to the party either in our heads or in actual fact, just to see what the world has to offer and if it's really as bad as some "narrow-minded" Christians say it is. Such curiosity ends up bringing trouble to everyone and disgrace to God.

TO READ: *Genesis 41:37-57*

READY FOR ANYTHING

Joseph named his second son Ephraim, for he said,
"God has made me fruitful in this land of my suffering."
GENESIS 41:52

J oseph was in his thirties when he named his son Ephraim—a name that sounds like the Hebrew word for "fruitful." Joseph had experienced his share of suffering through his teens and twenties. He had suffered the spiteful jealousy of his siblings from his youngest days. He had been kidnapped and sold to slave traders by his brothers (Genesis 37:28), then sexually assaulted by his boss's wife and wrongfully jailed for a crime he hadn't committed (Genesis 39:11-20).

Yet God was not absent from Joseph's turbulent years. He suffered the pit and the prison patiently, but then God placed him in charge of the whole land of Egypt and blessed him with a wife and children. Joseph's life had been planted in the soil of suffering so that he might blossom into godly manhood.

The real fruit was seen in Joseph's character—evidence of the Spirit of God in his life. Joseph showed love for his enemies, self-control with Potiphar's wife, and long-suffering with people who forgot all about him when they had promised to help him (Genesis 40:23). God's Spirit bore the fruit of righteousness through Joseph in Egypt. Could such fruit have been produced without the soil of suffering? Probably not. As James says, "When your faith is tested, your endurance has a chance to grow. So let it grow, for when your endurance is fully developed, you will be strong in character and ready for anything" (James 1:3-4).

Let God make you fruitful in the land of your suffering! Then you'll be ready for anything.

TO READ: *Genesis 47:1–12*

OUR BORROWED YEARS

*Jacob replied, "I have lived for 130 hard years,
but I am still not nearly as old as many of my ancestors."*
GENESIS 47:9

I n Old Testament times, long life was considered a sign of God's favor and was linked, very definitely, to obedience. When Pharaoh met Jacob, his only recorded question was "How old are you?" (Genesis 47:8). Pharaoh's query may have been prompted by appropriate awe in the presence of such an aged man. Jacob answered Pharaoh's question saying that he was not nearly as old as many of his ancestors.

In the end, it's not a question only of how many years God gives us but of how we live them. A long life may not necessarily mean a good life or a happy life, even if we enjoy God's favor. For Jacob it meant a hard life, but he did not allow his later years to be bitter ones. When Jacob was 130 years old, he blessed Pharaoh. Seventeen years later, as he lay dying, Jacob gathered his twelve sons around him and blessed them.

The point is that Jacob's old age was crowned with blessing and worship. Jacob used his borrowed years for God—he was a blessing to those around him.

So how do you and I live out our lives, whatever the years bring? Do we seek to live them as Jacob did—growing our souls upward toward the light in the fertile soil of adversity? Do we strive to be obedient, enriching other people's lives? Jacob was a blessing; we should be, too.

WHEN TROUBLE
TROUBLES YOU

*Pharaoh quickly sent for Moses and Aaron. "I confess my sin against the
LORD your God and against you," he said to them. "Forgive my sin only this
once, and plead with the LORD your God to take away this terrible plague."*
EXODUS 10:16-17

D oes something really bad have to happen to you before you let God
have his way in your life? Sometimes plagues of trouble bring
people to their senses, and they truly repent and come to the Lord. Others
repent for a moment, but when a reprieve comes, they, like Pharaoh, put
the whole thing out of their minds (Exodus 7:23).

When God sent a plague of frogs on the land of Egypt, Pharaoh
began to soften, so God removed the plague. "But when Pharaoh saw that
the frogs were gone, he hardened his heart" (Exodus 8:15). When the next
plague hit Pharaoh, he pled with Moses, "Now hurry, and pray for me"
(Exodus 8:28). But after God had removed the plague, Pharaoh again
hardened his heart. Pharaoh was given many opportunities to deal with
his sin, repent, and acknowledge the Lord. But he was never sorry for his
sin—merely sorry for himself. He repeatedly hardened his heart, and in
the end, God took over and hardened it for him. God has warned us that
his Spirit will not always "put up with" people (Genesis 6:3). If we resist
the promptings of God's Spirit pointing out our sin and our dire need of a
Savior, there may come a time when it will be too late. If God has allowed
trouble to trouble you, it may be a stimulus to let his Spirit do his
convincing, convicting, and converting work in your life.

TO READ: *Exodus 15:22-27*

JEHOVAH-RAPHA

"If you will listen carefully to the voice of the LORD your God and do what is right in his sight, obeying his commands and laws, then I will not make you suffer the diseases I sent on the Egyptians; for I am the LORD who heals you."

EXODUS 15:26

If the name *Jehovah-Jireh* revealed God's concern for people's spiritual health, the name *Jehovah-Rapha* revealed his gracious concern about Israel's physical health. Moses led the children of Israel to a place where they saw God heal bitter waters, making them fit to drink (see Exodus 15:23-25). God then used this as a little object lesson, saying: "If you will listen carefully to the voice of the LORD your God and do what is right in his sight, obeying his commands and laws, then I will not make you suffer the diseases I sent on the Egyptians; for I am the LORD who heals you." (Exodus 15:26).

It was at Marah, which means "bitter," that God showed the children of Israel that he was the source of all health.

Does God really care if I am sick? Does he notice when my child's life is threatened by some dreaded disease? Nowhere does Scripture tell us he will heal *all* people of *all* diseases; but he will heal *many* people of *many* diseases. There is no health without the healthy God. In his wholeness, we find a measure of health on earth and a full measure of health in heaven. Revelation 21:4 tells us no one is ever sick in heaven.

God heals, of that there is no doubt. Sometimes he allows the body to heal itself, and at other times, he miraculously quickens the process. Either way, he is Jehovah-Rapha, the healing God! This should be enough to turn our bitter waters to sweet.

TO READ: *Exodus 20:1-18; 24:12-18*

GOD'S TOP TEN

And the LORD said to Moses, "Come up to me on the mountain.
Stay there while I give you the tablets of stone that I have inscribed
with my instructions and commands.
Then you will teach the people from them."

EXODUS 24:12

I n the Ten Commandments, God gave Moses a pretty substantial message
for us. On tablets of stone were written ten things he wanted us to do.
These laws were given to the Jewish people to give to the world. While some
in today's culture don't want to admit it, these Ten Commandments form
the foundation of our society, the bedrock of our system of law and order.

The Ten Commandments are expanded and explained in the books
of Moses that form the Pentateuch. The statutes that Psalm 119 extols are
the civil and religious applications of the Mosaic Law.

The Bible is a whole book. The Old Testament is the preparation for
the Gospels, which contain the manifestation of the living Word of God;
the Acts of the Apostles, the propagation of his message; the Epistles, the
explanation; and the Revelation, the consummation of all things. The
Bible is God's library, yet some don't even bother to join! God in Christ
intervened in human history. The Old Testament sets the stage for it, and
the New Testament describes it as it happened.

The Ten Commandments are not ten suggestions; they are the
foundation of all the laws of life. They have to do with our relationship
to God, to other people, and even to ourselves. Psalm 119 tells us that his
laws are good, fair, and true (Psalm 119:68, 137-138, 151). Jesus said,
"Heaven and earth will disappear, but my words will remain forever"
(Matthew 24:35). Words *that* substantive are worth investigating, don't
you think?

TO READ: *Exodus 33:1-23*

FACE TO FACE
WITH A FRIEND

Inside the Tent of Meeting, the LORD *would speak to Moses face to face,
as a man speaks to his friend . . . And the* LORD *replied to Moses,
"I will indeed do what you have asked, for you have found
favor with me, and you are my friend."*

EXODUS 33:11, 17

M oses and God were friends! Have you ever thought of your
relationship with God in terms of a friendship? What were the
elements of this friendship between God and Moses?

The first element clearly was determination. Moses had a very busy
schedule, yet he was determined to spend time with God (Exodus 33:7-11).
God watched over his servant Moses, for Moses had been given the over-
whelming task of leading an entire nation from one country to another!
In turn, Moses knew that he could not possibly handle the task of leading
God's people without constant guidance from the Lord.

Second, Moses did not exclude others from his friendship with God.
"It was Moses' custom to set up the tent known as the Tent of Meeting far
outside the camp. Everyone who wanted to consult with the LORD would
go there" (Exodus 33:7). Moses knew that he was not the only one to
whom God could speak. Moses wanted others to know God's friendship,
too.

Third, the phrase *face to face* gives us the sense of openness, honesty,
and delight. Moses was not afraid to ask God anything. Moses spoke
honestly, showed his true needs, and expected God to answer.

We need to nourish our prime relationship with God! As we meet
him regularly "face to face," he will fill our lives to overflowing, and out
of that overflow our human friendships will flourish.

Do you lack friends? Start with God, and he will show you how to be
a friend to others.

PREJUDICE

*"Always judge your neighbors fairly, neither favoring the
poor nor showing deference to the rich."*
LEVITICUS 19:15

F ew of us would admit to being prejudiced. A dictionary defines
prejudice as suspicion, intolerance, or hatred of other races or creeds.
This type of unfair judging goes against God's law in the Old Testament
(Leviticus 19:15). It is also forbidden to the followers of Jesus (Matthew
7:1-2).

Consider the New Testament story of a man called Cornelius, who
was a high-ranking Roman officer. Cornelius was "a devout man who
feared the God of Israel" (Acts 10:2). Honoring Cornelius's religious
sincerity, God sent Peter to show him the way of salvation. But first God
needed to deal with Peter's prejudice. You see, Peter, like all Jews in his
time, would refuse to fellowship in the home or at table with a Gentile
(that is, a non-Jew). So God used a Gentile soldier—the very type of
person that Peter was prejudiced against—to teach Peter some important
lessons! First, God calls no human being common or unclean and offers
salvation to all (Acts 10:15, 34-35). Second, if God isn't prejudiced, we
certainly must not be. Peter was a man of principle, but his religious
traditions were in danger of overshadowing the truth that is in Jesus.

Do you have "people prejudices"—even subtle ones? Prejudice can
be a big barrier to our willingness to share the gospel with people who
need it. Many, like Cornelius, have not rejected Jesus; they just haven't
had an opportunity to receive him. Beware of prejudice!

TO READ: *Numbers 4:1-20*

CALLED TO CARRY

*"When Aaron and his sons have finished covering the sanctuary
and all the sacred utensils, the Kohathites will come
and carry these things to the next destination."*

NUMBERS 4:15

How many people does it take to run a large church? It took 8,580 Levites (Numbers 4:47-48) to care for and carry the Tabernacle under the direction of Aaron and his sons, whom God had put in charge. Aaron and his sons prepared the holy things to be moved when God said so, and then the Kohathites came to do the carrying.

Two generations later, Korah, Kohath's grandson (Numbers 16:1), and others of his peers became insolent and incited a rebellion along with 250 community leaders. They wanted to be in charge, to be the leaders—the priests, not the grunt workers (Numbers 16:1-10). Being in charge looked like so much more fun than being called to carry! Moses reminded them, "Does it seem a small thing to you that the God of Israel has chosen you from among all the people of Israel to be near him as you serve?" (16:9). But they wanted more. God punished their insolence and rebellion with death (Numbers 16:16-35).

There is great joy in accepting the place God has assigned us among his people. Paul tells us in the New Testament that confusion and divisions come when we write our own job descriptions (1 Corinthians 12:4-31). A sense of contentment and belonging comes when we discover our niche. No ministry should be seen as a small thing, for God has given a special ministry only to you. Have you been "called to carry"? Then carry with joy and pride. For God chose you for that special task.

GRUMBLER'S GRIPE

The people soon began to complain to the LORD about their hardships;
and when the LORD heard them, his anger blazed against them.
Fire from the LORD raged among them
and destroyed the outskirts of the camp.

NUMBERS 11:1

M oses was the pastor of the "First Church of the Wilderness." This popular church had thousands of members, but many of them were chronic complainers who displeased the Lord. The mixed multitudes, or the rabble who were with them, started it all. "Then the foreign rabble who were traveling with the Israelites began to crave the good things of Egypt, and the people of Israel also began to complain" (Numbers 11:4). What did the members of Moses' church have to complain about? They complained about the manna they were eating. Soon they began to pine for the good old days! They didn't like anything about the church—the location or the preacher—and they said so.

Every church has to contend with the rabble-rousers. The problem is, their grumbling grows, and before you know it, the members have begun to grumble, too!

It's hard for a pastor to cope with that sort of talk. When church people begin to talk about the previous pastor, or to pine for the food they were fed at their last church, there is little he can do about it. Complaining, grumbler's gripe, is caught like measles. Once started, it spreads like wildfire. It can become very discouraging.

Moses fell into the trap that many pastors fall into. He caught the disease and began griping too. The Lord is displeased with such behavior; he gripes about gripers, and that should be enough to stop it!

TO READ: *Numbers 11:10-23*

A BUTCHER'S SHOP IN THE MIDDLE OF A DESERT

"I can't carry all these people by myself! The load is far too heavy!"

NUMBERS 11:14

M oses had a terrible sense of isolation born of desperation. He felt that he was carrying the burden of the whole world on his shoulders. His ministry had become a punishment instead of a privilege.

"Why are you treating me, your servant, so miserably? What did I do to deserve the burden of a people like this?" he asked the Lord (Numbers 11:11). Moses was angry. "It isn't fair!" he raged. "Why should I have to take this? I don't need it!" Moses felt isolated from God and also from his people. "They are so unreasonable! Why, they expect me to find them a butcher's shop in the middle of the desert!" Moses almost became irrational with the weight of it all. "I'd rather you killed me than treat me like this. Please spare me this misery!" he cried (Numbers 11:15).

God answered Moses' complaint. He didn't baby Moses, defend himself, or let his servant off the hook. He simply gave Moses the solution to his problem. He advised him to delegate his responsibility, pointing out that there were plenty of good men around who could be trusted to share his heavy charge with him. He told Moses to choose leaders who had proved themselves and to set them apart for the ministry (Numbers 11:16-17). God promised that he would give them the same spirit of power and enabling that he had given to Moses himself.

Delegation is one answer to effective ministry. A shared ministry results in shared blessings.

TO READ: *Numbers 12:1–16*

MEEKNESS ISN'T WEAKNESS

Now Moses was more humble than any other person on earth.

NUMBERS 12:3

M oses' humility amazes me. He seems to have been a "gentle giant." Here was a man who had sat and talked with God—literally! God had spoken to him in a burning bush (Exodus 3:2, 6), used him in bringing plagues upon Egypt (Exodus 5–12), and even asked him to climb a mountain "to appear before God" (Exodus 19:3). Moses received the Ten Commandments directly from God. Here in Numbers 12, however, Moses' own brother and sister criticized him. Yet when God placed judgment on Miriam, Moses interceded and begged for God to heal her.

Moses remained close to God, while the people in his charge constantly rebelled. But Moses was never above interceding for them with God. His personal greatness and strength were controlled by God, and the prevailing attitude of his life was humility.

Jesus Christ was a superb model of humility. It took great power to exercise humility in redeeming sinful, uncaring, disobedient people. Yet when we study Jesus, we see a man moving among people in eternal strength, wrapped in earthly humility.

Jesus provides the perfect example, for he never failed to be humble. Moses provides an earthly reminder that humility can be found in people who have great ability and great responsibility. Yet those human beings will sometimes fail too. We must always look to the One who showed us how to live in humility as children of the King. Let us follow in his steps.

TO READ: *Numbers 21:4-9*

SNAKEBITE

Then the people came to Moses and cried out, "We have sinned by speaking against the LORD and against you. Pray that the LORD will take away the snakes." So Moses prayed for the people.

NUMBERS 21:7

D ealing with people's gripes and grumbles can wear you down. Moses and Aaron were constantly dealing with discontented people. The children of Israel became impatient with their leaders and with the direction the Lord was taking them. They had just won a major military victory (Numbers 21:3), and they became self-confident. They blasphemed God, rejected Moses, and complained about the manna, the bread from heaven. "We hate this wretched manna!" they said (Numbers 21:5). By rejecting the food, they were rejecting God's gracious provision (John 6:32-35, 48-51, 58). God's response was to send poisonous snakes among the people, and many died (Numbers 21:6). God judged their complaining attitude but also provided a way of escape. God's remedy was a bronze snake on a pole. All who looked at the bronze snake lived (Numbers 21:8-9).

It's easy to complain, but it's wrong. The Bible says we mustn't do it. Paul warned the Corinthians not to "put Christ to the test, as some of them did and then died from snakebites" (1 Corinthians 10:9). We are to "stay away from complaining and arguing" (Philippians 2:14).

Once we have received eternal life, we don't stop complaining overnight. Yet complaining has no place in believers' lives. Complaining is habit-forming and can be self-destructive. We should stop grumbling about our husbands, children, church, or friends. Life may feel like a desert, and we may be hot and tired and anxious for a new place to live and work, but beware of complaining about anything or anyone—it's like a poisonous snakebite!

TO READ: *Deuteronomy 1:1–8*

BREAKING A
FORTY-YEAR HABIT

*"When we were at Mount Sinai, the L*ORD *our God said to us,*
'You have stayed at this mountain long enough.
It is time to break camp and move on.'"

DEUTERONOMY 1:6

M oses reminded the Israelites that God wanted them to move on.
The ultimate goal for the children of Israel was the land of Canaan,
and they were not there yet. Forty years earlier, God had charged the
Israelites to go and take possession of the land. They had spent forty years
wandering in the desert as God dealt with their sin. They were forty years
behind schedule! It was time to move in.

Some of us would have to admit that we are like the Israelites. We are
behind the divine schedule—not growing as God would have us grow! We
need to move on with our Christian life. The Lord is saying to us, "You have
stayed at this mountain long enough. It is time to break camp and move
on"! Breaking camp is as hard as breaking a habit! Maybe we need to break
camp in the matter of Bible study and prayer. Perhaps we have lost our
vision of witnessing and winning the lost. Moving on requires resolve,
obedience, faith, prayer and fasting, Bible study, service, fellowship,
and discipleship. It's hard to break a forty-year habit, but it can be done.
Israel got moving, and God moved with the nation. God's challenge in
Moses' day was taken up by a new generation. He was gracious enough to
give them another chance.

God wants you to keep growing in your Christian life. Why don't
you break camp and move on? "You have stayed at this mountain long
enough"!

TO READ: *Deuteronomy 6:10–25*

SECOND FIDDLE

"You must fear the LORD your God and serve him.
When you take an oath, you must use only his name."
DEUTERONOMY 6:13

G od's clear command in Deuteronomy 6:13 is that his people are to "serve him." But in order to serve, people need to be willing to step out of the limelight and play second fiddle.

A little couplet says, "It matters more than tongue can tell, to play the second fiddle well." Playing second fiddle is a marvelous way to start serving others. There are so many second-fiddle positions to fill. If we would only roll up our sleeves and "have a go at it" (as we say in England). If we would but get involved wherever there is a need, then God could accomplish great things.

Just as you can't guide a stationary car, God can't guide a stationary Christian. We need to start going somewhere, doing something, soon! You may complain, "But it isn't my thing to teach Sunday school, help with the food collection, mow yards, pick up old folks, count money, wash dishes, give my testimony." Maybe not, but have you ever considered it might be *his* thing for you? The Lord taught me years ago that if I would stop worrying about playing first fiddle and start with second and do it well and to his glory, I would stumble over those prepared works along the way!

It starts with the fear of the Lord—which involves a hatred of individualism and pride—and with a servant's spirit. God will work this in the human heart if we ask him to. Are you willing to play second fiddle in God's orchestra?

TO READ: *Deuteronomy 10:12-22*

LOVE IS A DECISION

"And now, Israel, what does the LORD your God require of you?
He requires you to fear him, to live according to his will, to love
and worship him with all your heart and soul."
DEUTERONOMY 10:12

Wouldn't it be great if we could require someone to love us? "But," I can hear you say, "how can you require love? Love is a feeling—you can't require someone to have a certain feeling!"

If love were a feeling, I would agree. But feelings are only a part of love—and a very unreliable part at that. Jesus *did* say, "I command you to love each other in the same way that I love you" (John 15:12). Therefore, love has to be more than a feeling.

The love God requires from us for himself and for each other is the highest form of love—*agape* love—love like his. It is a love of the head rather than a love of the heart. A love that determines to be concerned, first and foremost, for the loved ones' well-being in every dimension of their lives—whatever the cost to ourselves and irrespective of their reaction.

So how can we know that we love God? By being obedient. Jesus said, "Those who obey my commandments are the ones who love me" (John 14:21). This verse relieves my anxiety, as I've always worried that I wasn't loving God enough. My fears were based on my erratic feelings toward him. These words of the Lord take the whole thing out of the realm of feelings and into the realm of doing. Now *that* I can handle! And what can I *do* to show God I love him? I can *do* for others. This is what he requires.

TO READ: *Deuteronomy 20:1-9*

DOING RIGHT
IN A WRONG WORLD

"When you go out to fight your enemies and you face horses and chariots and an army greater than your own, do not be afraid. The LORD your God, who brought you safely out of Egypt, is with you!"

DEUTERONOMY 20:1

The Israelites were facing the biggest fight of their lives, yet there was a bigger conflict going on behind the one for the land of Canaan. That conflict was a war between good and evil, and God was out to get the best possible army to fight it. He was interested in spiritually powerful people— not just military might. Those involved in this conflict could have absolute confidence in God's strength and ability to win any and all wars.

In the New Testament the language of warfare is often used in a figurative sense (2 Corinthians 10:3-4; Ephesians 6:12). This otherworldly war is to be fought with otherworldly weapons. Faith will embolden us to give ourselves fully to God's cause, knowing, as the Israelites knew, that we are on the winning side. Through Christ's death and resurrection and our faith in him, we can disarm the principalities and powers of darkness in this world (Colossians 2:15).

What battle are you facing today? Is it the battle to do right in a wrong world? Are you fighting to save your marriage and your family? Are you struggling to influence some hard-hearted young people in your Sunday school class? Are you trying to change a crime-riddled neighborhood, a dishonest workplace, an anti-God college campus? Do the "horses and chariots" appear formidable to you? "Do not be afraid as you go out to fight today! . . . For the Lord your God is going with you!" (Deuteronomy 20:3-4). Take heart. You are on the winning side.

TO READ: *Deuteronomy 32:1-9*

NOT JUST IDLE WORDS

"My teaching will fall on you like rain; my speech will settle like dew.
My words will fall like rain on tender grass,
like gentle showers on young plants."

DEUTERONOMY 32:2

D oesn't that sound as though you are about to be so thoroughly soaked with satisfaction you'll never be thirsty again? What beautiful words! Those of us who teach must want to fall on our knees before this verse! Moses had a message that would thoroughly refresh his hearers. Part of this fresh message was the concept of God as our Rock: "He is the Rock; his work is perfect. Everything he does is just and fair. He is a faithful God who does no wrong; how just and upright he is!" (Deuteronomy 32:4).

The picture of God as our Rock is firmly embedded in the ground of the Old Testament. Moses says that God is a perfect Rock, a faithful God who does no wrong. He is always right, and we must measure our little ideas of rightness against his eternal truth.

Moses mourned the times the children of Israel rejected the Rock, their Savior, and his ideas of rightness. Deserting the Rock who fathered them, Israel became like other nations whose dependence on lesser rocks had let them down—nations whose rock had sold them. "But the rock of our enemies is not like our Rock, as even they recognize," he reminded them (Deuteronomy 32:31).

Moses sang a fresh song, calling his people to a renewed commitment to the Rock of their salvation. When he had finished he warned, "These instructions are not mere words—they are your life!" (Deuteronomy 32:47). Have you deserted the Rock who fathered you? Return to him. You can depend upon his renewal.

TO READ: *Joshua 6:1–27*

GOING AROUND JERICHO

"Your entire army is to march around the city once a day for six days."

JOSHUA 6:3

W hen I have a problem in my life, it can look as big as Jericho. The walls may look formidable. In my waking moments, I find myself going around and around my dilemma.

God told Joshua to go around Jericho *once* every day (Joshua 6:3). I learned to discipline myself to go around my particular Jericho only once! True, there was an appropriate time for Joshua and his men to circumnavigate the city seven times (Joshua 6:4, 15), and there is an appropriate time for me to spend special effort in focused prayer about my difficulty. But I learned to wait for God to direct me into such a time.

The priests carried the Ark of the Lord representing the presence of Yahweh with his people. Each day as I went around my own Jericho, I took "the Ark" with me, reminding myself of God's presence and his word that had the power to pull down strongholds.

The walls *will* crumble one day, and it will all be over. God will get the glory, and the hard marches in the heat of the day will be forgotten in the sweet taste of victory. Until that great day when our particular Jericho falls, God grant us the perseverance and the endurance to go "once around Jericho" with our God and fellow travelers in the faith—believing that however high the walls, fortified the gates, or strong the enemy, it's only a matter of time!

TO READ: *Joshua 20:1-9*

A PLACE TO RUN TO

*"Now tell the Israelites to designate the cities of refuge,
as I instructed Moses."*

JOSHUA 20:2

G od had told Moses to set aside six "cities of refuge" placed
strategically throughout the land (Numbers 35:10-15). These cities
belonged to the Levites, who were the guardians of the law. Refuge was
offered to those who had caused accidental death (Joshua 20:3), not to
those who had committed premeditated murder (Numbers 35:16-21).
Once in the safe city, the man who had killed someone accidentally
would stand trial by the community (Joshua 20:6). Those found innocent
were given a place to live among the people there.

What a picture! There are things we do that we know are wrong, and
there are sins we commit by accident. When this happens, God is our just
judge. We may flee to him, for he has provided a "city of refuge" for us.
Just before he died, Moses told Israel, "The eternal God is your refuge, and
his everlasting arms are under you" (Deuteronomy 33:27). Psalm 9:9 tells
us "the Lord is a shelter for the oppressed, a refuge in times of trouble."
The prophet Nahum wrote, "The Lord is good. When trouble comes, he is
a strong refuge" (Nahum 1:7).

Are you in trouble? Are you a victim of circumstances? Have you
done something wrong by accident? Then flee to your "city of refuge."
God himself is that city, and God himself is your judge. Talk to him. He
may want you to right a wrong, to settle a misunderstanding, or to simply
wait patiently with him for the storm to pass.

FEBRUARY

TO READ: *Joshua 24:1-15*

A GODLY HERITAGE

"But if you are unwilling to serve the LORD, then choose today whom you will serve. . . . But as for me and my family, we will serve the LORD."

JOSHUA 24:15

Joshua had made up his mind. Knowing he was responsible to give an account of his life to God, he had decided to serve the Lord. Furthermore, as head of his household, he had set himself the task of leading and influencing his family to do the same.

David said, "I will be careful to live a blameless life . . . in my own home" (Psalm 101:2). The word *blameless* does not mean that David considered himself sinless; rather, it means that he was determined to be mature. He desired to grow up in God.

I often talk to women who envy the godly heritage of others—a heritage they themselves do not have. They seem to think that those born into Christian homes have had a somewhat unfair advantage. Don't let other people's blessings paralyze you. *Start* a godly heritage. Let it begin with you. Say, as Joshua said, "As for me and my family, we will serve the Lord" (Joshua 24:15).

I'm sure that Joshua's vibrant faith helped his family to follow his lead. The best possible thing we can do is to be sold out to God—at home. Joshua made loving God with all his heart a daily habit. His lifelong obedience set him and his family apart. I'm sure that many people chose the Lord that day—simply because of Joshua's testimony. Be encouraged to soldier on, even if those nearest to you, even a husband or a child, do not believe.

TO READ: *Judges 6:1-24*

JEHOVAH-SHALOM

And Gideon built an altar to the LORD *there and named it
"The* LORD *Is Peace." The altar remains in Ophrah in the land
of the clan of Abiezer to this day.*

JUDGES 6:24

The Lord is peace, as Gideon discovered, and he built an altar to the
Lord with that very name. The Midianites were harassing Israel and
destroying and plundering its crops. Gideon must have been scared to bits
because he was threshing wheat in a winepress, and no one normally does
that (Judges 6:11). People usually threshed wheat on the top of a hill so
that the wind would carry the chaff away.

The angel of the Lord came and sat under a tree and watched him.
After a bit the angel said, "Mighty hero, the LORD is with you!" (Judges
6:12). (He must have said that with a smile!) Then the angel of the Lord
told Gideon he was going to use him to save Israel from the Midianites.

If you think Gideon was frightened before, you should have seen
him then! He began to come up with all sorts of excuses. Then the angel
of the Lord revealed his power. Realizing that he had been arguing with
God himself, Gideon was paralyzed with fear. Then the Lord said to him,
"It is all right. . . . Do not be afraid. You will not die" (Judges 6:23).

Fear petrifies, punishes, and paralyzes us. Fear of what others may do
to us, fear of what we cannot do for others, or fear of what God may do to
us if we do not do for others—all can be dealt with by *Jehovah-Shalom,*
who is our peace.

TO READ: *Judges 9:22-57*

TRUTH AND INTEGRITY

Thus, God punished Abimelech for the evil he had done against his father by murdering his seventy brothers.

JUDGES 9:56

A bimelech was the son of Gideon's concubine from Shechem. He had seventy half brothers and fought with them all. In every aspect of his life, Abimelech rejected truth and integrity. He went to his mother's hometown of Shechem—a city that had lived in peace with Israel up to that point. Once Abimelech arrived, he schemed to get the people of Shechem to make him their king and then persuaded them that all seventy of his Israelite half brothers needed to be eliminated. So the people joined Abimelech in returning home and slaughtering all but one of his brothers.

But Abimelech's actions would not go unpunished. God makes it known that he is angry with those who abandon truth and integrity. It took an unknown but determined woman to finish off Abimelech. From the top of the tower that Abimelech was attacking this woman threw down a millstone on his head (Judges 9:52-53).

The story of Abimelech highlights what happens when pride rules a person's heart. Too often truth and integrity are sacrificed to the god of pride. Truth and integrity ought to have been the mark of the people of God—especially their leaders. Abimelech had no truth or integrity whatsoever.

God always honors people who are on his side—the side of truth and integrity. He will search for, find, and use men and women ready to live by grace and faith and drop truth's millstones on the head of untruth and dishonesty, smashing them to smithereens!

35

TO READ: *Ruth 4:1-22*

SUCH LOVE

"May this child restore your youth and care for you in your old age.
For he is the son of your daughter-in-law who loves you so much
and who has been better to you than seven sons!"

RUTH 4:15

I t is said that you don't choose your relatives—and that is true. But with God's help, you can choose to love the ones you don't choose!

Ruth knew what it was to mourn the deaths of husband and brother-in-law (Ruth 1:4-5). She chose to leave her family heritage in Moab for a foreign land (Ruth 1:14-17). Once in Bethlehem, Ruth toiled diligently at menial work, willing to cast herself on the charity of others—and all for love. And this, not because of her love for a man, but because of her love for her mother-in-law!

Such love is attractive, winsome, noticed—especially by men of character such as Boaz (Ruth 2:11-12). Such love was "as strong as death" (Song of Songs 8:6) and loyal. As Paul puts it, "Love never gives up, never loses faith, is always hopeful, and endures through every circumstance" (1 Corinthians 13:7).

Like Ruth, we can discover the source of such love. It is found in God. The force of such love is the Holy Spirit, who pours it into our hearts (Romans 5:5). The course of such an overflowing river of blessing will drench those close to us with delight.

We do not have it within ourselves to love anyone whom we might find different or difficult. But God will give us his love with which to love that person. God understands our differences and loves the unlovable. Remember, he loves *us!* Such love is ours for the asking, the taking, the loving.

TO READ: *1 Samuel 1:1-28*

A PENINNAH PROBLEM

But Peninnah made fun of Hannah because the LORD *had closed her womb.*
Year after year it was the same—Peninnah would taunt Hannah
as they went to the Tabernacle. Hannah would finally be reduced
to tears and would not even eat.

1 SAMUEL 1:6-7

Hannah had a Peninnah problem—a person in her life who, year after year, taunted her about her childlessness. This would go on until Hannah would be "reduced to tears and would not even eat" (1 Samuel 1:7). It's no fun to have your life intricately bound with a Peninnah-type person. Perhaps you, too, have such a problem. Maybe you have to put up with someone in your family who provokes you relentlessly, taunting you with cruel words.

Hannah did the wisest thing. First, she prayed (1 Samuel 1:9). She went to the Tabernacle and poured out her heart to the Lord. She laid her load of heaviness down and returned to her family a different woman. She was "no longer sad" (1 Samuel 1:18). Oh, if we could so easily let all the dark nights of our soul be dealt with in such a manner!

Not only had Hannah prayed for a child, she had also promised the child to God's service "for his entire lifetime" (1 Samuel 1:11). When God gave Hannah a son, she kept her word, testifying, "My heart rejoices in the Lord! Oh, how the Lord has blessed me!" (1 Samuel 2:1). Her heart rejoiced first in the Lord, not in her beloved husband or her precious son.

Prayer, trust, and worship will help you deal with your Peninnah problem—no matter how hard it is for you. Give your burden to the Lord, and don't pick it up again. Let him dry your tears and give you back your joy.

TO READ: *1 Samuel 3:1–20*

DOING OUR PART

*Samuel did not yet know the LORD because he had never
had a message from the LORD before.*

1 SAMUEL 3:7

S amuel had grown up in the Tabernacle, but that did not guarantee a
relationship with God. Even when we raise children who know of
God, in the end the Lord has to call, and each child had to respond. So
just how can parents set the stage for this divine confrontation?

First, we can pray. Hannah prayed for her little boy before he even
existed. She prayed that her boy would "belong to the Lord his whole life"
(1 Samuel 1:28). Second, we can provide an environment where our
children can meet God. Hannah placed Samuel into Eli's care to teach
him the ways of God. Eli gave him tasks to do in the Tabernacle and
began to train him to listen for the Lord's voice.

Can we have any assurance that God will call our children to
himself? I believe we can. We can do our part with confidence. We can
keep our children "near the Ark" by making sure they know God's rules.
We can keep our children in church, much as Hannah dedicated Samuel
to the Tabernacle. Our children can be taught to serve and help as part of
Christ's body (1 Samuel 2:18). And we can keep them in our prayers.
Doing our part is doing everything we can to make sure, as Hannah did,
that our children grow up "in the presence of the Lord" (1 Samuel 2:21).
Then we let them go. After that, it's up to God and them!

TO READ: *1 Samuel 12:1-25*

PRACTICING WHAT WE TEACH

"As for me, I will certainly not sin against the LORD by ending my prayers for you. And I will continue to teach you what is good and right."

1 SAMUEL 12:23

P raying is a spiritual discipline. It takes work. Yet God expects us to pray! Samuel told the children of Israel that he considered it a sin against the Lord if he failed to pray for them. How easy it is to stop praying for people who never seem to change. After all, if our prayers aren't working, why go on praying?

Samuel was called by the Lord to serve as a prophet to Israel (1 Samuel 3:20), and this he did faithfully. Although the people's habitual turning away from the Lord had wearied Samuel, he persevered and promised that he would continue in his prophetic office. To pray and to teach those who wander from the truth takes spiritual tenacity. Samuel practiced such endurance. He had been Israel's leader from his youth (1 Samuel 12:2); and now, old and gray, he committed himself to continue praying faithfully for the obdurate children of Israel.

It is also a spiritual discipline to teach others "what is good and right" (1 Samuel 12:23). It is an all-absorbing task to teach our families. It's a sacrifice to prepare a Sunday school lesson or put time aside to meet young Christians and encourage them in the Lord. It also takes self-discipline to live a holy life, to hold people accountable, and to warn them that actions have consequences (1 Samuel 12:25). In other words, we need to be spiritually disciplined ourselves if we are ever to be used to teach others. We must earn the right to be heard. We must practice what we teach.

TO READ: *1 Samuel 21:1-15*

YOU DON'T KILL A GIANT EVERY DAY

*David heard these comments and was afraid of what
King Achish might do to him.*

1 SAMUEL 21:12

W e all have good days and bad days. Often, a really bad day follows a really good day. God, however, is always the same, whatever our days may bring. David found that out.

One day young David had arrived at the battle scene where he heard the giant Goliath, from the Philistine city of Gath, defying God's people. So David bravely killed him (1 Samuel 17:32-51).

King Saul took David to his palace as his servant, but became madly jealous of David and tried to kill him (1 Samuel 19:9-10). So David became a fugitive. He traveled to the camp of Achish, the king of Gath, and threw himself on his mercy. The servants of King Achish did not trust David, and David was afraid.

David had killed the king's giant, yet he was afraid of the giant's king! How can we do so well one day and so badly the next? I know, don't you? David gives me courage to know that I don't kill a giant every day. Some days the giant gets us, and we fail badly. Then we may feel like running away. We may lose all sense of focus and feel so down that we have no energy to do *anything*. As with David, our days will be filled with victories and defeats. But remember, God didn't give up on David, and he won't give up on us. So *we* mustn't give up! We need to repent, redo, regroup—whatever it takes—but not let the giant drag us down. God loves us, even in our failures. Don't ever forget that.

TO READ: *1 Samuel 30:1–31*

GOD IS GOD ENOUGH

David was now in serious trouble because his men were very bitter about losing their wives and children, and they began to talk of stoning him. But David found strength in the LORD his God.

1 SAMUEL 30:6

David was in the depths of despair. He had been living in Philistine territory for over a year (1 Samuel 27:7) while he hid from Saul. This meant that by accepting sanctuary, he was obliged to serve the king (1 Samuel 28:1). When the Philistines prepared to fight Israel, David and his men were put in a difficult position by having to go out with the army to fight against their own countrymen. But the Lord kept them from having to do this—King Achish sent them home (1 Samuel 29:1-11). Returning home to Ziklag, however, David and his men discovered that in their absence all their families had been taken captive by the Amalekites. David's closest friends were ready to stone him (1 Samuel 30:6)!

That's the pits! "But David found strength in the Lord his God" (1 Samuel 30:6). How did he do this? By bringing to mind that God was God enough. What did David discover? The answer can be found in Psalm 40, a psalm in which David records how God was God enough to lift him out of his pit, from the mud and mire; to set his feet on a hard, firm path; and to steady him as he walked along (Psalm 40:2).

What sort of pit are you in? Do you feel like David? Spend time in Psalm 40, and remember that God is God enough to deliver us from all our pits of despair.

TO READ: *2 Samuel 11:1-13*

GET OFF THE ROOF!

*Late one afternoon David got out of bed after taking a nap and went for a
stroll on the roof of the palace. As he looked out over the city,
he noticed a woman of unusual beauty taking a bath.*

2 SAMUEL 11:2

The Bible tells us that sin begins right in our heart. The sin of adultery
begins with the eyes. The Bible also gives us examples of people who
let themselves fall into the sin of adultery. One of these was King David.
You may remember him as the king of Israel, the great warrior, the writer
of psalms, the man after God's own heart (Acts 13:22). Yet even David
was vulnerable in this area.

At some point, David, the middle-aged king, had let himself become
lazy. So it's not surprising to find him on the roof watching Bathsheba
bathing. When David saw Uriah's beautiful wife bathing, David committed
adultery on the roof. Long before he took Bathsheba to bed, the deed was
done. It starts in the eyes, works its way to the heart and emotions, and then
moves to the rest of the body.

The sin of adultery begins with the first look, which too often leads
to the second and third and fourth. You need to get yourself out of the
way of temptation—you need to refuse to remain in a situation that might
cause you to sin. Even though God promises to give strength to withstand
temptation (1 Corinthians 10:13), you ought to do what you can to stay
out of its way. You need to do what David should have done—*get off the
roof!*

TO READ: *2 Samuel 15:1–14; 16:15–22*

GOD WOULD SPARE US

Ahithophel told him, "Go and sleep with your father's concubines,
for he has left them here to keep the house. Then all Israel will know
that you have insulted him beyond hope of reconciliation,
and they will give you their support."

2 SAMUEL 16:21

D o you ever think you can sin and get away with it? "Nobody will know," we say to ourselves and then try to cover up our trails. But it can't be done. God has decided that we won't get away with it. "You may be sure that your sin will find you out" (Numbers 32:23).

King David had thought he could cover up his sin with Bathsheba, but God made sure David didn't get away with it. David confessed his sin and received forgiveness (2 Samuel 12), but that didn't stop the consequences of sin in his own life, or the repercussions of his sin that rippled through his family.

Absalom, one of David's sons, revolted against his father, raped his father's concubines in public, and tried to kill him (2 Samuel 13–18). Could this have been merely a reflection of David's sin?

Joab, David's general, had received David's message delivered by Uriah, Bathsheba's husband: "Station Uriah on the front lines where the battle is fiercest. Then pull back so that he will be killed" (2 Samuel 11:15). Did General Joab's decision to kill Absalom come from watching his boss's coldheartedness (2 Samuel 18:14)? Did Joab later join Adonijah's rebellion against Solomon as a reflection of his disillusionment with King David's leadership (1 Kings 2:28)?

You reap what you sow. The far-reaching results of sin are appalling, and God would spare us.

TO READ: *2 Samuel 18:19-33*

FEAR OF A FAMILY FEUD

*The king was overcome with emotion. He went up to his room over the
gateway and burst into tears. And as he went, he cried, "O my son Absalom!
My son, my son Absalom! If only I could have died instead of you!
O Absalom, my son, my son."*

2 SAMUEL 18:33

There's nothing like a family feud to crush your spirit! David knew all
about that. To the boy David, a giant's wounds were nothing compared
to the hurt his older brother Eliab's angry words caused. "What are you
doing around here anyway? . . . What about those few sheep you're
supposed to be taking care of? I know about your pride and dishonesty.
You just want to see the battle!" (1 Samuel 17:28).

You get the picture: a long-standing family problem—a big brother
with a complex about his little brother, perhaps. Something like that can
break your heart. Much later in his life, David was to have his heart
broken yet again by another family feud. This time it was to be his own
son—his favorite son—Absalom, who would steal away the people's
hearts, pursue his father to death, and try to seize his throne.

If anyone could talk about being brokenhearted, it was David. But,
oh, "The LORD is close to the brokenhearted; he rescues those who are
crushed in spirit" (Psalm 34:18). After David had mourned for Absalom,
perhaps he took that psalm out of the scroll shelf and reminded himself
of the words he had penned.

Which of us does not know what it is like to lie awake all night
worrying ourselves sick over members of our families who are at odds
with each other? No one can hurt you like your family can. If such is our
case, we can do the same as David!

TO READ: *1 Kings 3:1-15*

EXCEPTIONS

Solomon loved the LORD and followed all the instructions of his father,
David, except that Solomon, too, offered sacrifices and
burned incense at the local altars.

1 KINGS 3:3

How do we show our love for the Lord? Will it be written of us that we loved the Lord and followed him "except . . ."? Nobody's perfect, that is true, yet some exceptions should be excepted! Sometimes we pamper ourselves, allowing too much spiritual leeway. We could and should show our love to the Lord more by dealing with our "Solomon tendencies."

Solomon excelled as no other king before or since—but there were some "exceptions" in his life. "Solomon loved many foreign women. . . . They turned his heart to worship their gods instead of trusting only in the Lord his God, as his father, David, had done" (1 Kings 11:1, 4). Little by little throughout his long life, Solomon allowed himself the indulgence of exceptions.

Whether it be the opposite sex, material possessions, wealth, fame, success, or anything else, each of us has to deal with our own "Solomon self." It's easy to let things slip little by little. A little flirting here, a little self-indulgence there, and the evil one establishes a beachhead in our thinking and in our disciplines. It's when we let go of godliness and hold fast to ungodliness that we lose direction and let others take control of our lives. Erosion in dearly held values often begins almost imperceptibly with a seemingly small decision. God will help us keep alert to the dangers and notice each evil incursion. If we persist in listening to and obeying his word, we will hear his still, small voice reminding us, "No exceptions."

TO READ: *1 Kings 18:20-40; 19:1-6*

I QUIT!

*Elijah was afraid and fled for his life. He went. . . . alone into the desert,
traveling all day. He sat down under a solitary broom tree and prayed that
he might die. "I have had enough, LORD," he said. "Take my life,
for I am no better than my ancestors."*

1 KINGS 19:3-4

E lijah had just experienced a real "high." He had just given the idol-
worshiping Israelites an astounding reminder that the one true God
still reigned. God's power in response to Elijah's prayer had been an
astonishing experience for all those who stood on Mount Carmel that day
(1 Kings 18:36-39).

But a certain king and queen held power in Israel—Ahab and Jezebel,
two of the most evil rulers ever to sit on the throne. Ahab and Jezebel
already hated Elijah. When Jezebel heard that Elijah had killed all the
prophets of her god, Baal, she threatened to kill him (1 Kings 19:2). And
Elijah ran away—he quit!

There are times when we've all had enough. We want to get away
when life gets to be too much. God will allow the time for rest and
refreshment so we can get up and get going again. That strength comes
to us through the Holy Spirit.

There is wonderful gentleness in the way God dealt with his exhausted
prophet. It's easy to lose perspective when we are flat on our face under
our particular broom tree. God did not rebuke or exhort Elijah but simply
told Elijah that he knew that the journey was too much and that he
understood. What spiritual provision at such a low point in Elijah's life!

God tells us the same thing. Go ahead, take a break. But use it to let
God refresh you. You can't quit now—he has work for you to do!

TO READ: *1 Kings 19:7-18*

THE PLACE OF BEGINNING AGAIN

Then the LORD told him, "Go back the way you came,
and travel to the wilderness of Damascus. When you arrive there,
anoint Hazael to be king of Aram."

1 KINGS 19:15

W hat does God's gentle whisper sound like? How can we know if a voice in our head belongs to God or if it is a product of our own fertile imagination?

First of all, God's "voice" will never contradict his written word. If I put my inner thoughts through the filter of Scripture in context, and my thoughts "line up" with God's word, then I am safe to believe that I am hearing his whisper.

Second, we will know God's gentle whisper because it will always bring grace to our raw spirit, mercy to our sorry heart, and love to our discouraged soul. Elijah had run away from God's work in fear, but God met him and offered him bread and water. That's grace. However, God didn't say, "You can just stay here as long as you want. Enjoy your pity party." Instead, God told his prophet, "Go back" (1 Kings 19:15), and "Elijah went" (1 Kings 19:19). God tells us, his children, to go back. Back to that painful situation and those difficult people. Back to the service that each of us has been equipped to complete.

But God doesn't send us back alone. He sends us in the power of the Holy Spirit and with the gentle whisper of his love and encouragement. The gentle whisper reminded Elijah that, as far as God was concerned, the place of discouragement could become the place of beginning again.

47

TO READ: *2 Kings 5:1–19*

SHARED FAITH

One day the girl said to her mistress, "I wish my master would go to see the prophet in Samaria. He would heal him of his leprosy."

2 KINGS 5:3

Have you ever found yourself alone in what you believe? Perhaps at work or in the neighborhood your faith makes you stand out. The fear of what others may say or do to you may make you keep quiet. But such was not the case for a young woman in Naaman's employ. She gives us a brave example of sharing her faith in such a situation.

Naaman was the commander of the army of Aram, an enemy nation of Israel. He also suffered from leprosy. Naaman's wife had a little maid, who had been taken captive from Israel. This young girl found herself very much alone in a foreign land. Instead of feeling sorry for herself, however, she set about making some more believers like herself. It was a real miracle that this little girl, despite unspeakable hurt done to her, was able to reach out in love to those who had harmed her and point them to salvation. She had no desire for revenge against her master. Instead, she loved her enemies, forgave the wrong done to her, and set about pointing her master and mistress to Yahweh as their only hope.

I'm quite sure that Naaman and his wife wouldn't have listened to the advice of their little slave girl if her life had not backed up her words. We should live such a life among unbelievers, however they treat us, so that they might listen to our words. You never know where sharing your faith will lead!

TO READ: *2 Kings 6:8-23*

AGAINST ALL ODDS

Then Elisha prayed, "O LORD, open his eyes and let him see!" The LORD
opened his servant's eyes, and when he looked up, he saw that the hillside
around Elisha was filled with horses and chariots of fire.

2 KINGS 6:17

Are you ever greeted in the morning with a situation where you feel
you are facing unbelievable odds? Do you feel surrounded by
unfriendly faces? Perhaps you, too, have cried out, "Ah, Lord, what will
I do now?"

Christ, who is captain of the Lord's host, encamps around those
who fear him. Sometimes the Captain commands those unseen hosts to
intervene, as in Elisha's case, and a miracle of deliverance takes place. At
other times, in God's infinite wisdom, the heavenly host is restrained. But
it's still a comfort to know that they are there!

We can learn to "see" God's resources for ourselves through faith and
revelation. Reading the Word of God helps us when we are overcome with
fear. We learn that many people who served God were frightened. Elisha's
servant was frightened when he saw the Aramean army. Joshua must have
been frightened when Moses died and he had to take over (Joshua 1:6-9).
David must have been frightened when Saul was chasing him and all he
could see was the human army (1 Samuel 23; Psalm 35). In each instance,
God encouraged his servants and told them not to be afraid. Once God
gives us courage, we can then become an Elisha for our friends and family
when they are frightened or worried. We can pray, "Oh, Lord, open their
eyes, and let them see!" God is on our side, and it will be all right.

WHEN PEOPLE REMEMBER ME

As soon as the body touched Elisha's bones,
the dead man revived and jumped to his feet!

2 KINGS 13:21

W hen good people die and are buried, is that the end of them? Not at all. The Bible records that a miracle occurred involving Elisha's body after his death. Later that spring when a man's dead body was hastily thrown into Elisha's tomb, it touched Elisha's bones and immediately "the dead man revived and jumped to his feet!" (2 Kings 13:21). That was true resurrection power manifesting itself through contact with a holy man's bones!

When I look at Elisha speaking up for the Lord even on his deathbed and his body showing God's power even after his death, I am reminded that God's calling on our lives does not falter at the door of death! Aging is but the birth pang of a new dimension of life and influence that can continue far beyond the grave. Elisha left behind a legacy of words, God's words. God's words were recorded for our good. The Bible records Elisha's teaching, his miracles, and his dealings with both kings and commoners. To leave behind a legacy of words and actions should be the aim of a holy life! We should ask ourselves, "When people think of my life, what will happen? Will they feel the Spirit's power?"

What legacy will I leave? What evidence will show that I spent my life serving and honoring God? Elisha's life was stamped by courage and perseverance. Such holy consistency is attainable today by the same Spirit that inspired and sustained Elisha.

TO READ: *2 Kings 19:1-19*

LETTING GOD READ YOUR LETTERS

After Hezekiah received the letter and read it, he went up to the LORD's Temple and spread it out before the LORD.

2 KINGS 19:14

Threatening letters can frighten us out of our minds. What do we do with such a letter? King Hezekiah took a frightening letter to the highest power of all—the King of kings. He took his fear to his Lord.

Sennacherib, king of Assyria, had arrived at the gates of Jerusalem. He threatened to put the city under siege and starve all the people to death. In a letter to Hezekiah, Sennacherib tried to scare all the people of the city into turning against Hezekiah and against the Lord (2 Kings 18:27-30).

Hezekiah took the frightening letter to the temple. In a quiet time with the Lord, Hezekiah prayed. He reminded himself of the power and majesty of God. He asked God to listen and look. Hezekiah knew God and God's power, so Hezekiah petitioned God to show the world his power over the gods of the Assyrians. The Lord heard and answered Hezekiah's prayer (2 Kings 19:20, 35-36).

When you're frightened, your quiet time is an excellent place to begin to deal with whatever is troubling you. Start by reminding yourself that God rules over all the kingdoms of the earth. Then take the news to your upper room of prayer and spread it out before God. Face the facts with him, then call on him to defend his name. Let God take care of your fears. Listen for his answer. Ask him to show you what action you should take. Time alone with the Lord will give you peace of mind as nothing else can.

TO READ: *1 Chronicles 1:10; 2:3-7; 4:9-10; 5:18-20*

ROOTS

*Cush was also the ancestor of Nimrod, who was known across
the earth as a heroic warrior.*

1 CHRONICLES 1:10

S cattered throughout a long list of names in 1 Chronicles are several vignettes—small portraits of people the chronicler believed were important enough to mention. Some of these people, otherwise unknown, are noted for their faith in God (1 Chronicles 4:9-10; 5:18-20). These people have found their place among the mighty—the Noahs, the Abrahams, the Isaacs, and the Jacobs!

The writer tells about Er and Achan (1 Chronicles 2:3, 7), who disregarded their heritage and brought trouble on Israel. There is also a record of Nimrod (1 Chronicles 1:10). Like Er and Achan, he did not stand out for his faith in God. Yet he deserved mention as someone who had changed the course of civilization. (He founded the city of Babel for one thing; Genesis 11 records what happened there.) Nimrod had been the world's first conqueror, a mega-monarch. The Bible does not record him for his faith, but he was known for mighty deeds (Genesis 10:8-12).

Reading this list of names, the Israelites would have been reminded of their family roots and of those whose lives made a difference—for good or bad. Do you want your life to count long after you've gone? Then revisit your spiritual heritage. This is your spiritual family tree, too! These people had their place in God's plan, and so do you. You will be remembered. Ask God to help you be remembered for great faith in God.

TO READ: *1 Chronicles 2:7; Joshua 7:1-21*

A DOOR OF HOPE IN THE VALLEY OF TROUBLE

Achan son of Carmi, one of Zerah's descendants, brought disaster on Israel by taking plunder that had been set apart for the LORD.

1 CHRONICLES 2:7

W hen we've brought trouble on ourselves through our own bad choices, there may seem to be no way out. While some may try to hide or ignore their sin, it is far better to confess to God and ask him to show us a door of hope in our valley of trouble.

Achan's epitaph in the chronicles of the Jewish nation is that he "brought disaster on Israel" by violating the ban on taking devoted things from Jericho (1 Chronicles 2:7). God required that his people destroy some cities without taking any plunder for themselves. But one man disobeyed.

It all began with Achan's "greed need." He saw, he coveted, and he took (Joshua 7:21). Achan tried to bury the consequences of his actions, but his sin found him out. His wrongdoing affected himself, his family, and Israel, and resulted in death in the valley of Achor, the valley of trouble—for "Achor" means trouble.

We can be sure that whatever disobedience we try to hide has been discovered by God. It will only be a matter of time until our sin affects others. Yet God is a God of forgiveness and reconciliation. He promised: "I will . . . transform the Valley of Trouble into a gateway of hope" (Hosea 2:15). When we admit and deal with our hidden sin, God will open a door of hope right in the middle of our valley of trouble. Then the choice is ours to walk through that gateway into the blessing of his love and forgiveness.

TO READ: *1 Chronicles 5:18-22*

PEACE IN OUR TIME

*They cried out to God during the battle, and he answered
their prayer because they trusted in him.*

1 CHRONICLES 5:20

When you're in the middle of conflict, it's not hard to remember to cry out to God. These men of Israel were "skilled warriors" (1 Chronicles 5:18). They waged war in their endeavor to possess the territory God had given them (1 Chronicles 5:19). They were armed with shields, swords, and bows, but their greatest weapon was prayer.

As soon as we cry out to God during battle—whatever that battle may be—the battle becomes God's and not ours! Our part is to fight, to learn the skills of standing up against God's enemies, and to wield the sword of the Spirit (which is the Word of God—Ephesians 6:17). As we trust God and thrust our sword, we gain ground.

All of us need to gain ground in the battle between good and evil. Some of us are fighting for our homes and families. Some of us are fighting despair, fear, worry, or depression. Some of us are fighting to gain confidence. If we will only cry out to God during the battle, we will occupy the "land."

However, once the battle is "won," you must then sustain the victory. You need to keep on crying out and God will keep on giving you victory and peace! Prayer helps you to remember that, above all, the battle is God's (1 Chronicles 5:22)—he will fight for you.

TO READ: *2 Chronicles 6:12-42*

TRUE BLESSING LIES IN SELF-FORGETFULNESS

He prayed, "O LORD, God of Israel, there is no God like you in all of heaven and earth. You keep your promises and show unfailing love to all who obey you and are eager to do your will."

2 CHRONICLES 6:14

D o you ever wish that you knew the secret of privately praying for people so that their lives are really changed? Solomon shows us how.

First, Solomon praised God. Second, he prayed that God would help his people. Solomon knew that the promise to his father, King David, of his line continuing on the throne ("they will always reign over Israel") hinged upon the people's obedience (2 Chronicles 6:16). But people cannot be sinless (2 Chronicles 6:36), so Solomon asked God to "hear . . . from heaven" when his people confessed their sin, and when he heard, to forgive them (2 Chronicles 6:21-39). We also can pray for others by asking God to help them obey him, which he is always delighted to do, and then to pray that God will hear *their* prayers.

In your times of quiet, you also can intercede for others. Faith in who God is must precede all asking. In your quiet time, as you affirm God's holiness and transcendence, you can humbly present your requests to the one who *can* make a difference in the lives of those for whom you are praying.

Intercession means using our quiet time to turn our attention away from our own needs and toward the needs of others. In this way our prayers not only bless others, but bless us too. In the end, true blessing lies in self-forgetfulness and concern for others. Then your quiet time will truly make a difference—for you and for others.

TO READ: *2 Chronicles 14:1–15*

THE INTERFERENCE OF GRACE

Then Asa cried out to the LORD his God, "O LORD, no one but you can help the powerless against the mighty! Help us, O LORD our God, for we trust in you alone. It is in your name that we have come against this vast horde. O LORD, you are our God; do not let mere men prevail against you!"

2 CHRONICLES 14:11

How often have you looked at impossible situations and said, "Unless God does something, it's all over?" Asa had everything against him—an Ethiopian army of a million men and three hundred chariots (2 Chronicles 14:9). But in the middle of that impossible situation, Asa cried out to the Lord. God interfered with his grace and gave Asa victory over his enemies.

Obedience releases grace. How is it that Asa "remained fully committed to the Lord throughout his life" (2 Chronicles 15:17), when his father and grandfather were not such good examples? I call it the interference of grace! God interferes in Satan's working and brings grace to bear on grim realities. The notion that evil begets evil must at some point give way to the interference of grace, or the consequences would be catastrophic.

When Zerah the Ethiopian waged war against Asa, God fought for Asa when he was vastly outnumbered and virtually powerless. On Asa's return from victory, the word of the Lord came through Azariah, "The Lord will stay with you as long as you stay with him! Whenever you seek him, you will find him. But if you abandon him, he will abandon you" (2 Chronicles 15:2). Faith and obedience were reiterated as God's prerequisites for his interference of grace. When we trust the Lord and obey him, he will interfere in our impossible situations with his grace. That's the kind of interference we can welcome!

TO READ: *2 Chronicles 26:1-23*

HANDLING SUCCESS

But when he had become powerful, he also became proud, which led to his
downfall. He sinned against the LORD his God by entering the sanctuary
of the LORD's Temple and personally burning incense on the altar.

2 CHRONICLES 26:16

It's not how a woman starts her Christian life that's important; it's how she finishes it. King Uzziah began well—even as his father Amaziah had done (2 Chronicles 26:4). But also like his father before him, Uzziah later turned away from following the Lord. Amaziah had not followed God wholeheartedly; Amaziah had even set up his own gods and presented sacrifices to them (2 Chronicles 25:14).

Uzziah should have been warned by his father's example. Uzziah became very powerful, and his fame spread. Ultimately, this power and pride brought him down. Uzziah overstepped the spiritual boundaries laid down in the law when he burned incense on the altar—something only priests were allowed to do. So God's judgment fell upon Uzziah, and he became a leper. He lived out the rest of his days isolated and excluded from the temple of the Lord. He who had begun so well ended horribly.

Not too many of us can handle power and success—even spiritual power and success. Sometimes we find ourselves in a prominent position in public affairs and begin to believe the flattery we receive! It appears that when Zechariah died, Uzziah stopped growing spiritually. He seems to have grown ignorant and arrogant about God's word. May we take note and make sure we continue to seek the Lord and be instructed in his ways, even if power and fame come our way.

TO READ: *2 Chronicles 34:1-7, 29-33*

GOING IT ALONE

*During the eighth year of his reign, while he was still young, Josiah began
to seek the God of his ancestor David. Then in the twelfth year,
he began to purify Judah and Jerusalem, destroying all the pagan shrines,
the Asherah poles, and the carved idols and cast images.*

2 CHRONICLES 34:3

D id you ever think a king could be lonely? I think Josiah was—alone
in his faith as he began sweeping reforms in a nation that had
forgotten about God. Josiah "did what was pleasing in the Lord's sight. . . .
He did not turn aside from doing what was right" (2 Chronicles 34:2).
Josiah is painted as one of the finest of all the kings. "Never before had
there been a king like Josiah, who turned to the Lord with all his heart
and soul and strength, obeying all the laws of Moses. And there has never
been a king like him since" (2 Kings 23:25).

Judah's great kings were always those who reformed the nation,
bringing them back to God. Josiah's Judah did not follow their king's lead
with much enthusiasm, however. In fact, Josiah had to require the people
to obey the terms of God's law as read in the newly discovered Book of
the Covenant (2 Chronicles 34:31-32). Yet Josiah knew how the kingdom
needed to go and he did what had to be done—whether the people
enthusiastically followed or not.

So how do you do it alone? How do you try to make a difference for
God when everyone else is complacent? You take responsibility yourself.
You seek to please the Lord. You live openly and with integrity. Josiah's
spirituality and disciplined life meant going it alone. Will you go it alone
if necessary? God will go with you if you do.

TO READ: *Nehemiah 1:1—2:8*

TELEGRAM PRAYERS

The king asked, "Well, how can I help you?" With a prayer to the
God of heaven, I replied, "If it please Your Majesty and if you are
pleased with me, your servant, send me to Judah to rebuild the city
where my ancestors are buried."

NEHEMIAH 2:4-5

N ehemiah had heard, through the grapevine as it were, that even
though some Jews had returned to their homeland from captivity,
the wall of Jerusalem was still in ruins (Nehemiah 1:1-3). Nehemiah
could hardly contain his sadness, but as the king's cup-bearer (Nehemiah
1:11), he had to appear often before the king. The record tells us that
Nehemiah was "badly frightened" when the king asked him why he
looked so depressed (Nehemiah 2:2). He was frightened because it was
dangerous to look sad in the service of the king, but Nehemiah bravely
replied honestly. To his amazement the king asked him, "How can I help
you?" There was a split second pause, and in that split second, Nehemiah
tells us, "With a prayer to the God of heaven, I replied" (Nehemiah. 2:4-
5). He then asked for the moon! He requested months of absence, letters
of safe conduct, and supplies for rebuilding (Nehemiah 2:5, 7-8). Now
that was quite an audacious mouthful for a slave! But the king granted his
requests.

"Telegram" prayers (crisis prayers) are legitimate and can bring great
results, but that was not the only way Nehemiah prayed. Such crisis
prayers should be borne out of a regular prayer habit. In other words,
crisis praying should not be the only praying that we do. To know *how* to
pray in a crisis, we need to be in the habit of talking to the God whose
gracious hand alone will help us as we instinctively turn to him.

TO READ: *Nehemiah 10:28-39*

FALLING SHORT OF OUR PROMISES

"The people and the Levites must bring these offerings of grain, new wine, and olive oil to the Temple and place them in the sacred containers near the ministering priests, the gatekeepers, and the singers. So we promise together not to neglect the Temple of our God."

NEHEMIAH 10:39

Nehemiah, the governor of Jerusalem while it was being rebuilt, had helped the people to find their roots again. After a reading of God's law, the people "bound themselves with an oath" (Nehemiah 10:29) to obey God and follow his commands, laws, and regulations. The people promised to support the priests and the Levites, and "not to neglect the Temple of our God" (Nehemiah 10:35-39). But at some point, Nehemiah had gone back to Babylon (Nehemiah 13:6), and when he returned to Jerusalem, he found that the people had not kept their promises. They had not supported the Levites who were to conduct the worship services, so the Levites had left their temple duties and returned to work their fields so they could eat (Nehemiah 13:10).

Nehemiah restored the Levites back to their proper duties, and then the people followed through on their promise and began bringing their tithes to the temple again (Nehemiah 13:11-12).

We all have a responsibility to our place of worship and to the people who have been called to serve there. God calls some people to lay down their secular work altogether and commit themselves full time to ministry. In the same breath, God calls those of us who retain gainful employment to provide materially for those who minister to us spiritually. When we join a church, we commit to this responsibility. But people cannot live just on our promises, so we must not fall short. May we follow through with our gifts and support that the work of the church may go forward.

MARCH

TO READ: *Esther 4:1–17*

DOING WITHOUT THE COURAGE

"If you keep quiet at a time like this, deliverance for the Jews will arise from some other place, but you and your relatives will die. What's more, who can say but that you have been elevated to the palace for just such a time as this?"

ESTHER 4:14

E sther knew a God who was all-powerful and completely trustworthy. Before Esther ever dressed herself in royal robes, she prayed and fasted for the courage to do what God had called her to do.

No big decisions should be made and no great changes should be undertaken without much personal prayer. Then, when you have your answer, where do you go for the courage to carry it out? Esther knew that for her to appear before the king without being summoned by him was punishable by death unless the king extended mercy. She needed great courage to do what she knew God wanted her to do. Courage is a very scarce commodity. Faith, however, is doing something without having the courage to do it. Faith trusts God as we do something courageous without wanting to. Faith says, "It shall be done—look out, devil, here we come!" Faith is very practical. It enlists our minds and helps us believe that we were born for a purpose. We should have a sense of destiny that says, "I was created for just such a time as this" (Esther 4:14).

Faith believes God when he says, "I am with you always, even to the end of the age" (Matthew 28:20). Faith doesn't say, "Courage is with me," but rather, "God is with me"—even when your courage isn't. Like Esther, we must not allow fear to dictate our actions, but let Christ direct us wherever he wants. In the end, faith is being able to do without the courage!

TO READ: *Job 2:1-10*

THE SURE HARBOR
OF SAFE FAITH

His wife said to him, "Are you still trying to maintain your integrity?
Curse God and die."

JOB 2:9

At times we may feel like a ship that has been overloaded to the point of capsizing. Job did. All in one day he had enough trouble loaded onto his boat to take him right to the bottom of the ocean! Terrible circumstances and disastrous events had combined to rob Job of his tranquil life. He lost all of his wealth, then all of his children, and finally his health.

The same trouble hit Mrs. Job as well. She lost her children, too—all ten of them. She lost her servants, her wealth, and all she held dear, just like Job did. She then had to watch helplessly as her husband succumbed to "a terrible case of boils from head to foot" (Job 2:7).

The burden of these dreadful experiences eventually brought her husband's little craft into the safe harbor of God's arms. Job's suffering led him to God's grace. But Mrs. Job felt too hurt to make for such a secure destination. She chose instead to toss aimlessly on a sea of doubt and disbelief, like a little boat adrift. She advised her husband to "curse God and die" (Job 2:9). Fortunately, Job chose to live through the suffering and learn God's lessons for him.

Are you carrying such a burden of doubt on your decks that you feel a "sinking" sensation that has no equal? Are your troubles overwhelming you? You can decide that God doesn't care, or you can let the winds of adversity drive you to the sure harbor of safe faith.

TO READ: *Job 2:11–3:26*

THE SOUND OF SILENCE

Then they sat on the ground with him for seven days and nights. And no one said a word, for they saw that his suffering was too great for words.

JOB 2:13

Listening works wonders! Loving silence has no sound but tells the one sitting next to you that you care. It can say to the hurting heart, "Because I love you and am interested in you, I am willing to be here and sit in silence with you."

Job's friends came to be with him during a difficult time. When they arrived, they were rendered speechless by Job's obvious sickness and pain. So they simply sat, not saying a word. They had the ministry of presence, and they showed that they cared enough to be there. (If only they had *remained* quiet, but that's another story!)

There is such a thing as the ministry of presence, and there is also such a thing as the ministry of silence. Ecclesiastes 3:7 tells us there is "a time to be quiet and a time to speak up." Can you sit with a friend in silence? When a person is going through a difficult time, can you let her vent and spill and cry while you simply listen? Or do you complete all of her sentences for her? Do you feel that you must give her the answers to all her problems? Perhaps you feel the necessity to fill the air with words. Do you half listen to what she's saying, waiting to begin on what *you* want to talk about, the troubles *you* want to share? In reality, she needs you simply to listen—not give answers, not back away, not talk too much yourself—just listen.

TO READ: *Job 16:1-22*

LIVING WORDS FROM THE LIVING GOD

"I have heard all this before. What miserable comforters you are!
Won't you ever stop your flow of foolish words?
What have I said that makes you speak so endlessly?"

JOB 16:2-3

What turned Job's masterly comforters into miserable ones? How could these who had consoled him without words (Job 2:13) later crush him with words (Job 19:2)? Words are instruments for good or weapons for ill. Job wished his words about the comfort he was receiving from the Lord could be recorded—written down, carved with an iron chisel (Job 19:23-26). Little did he know they would not only be recorded, but thousands of years later they would be published in the Bible and other books and sung by great choirs around the world.

Job's comfort came from God, the living God. Job knew that his Redeemer lived (Job 19:25). This God is "the source of every mercy and the God who comforts us" (2 Corinthians 1:3). Job said, "I have treasured the words of his mouth more than my daily bread" (Job 23:12, NIV).

By continually emphasizing that Job was sinful and far from God, his friends—Eliphaz, Bildad, and Zophar—misrepresented God to Job, and they misrepresented Job to God. Therein lay their error (Job 26:4). They were not speaking living words from God; instead, they spoke their own opinions that proved wrong. We must be very careful to speak what is right about God to people and what is right about people to God. God rebuked these three men for their mistakes (Job 42:7-9).

God comforted Job with his living, loving words. Let us ask God to help us comfort others with words from him.

TO READ: *Job 20:1-29*

KEEPING YOUR JOY

*"Don't you realize that ever since people were first placed on the earth,
the triumph of the wicked has been short-lived and the joy of the
godless has been only temporary?"*

JOB 20:4-5

People look for joy in all the wrong places. Real joy can be found only in the presence of God. The joy of the presence of God is a joy that lasts, not just for certain moments, but forever. One of the problems is that people get happiness and joy all mixed up, yet they are very different things. Happiness depends on happenings while joy doesn't. Happiness doesn't maintain well and often relies on "pleasure feelings" to fuel it. The pleasures of this world and the pleasures of sin last only for a moment, as Job's friend Zophar pointed out.

Sin, of course, never tells you it is fickle. Sin wants you to believe that it's all flowers and sunshine. But if you're looking for real pleasure, you'll find that sin may be fun but is always fleeting. The flowers and sunshine turn to cold winter very quickly.

God is a God of joy, so we need to start by finding him and knowing him. Keeping our joy means realizing that the pleasures found in wickedness are only temporary. We must choose to side with the people of God rather than those who enjoy the fleeting pleasures of sin, even if it means suffering. We may have to put aside some pleasures in order to find true joy. We may have to become a very different person as we turn away from certain activities to obey God. We might not keep our friends, but we'll certainly keep our joy!

TO READ: *Job 26:1-14*

HANDLING CRITICISM

"Where have you gotten all these wise sayings?
Whose spirit speaks through you?"

JOB 26:4

It's hard not to criticize others for criticizing us, isn't it? It is difficult to take criticism graciously. One of the problems is that criticism often comes to us when we are at our lowest ebb—like Job.

Job was sick and sorrowing. The three friends who came to bless him ended up breaking his heart with their words. Eliphaz criticized his integrity; Bildad criticized his worth as a person; Zophar criticized his faith.

Eliphaz, the oldest and first to speak, had used scriptural language, saying that a spirit had visited him with a message for Job (Job 4:12-17). It's hard to know what to say when someone comes to us and says, "God told me to tell you" such and such. How do we know when to take criticism to heart and when to simply walk away graciously?

Job was astounded by his friends' harsh words. "Whose spirit speaks through you?" he asked (Job 26:4). Job told his friends that God was his judge, not they. Job knew that his worth lay in what his Redeemer thought about him and not what his friends thought! Job had his share of criticism, but, in the end, God was angry at his friends, for they had not been right in what they said about God to Job (Job 42:7).

We must deal with criticism honestly. We need to have personal integrity with God, with ourselves, and with others! Remember, in the end we answer to God—not Eliphaz, Bildad, or Zophar!

TO READ: *Job 33:1-33*

THE APPARENT
SILENCE OF GOD

"But God speaks again and again, though people do not recognize it."

JOB 33:14

E lihu, one of Job's comforters, found the right words at the right time and said them in the right way. Job's three friends—Eliphaz, Bildad, and Zophar—had done their best to comfort Job, but their words had been full of anger and accusation.

Elihu answered Job's complaint about God's silence by reminding him of the many ways that God speaks to his people (Job 33:13-19). In reality, Job was only complaining about God's silence in his present circumstances, but Elihu did the right thing by pointing out that although we may not hear God for a time, it does not mean that he is far away from us.

At a particularly dark time in my life, it seemed that God had nothing more to say to me. Like Job, I became terrified by the apparent silence of God. At that time, God sent a sweet Elihu my way to remind me of God's presence, protection, and promises. God spoke through Elihu to Job, and God encouraged me to wait patiently. It was not long before I heard his voice again.

If you are hearing only the silence of God, perhaps you need to listen for his words from other places. Someone may be an Elihu for you. When you know your friend feels abandoned by God, you may be an Elihu to her. You need to make sure your words line up with Scripture; then your words of comfort can remind her of God's promises and provision in the Bible and about his promises and provision for her.

TO READ: *Job 35:1-16*

THE SONGWRITER

"Yet they don't ask, 'Where is God my Creator,
the one who gives songs in the night?'"

JOB 35:10

☆

When the young Elihu finally got a chance to speak to Job, he pointed out that even in the middle of Job's suffering, God was still there and still concerned. Elihu may not have had all the right answers, but he did remind Job of God, the Creator, "the one who gives songs in the night" (Job 35:10).

Do you sometimes need songs in the night? I know I do. When the darkness descends upon my worry and suffering, the pain only seems to intensify. In the dark, I need God to send me a song. The psalmist exhorted people to "sing for joy as they lie on their beds" (Psalm 149:5)—and for good reason. Songs can lift the downcast soul and help ease the suffering.

It is comparatively easy to whistle a tune under a cloudless sky. In fact, I seldom suffer from insomnia when all is well. It is trouble that chases sleep away. When I can't sleep, when I am afraid and find no comfort, when my thoughts run around in my head and refuse to let me rest, then I need to ask God to fill my nights with joyful songs. I need to remember other sleepless nights—how the day dawned and the shadows flew away when he gave me a song to sing.

There have been sleepless nights, but never a night unmatched by a song! God brought me words of comfort—songs in the night. God is the songwriter. It is up to us to listen, learn, and then to sing!

TO READ: *Job 42:1-17*

SEEING THE POINT OF PAIN

"I had heard about you before, but now I have seen you with my own eyes."

JOB 42:5

H ave you ever wondered about the point of your suffering? The darkness of the depression that surrounds grief or difficulty can be so deep that it seems no light will ever penetrate, that no end is in sight. Job wondered aloud why life is even given to those who must suffer. It seemed to him that death would be far better than depression (Job 3:20-23).

However, there *was* a point to Job's pain. Job learned lessons through his suffering that he couldn't have learned any other way.

Job learned that he had an intercessor and a witness in heaven, an advocate on high who counted his tears (Job 16:19-20) and could lift him out of depression.

Job also learned that God is the living Redeemer (Job 19:25), who would stand upon the earth at last. Job seemed to understand that he would experience life beyond the grave. He knew that one day he would have a new body instead of the terribly painful, disintegrating one he suffered with in this present world.

Job came out of his dark tunnel with new insight. In fact he said, "I had heard about you before, but now I have seen you with my own eyes" (Job 42:5). Somehow you see God in the dark in a way you seldom see him in the light. That glimpse of God's glory, as Job discovered, made a terrible ordeal worthwhile. In other words, God's presence became more important than God's protection. God's presence was enough.

TO READ: *Psalm 1:1–6*

DELIGHTFUL DESIRES

But they delight in doing everything the LORD wants;
day and night they think about his law.

PSALM 1:2

S ome people believe you are at the mercy of your feelings. I don't
believe that! I believe you are at the mercy of the Lord, and when you
know that, he will give you the very feelings of delight that your heart
desires.

Are you looking for happiness? The woman who looks for delight in
all the wrong places needs to be told where true happiness lies. According
to Psalm 1, the truly happy person delights to think about or meditate on
the truth of God.

Delighting in his Word brings a deeper delight, a delight in the Lord
himself. The Word, after all, speaks of him. How can you ever get to know
God apart from his self-revelation? For many, reading the Bible is a
drudgery—a drag. But when you are weary of the words of cynical people,
try delighting in his words and see the difference it will make in your life.

Psalm 37:4 tells us: "Take delight in the LORD, and he will give you
your heart's desires." When our delight is in the Word of the Lord and in
the Lord of the Word, it follows quite naturally we will delight to do his
will. Speaking prophetically of Jesus, the psalmist wrote, "I take joy in
doing your will, my God, for your law is written on my heart" (Psalm
40:8). Jesus would have us say the same.

TO READ: *Psalm 1:1–6*

EVER GREEN

*They are like trees planted along the riverbank, bearing fruit each season
without fail. Their leaves never wither, and in all they do, they prosper.*

PSALM 1:3

A tree with roots in the riverbank will be ever green. The leaves are green, the branches are strong, the trunk is solid, the roots are deep. Similarly, the woman who chooses to live a spiritually vibrant life will choose to be a "planted" person, like a tree planted in a channel where the water never stops flowing. God's grace plants his followers in running streams of his love. These "trees" *have* to flourish, for they have all they need.

The desert crowd, on the other hand, is a secular bunch of scrublike bushes, parched and dry. Politically correct maybe, yet scoffing at the God of all things and all the things of God. Such people "are like worthless chaff, scattered by the wind" (Psalm 1:4).

We need to find out what sort of people we are—planted by the riverbank or blowing across the desert. If we are God's people, he plants us in his river of salvation, where our roots are bathed in the water of eternal life. Then, as the psalmist says, we will prosper spiritually. We need to let our roots drink deeply of this living water so we can be transformed. If we are truly planted, we will be productive, however hot the desert sun or barren the wilderness around us. Planted people are joyous people (Psalm 1:1). Our soul, like the tree with its roots in the river that flows from the throne of God, will be ever green.

TO READ: *Psalm 1:1–6*

THE NOWHERE WOMAN

But this is not true of the wicked.
They are like worthless chaff, scattered by the wind.

PSALM 1:4

W e ought not get our advice from people who don't care about God. Do you listen to the opinion makers of the day—film stars, models, important women in top jobs, glossy-magazine editors? Do you do things you'd rather not do, go places you'd rather not go, and say things you'd rather not say to be accepted among your nowhere friends? Do you stay silent when your peers make a mockery of everything sacred?

Do you feel you are a "nowhere person"? Do you know you are going nowhere in life, and, in death, somewhere that's like nowhere forever?

Nowhere men and women follow the advice of the wicked, stand around with sinners, and join in with scoffers (Psalm 1:1). The psalm tells us nowhere people are "worthless chaff"—used throughout Scripture as a symbol of the weak and worthless. These people have no substance to them. In the Middle East, grain is thrown up in the air in an open space to allow the wind to winnow out the residue. But when the fan or shovel of God's power throws nowhere people up to the wind of his judgment, they will not be found again. The psalmist knew that "they will be condemned at the time of judgment" (Psalm 1:5). However, the moment a nowhere person decides to go somewhere with God, she will be taken by the hand and led home!

TO READ: *Psalm 5:1–12*

REWINDING
THE UNRAVELED

Listen to my voice in the morning, LORD.
Each morning I bring my requests to you and wait expectantly.

PSALM 5:3

⑤

The young mother asked me how she could keep sane when she lacked adult company all week long. "Does anyone else feel the way I do?" she wondered aloud.

I told her about the time my husband and I lived in a very tiny house in England, and I was shut in with three preschoolers. By the end of each rainy day, I felt like an unraveled ball of yarn!

Prayer winds up the unraveled ball of yarn. But I had to find a place and a time for that to happen. I looked around my tiny house and found the place—then I had to find the time.

My packed calendar showed me that a regular time for prayer was impossible since each day's schedule was so different. But I found twenty minutes here and ten minutes there and blocked them off. Writing on my calendar helped me to keep the divine appointment. God and I needed to be alone long enough for him to wind the ball of yarn up again. It was good advice to seek more "adult" time, but I needed, above all else, to find more "God time." And that, in the end, was what kept me sane!

Are you feeling unraveled and hungry for time alone with God? Make a cup of tea, take your calendar, and mark those divine appointments along the way. Then, having found the time, why not pray about the place? After that, you can look forward to God winding you up again.

TO READ: *Psalm 19:1-14*

THE GOLD RUSH

They are more desirable than gold, even the finest gold. They are sweeter than honey, even honey dripping from the comb.

PSALM 19:10

Why is it that people seem to be so discontented? Maybe they are looking for the wrong kind of wealth. The world is full of people trying everything they can to accumulate material wealth. The lifestyles of the rich and famous are fascinating. Many people hope that their own gold rush will give such sweet results. Along with the desired rewards, however, comes the effort to protect the gold they've got. Security systems lock them in and the rest of the world out. Accumulating wealth can put people at risk.

No wonder the psalmist uses the symbols of gold and honey to point out the value of God's word. While accumulating wealth puts us at risk of losing it, accumulating knowledge and understanding of God's word only enriches us. Mere gold cannot substitute for any God's riches.

God's laws are also described as "sweeter than honey" dripping from a honeycomb because they warn us away from harm, and "there is great reward for those who obey them" (Psalm 19:10-11). That is sweet! Spiritual riches are found in biblical knowledge. Sweet success lies in living out that knowledge! What are you "rushing" after? Oh, to be involved in a gold rush with eternal dividends!

My human father was wealthy. I grew up with every material blessing. When I came to faith, I began to discover that Christ was my greatest treasure and in him alone lay satisfaction. There are eternal riches in knowing him. Only then can we find true contentment.

TO READ: *Psalm 22:1-21*

THE LION GOT HIM

Like roaring lions attacking their prey, they come at me with open mouths.
PSALM 22:13

T he Greek poet Homer said, "All kings are shepherds of the people."
Shepherds and kings went together in the minds of the ancients.

The writers of Scripture use the shepherd picture constantly. God is shown to be shepherd King of Israel. The writer of Psalm 80 prays, "Please listen, O Shepherd of Israel, you who lead Israel like a flock" (Psalm 80:1).

Psalm 22, graphically portrays the shepherd's cross. Jesus Christ told us he was the Good Shepherd who had come to give his life for the sheep (John 10:11).

In David's time, the shepherd would count his animals into the fold, then lay himself down across the opening, becoming the "gate." If any wild animal would have lamb for dinner, he would have to deal with the shepherd. Therefore, Jesus is the gate by which if anyone enters in, he or she shall be saved (John 10:7).

We all know the gospel story. The Good Shepherd came to "seek and save those . . . who are lost" (Luke 19:10). He gathered his flock, lay down in the gate, and the lion got him! You can read in Psalm 22 about the fight that ensued. The shepherd fought alone, feeling forsaken by his God. The psalmist wrote: "For he has not ignored the suffering of the needy. He has not turned and walked away. He has listened to their cries for help" (Psalm 22:24).

The lion got him, but on Easter Sunday morning, he got the lion!

TO READ: *Psalm 23:1–6*

GOD'S GRASS

He lets me rest in green meadows; he leads me beside peaceful streams.

PSALM 23:2

W hy does the grass on the other side of the fence always look greener than God's grass?

"I don't love my husband anymore," a young wife confided in me. "Everyone else's husband looks more desirable than mine!" This woman left her husband and enticed a young father away from his children. After a short time, she grew restless again. "Older men look more appetizing than younger men," she said wistfully.

When I was a student, I couldn't decide what courses to take. Everyone else's major looked so much more interesting than mine. When I got married, other men seemed to have better jobs than my husband had. When I had children, other houses looked more useful for rearing a family. I kept studying that grass on the other side of the fence.

Even though the grass on the other side of the fence looks greener, it doesn't satisfy like God's grass! The Good Shepherd led his sheep to the good grass. The green meadow, or God's grass, is obedience. Feed on it, and you will find rest for your soul beside a peaceful stream. Like a happy lamb, you will lie down and find comfort in doing the shepherd's will. Through the years, I have come to realize that, when I follow the Shepherd and feed on his will for my life, I find all I ever needed, all I ever wanted, and all I ever imagined could be mine.

TO READ: *Psalm 23:1-6*

THE GREENEST GRASS

*Even when I walk through the dark valley of death, I will not be afraid, for
you are close beside me. Your rod and your staff protect and comfort me.*

PSALM 23:4

The Great Shepherd supports the sheep when they are frightened, but
he knows the greenest grass is found in the valleys. Do you believe
that? What dark valley are you traveling through just now?

Not long ago, my husband went away on business for five weeks. All
the children are grown now, so I was alone. This time, because the dog had
died a few years earlier, there was not another living, breathing soul in the
house with me! I am not usually nervous, but I found myself wondering
why I had never before noticed the veritable symphony of creaks and
groans in the timbers of the house! It may seem a small valley to you, but
it became a very big one for me.

I began to devise ways of staying out as late as I could after work,
rather than coming home to face that empty house. One day, when I
had had enough of my churning stomach, I simply put my hand in my
shepherd's and said, "Help me walk through this valley with you."

"Stop running," he replied. "You have been sprinting along, intent
on getting out of this situation as quickly as you can! Walk slowly and
take a long look around. See, here is some green, green grass."

Verse after verse of Scripture flooded my mind, bringing peace, and
calm, and a sensible acceptance of the situation. I ate my fill and was
satisfied. Yes, the greenest grass is *always* found in the valleys.

TO READ: *Psalm 23:1-6*

PICNICS

*You prepare a feast for me in the presence of my enemies. You welcome me
as a guest, anointing my head with oil. My cup overflows with blessings.*

PSALM 23:5

The Great Shepherd not only satisfies and sanctifies his flock,
supporting them in their valleys of fear; he supplies them with
picnics along the way! He gives us time for enjoyment of others, for
release from the strain of circumstance, for fun!

There is nothing that calms an English lady more than putting the
kettle on. I believe every crisis needs a pot of tea—a time to sit and
regroup; a kind friend to share the pause, to reach across the table of
trouble, take our hand and say, "Eat a little something. You'll feel better."
When fears fight us, trying to put us to flight, Jesus puts the kettle on!

Our great shepherd lays a table for us in the very presence of our
enemies. I have a picture of his covering a table in the dark valley with
a white cloth, finding a leaf for a plate, and picking some lovely green
blades of grass for his jumpy lamb! By the time the lamb has eaten his fill,
he will have had his head anointed with the oil of gladness, and his cup
of joy will overflow. He will be up and away to gambol about the valley,
sure his shepherd is big enough to keep the lions and bears away from
him.

Do you need a picnic right now? Jesus is waiting for you to say yes.

TO READ: *Psalm 23:1-6*

SURELY

*Surely your goodness and unfailing love will pursue me all the days of
my life, and I will live in the house of the LORD forever.*

PSALM 23:6

The words of Psalm 23:6 tell us that "surely [God's] goodness and unfailing love will pursue" us. *Surely*—not *maybe* or *perhaps*. The man who wrote those words, King David of Israel, experienced God's goodness and mercy all his days and nights. Whether the sun was shining, or it was midnight in his soul, David was able to say, "Surely your goodness and unfailing love will pursue me."

It's so much easier for us to say "most days" or "some days." Yet the text promises God's presence all the days of our life. This is not a promise that all our days will be good or happy but rather an assurance that the God of mercy will follow us through the good and the bad days, the rich and the poor days, the sick and the well days—*all* the days of our life.

When we believe this promise, we bring his presence into our problems. It is his presence in all of our nights that wrings from our lips the certain cry, "Surely!" His sweet friendship lights up good days and makes them even better. So we do not have a *maybe* or a *perhaps* or a *hopefully*, but a *surely* that is rooted in the proven promises of God. Such certainty in the reliability of the good and loving shepherd of our soul grows trust day by day, whether he leads us through the dark valleys in the shadows or on the high hills in the sunshine.

TO READ: *Psalm 23:1-6*

WHAT MORE COULD A LOVED LAMB NEED?

*Surely your goodness and unfailing love will pursue me all the days of
my life, and I will live in the house of the LORD forever.*

PSALM 23:6

"T hese days, houses aren't built to last forever," complained a home-
owner friend as he looked at some poor workmanship.

"I know of one that is," I ventured timidly.

"Really? Who is the builder?" my neighbor replied, looking
interested.

"God," I whispered.

"Who?" he asked, shooting me the strangest of looks.

I was able to share, somewhat clumsily I'm afraid, that those who
follow the shepherd have been promised a dwelling in heaven, "a home
in heaven . . . made for us by God himself and not by human hands"
(2 Corinthians 5:1). What's more, the shepherd has told us it is to be a
forever fold, having a firm foundation whose builder and Maker is God!

By this time, my friend had forgotten his repair job, obviously
thinking it was I that was falling apart! I grinned at him and changed the
subject. Much later I heard his wife had died. I knew she followed the
shepherd. Can you imagine my joy when the soloist chose to sing Psalm
23? Psalm 23 is used so often to bring comfort to the bereaved, people
forget that it is a psalm primarily for the living! It speaks of a relationship
with the great shepherd.

When the time comes to follow him into the heavenly fold, the
journey will be made that much easier for those who are used to
following him. What more could a loved lamb need?

TO READ: *Psalm 24:1-10*

THE SHEPHERD'S CROWN

Open up, ancient gates! Open up, ancient doors,
and let the King of glory enter.

PSALM 24:7

Psalm 24 speaks of the king of glory, our heavenly shepherd, entering heaven in triumph. He shall come to judge the living and the dead (2 Timothy 4:1). When he does appear, he will have crowns of glory in his hand for the shepherds of his flock (1 Peter 5:4). Hebrews tells us that the God of peace, who brought Jesus from the dead, will equip us with all we need for doing his will (Hebrews 13:20-21).

Those of us who have the priceless privilege of caring for the flock can know he will help us to do that. He is the great shepherd who has equipped us with great gifts. He does not ask us to chase after wayward sheep without a rod and a staff. He shows us how to prod people's consciences and rescue them from the folly of their own bad choices. Not only is he my model, he is my might. What greater joy than to have the crown of well-doing placed upon my head and see his smile?

I never thought of myself as a leader. It was only as I followed that I led. Unless we learn to follow, we shall never learn to lead. As I began to take opportunities and responsibilities in my church, I found myself with a flock that needed care. The sobering fact is I must answer for that privilege to God, who is determined to hold me to account!

TO READ: *Psalm 24:1-10*

JEHOVAH-SABAOTH

Who is the King of glory? The LORD *Almighty—he is the King of glory.*
PSALM 24:10

G od is the refuge for his people and the conqueror of nations. God commands a heavenly host—spirits that battle the abounding evil that threatens us. "The LORD Almighty is here among us" (Psalm 46:7).

God shows us his power, not only through his personal intervention, but by sending individual members of his host to empower, console, or encourage us in our earthly pilgrimage. People do not always recognize such heavenly visitors because they have the ability to appear as humans. Many of us have perhaps "entertained angels without realizing it!" (Hebrews 13:2). Usually the people in Scripture became aware that they were involved in an angelic visitation. Gideon didn't realize that the angel of the Lord (a pre-Incarnation appearance of Jesus himself) was God until he suddenly disappeared (Judges 6:21-22)! An angel strengthened Daniel after Daniel recognized his heavenly visitor: "'Don't be afraid,' he said, 'for you are deeply loved by God. Be at peace; take heart and be strong!' As he spoke these words, I suddenly felt stronger and said to him, 'Now you may speak, my lord, for you have strengthened me'" (Daniel 10:19).

The heavenly host sang a cantata at Christ's birth, succored Christ after his temptations, and hovered around his cross to rescue him if he called. They rolled away the stone on Resurrection morning and "sat on it" (Matthew 28:2)!

The hosts of the Lord are marvelous, but not nearly as marvelous as the Lord of hosts!

TO READ: *Psalm 34:1-22*

FEAR
OF THE FUTURE

*Let the LORD's people show him reverence, for those who honor him will
have all they need. Even strong young lions sometimes go hungry,
but those who trust in the LORD will never lack any good thing.*

PSALM 34:9-10

D avid had seen lions during his days as a shepherd protecting his
sheep. He knew their strength; he knew their ferocious protection
of their cubs; he also knew that even strong young lions went hungry at
times. So he compared God to "an indestructible lion," and as his "cub,"
David would never go hungry—never lack any good thing—while God
was looking after him!

Life is unpredictable, isn't it? Nobody's job is secure anymore. Even
presidents of large corporations cannot be certain they will be retained.

David knew what it was like to be a king one day and a fugitive
the next! He had lost a job as shepherd, a job at Saul's palace, and his
position as captain in Israel's army. Yes, David knew what it was to feel
very insecure about the future, even to the point of wondering if he would
starve to death! "The righteous face many troubles, but the LORD rescues
them from each and every one" (Psalm 34:19).

He who taught us to pray, "Give us our food for today" (Matthew
6:11), keeps a full larder for his hungry children. Of course, he expects
those of us with laden baskets to share with those with empty stomachs.
God used the priest Ahimelech to feed David. He doesn't send bread from
heaven any more than he sends pennies. He wants us to be part of the
answer to others' needs.

TO READ: *Psalm 34:1-22*

GOD IS ALWAYS WITHIN EARSHOT

The eyes of the LORD watch over those who do right;
his ears are open to their cries for help.

PSALM 34:15

D avid had the answer to all of his afflictions. He sat in his cave and counted his blessings. Blessings are very threatening to afflictions. Troubles tiptoe out of the door when praise bursts in. David began to praise God for being God, which is an excellent idea when you can't praise him for what he has allowed to happen in your life!

David said, "I prayed to the LORD, and he answered me" (Psalm 34:4). He believed God was near enough to hear his cry. We need to remember that, when trouble comes, God is always within earshot. "The LORD is close to the brokenhearted," insisted David (Psalm 34:18). A broken heart may feel only its brokenness, not his nearness. It's what we *know* of God, not what we *feel* of him, that brings his healing presence to our damaged lives.

"Where is God when it hurts?" cry the rejected wife, the mourning husband, the lonely teenager. God is near. David wrote in another place, "Do not stay so far from me, for trouble is near" (Psalm 22:11). When David insisted on believing trouble was near, God insisted on being nearer.

"But if I could only see him, feel him," we say. Will you believe he is near when you can do none of those things? If you will, you will be well on the way to growing faith in the soil of your troubles. After all, what is faith for? When we count the blessings of his nearness, sorrow and sighing flee away.

TO READ: *Psalm 34:1-22*

THE YEAR OF FAILURE

But the LORD will redeem those who serve him.
Everyone who trusts in him will be freely pardoned.

PSALM 34:22

H ave you ever been really disappointed with yourself? David was. He must have felt that he had really let the Lord down. Looking back to his brave beginning with Goliath, he may have found himself fearing he never again would attain such spiritual heights.

After he escaped from the Philistine king, he hid in the cave of Adullam and penned Psalm 34. He was able to say, "I prayed to the LORD, and he answered me, freeing me from all my fears" (Psalm 34:4). One of those fears must have been the fear of failure.

He reminded himself that: "Those who look to him for help will be radiant with joy; no shadow of shame will darken their faces" (Psalm 34:5). Was he thinking back to his desperate measure at Gath when he had scrabbled on the gate with his fingernails and had let saliva flow down his beard? If he came back to trusting the Lord, he told himself, his face would be ruddy and radiant again!

The fear of failure can keep you in a cave of self-recrimination forever. Or it can drive you to the One who said: "The LORD will redeem those who serve him. Everyone who trusts in him will be freely pardoned" (Psalm 34:22).

A good dose of Psalm 34 will help you confess your transgressions to the Lord who will forgive the guilt of your sin (Psalm 32:5). You will discover that failure is never final.

TO READ: *Psalm 40:6-10*

JOY IN THE DOING

"I take joy in doing your will, my God, for your law is written on my heart."
PSALM 40:8

To *know* the will of God and to *take joy* in doing it are two different things! Many of us do not *really* want to *know* what God wants us to do because we might not want to *do* it once we know it! If we are inwardly honest and sincere, we will determine to find God's will and then set about joyfully obeying.

While Jesus was on earth, he explained his mission: "For I have come down from heaven to do the will of God who sent me" (John 6:38). The Son of God was not talking about a trip around the world—a luxury cruise through the universe. He was talking about the will of God for him, which involved suffering. Yet he delighted to do it because God wanted it!

It isn't easy to do the will of God when his will for us is difficult or involves suffering. It isn't easy to say no to a relationship or a job, even when we know that it is not God's will for us. It isn't easy to say yes to a difficult step or a move across the world, even when we know it *is* God's will. Notice that the psalmist took joy in "doing" God's will, not just in "knowing" it. Yet can we obey God, knowing the joy "set before us" at the end of the day? It may not be easy at first, but God promises that we will have great joy in the doing.

TO READ: *Psalm 45:1–17*

BY INVITATION ONLY

You love what is right and hate what is wrong. Therefore God, your God, has anointed you, pouring out the oil of joy on you more than on anyone else.

PSALM 45:7

Jesus is the source of joy and he lives in our heart, so why are we miserable so often? With Jesus in our heart, it should follow that we would be overflowing with joy.

The psalmist, writing prophetically, described the coming one whom God would anoint with the "oil of joy" (Psalm 45:7). In the New Testament, Hebrews 1:8-9 quotes this psalm as referring to Jesus. Do you think of Jesus as a joyful person? Jesus is the absolute source of joy.

Jesus talked with his disciples about this great joy (John 15:11). In John 17:13 he prayed that his disciples would be filled with his joy. Then he added that he was praying not only for his disciples but also for all those who would become his followers through them (John 17:20)— that's us! Jesus wants us to share in his complete joy.

So how can we possess this wonderful joy of God? It can be ours when the Spirit of Christ, the Spirit of joy, invades our life. Joy is a fruit of the presence of the Holy Spirit in our life (Galatians 5:22). And how does the Spirit invade our life? By invitation only. He waits to be invited into our heart. What words should we use to issue such an invitation? We can address him as Savior and Lord, for that is who he is. We can simply say, "Come into my life, Lord Jesus, by your Spirit." We dare not keep him waiting—and why would we? Who would not want to know total joy?

TO READ: *Psalm 50:1-23*

BEAUTY

From Mount Zion, the perfection of beauty, God shines in glorious radiance.

PSALM 50:2

What is *beauty?* There is a beauty of form and figure that catches the breath by its sheer symmetry. Then there is the beautiful supple strength of the athlete. But we are thinking "outward." What about the "inward," the beauty of a bright mind, for instance? The writer of Proverbs 31 warned, "Charm is deceptive, and beauty does not last; but a woman who fears the LORD will be greatly praised" (Proverbs 31:30).

The most radiant beauty of all is spiritual beauty, that inner tranquility that comes from a meek and submissive spirit resting at the Savior's feet. Moses prayed that the beauty of the Lord would be upon his people. When David had placed the ark of God inside the tent that he had pitched for it, he offered burnt offerings and told the people to worship their Lord in the splendor and beauty of his holiness.

Romans 10:15 tells us that the feet that take the gospel to the lost are beautiful. But how perfectly beautiful is our Savior Jesus! Beautiful in love, holiness, forgiveness, and grace! If we will only pray the prayer of Moses as we worship Christ, the Lord will think us beautiful too. We will hear our Savior whisper, "How beautiful you are, my beloved, how beautiful!" (Song of Songs 4:1).

TO READ: *Psalm 50:1-23*

PRAISE OPENS OUR EYES

"But giving thanks is a sacrifice that truly honors me. If you keep to my path, I will reveal to you the salvation of God."

PSALM 50:23

The whole duty of people is to glorify God. We glorify God when we praise him. To praise or worship means to ascribe value or worth to someone or something—in other words, "worth-ship." We worship through our praise. The more we know about God, the more praise we will want to express. Then, the more praise we express, the more our eyes will be opened to who God is and what he has done.

If we would learn to truly worship, we must first have some understanding of the one true God. As we study the Scriptures, we can begin to understand God's worth through a realization of his character. We find him revealing himself in various ways in the Old Testament; we see him fleshed out in Christ as we watch him in action through the Gospel narratives. Above all, through quiet contemplation of his work on the cross for us, we will find ourselves responding in praise and thanks.

Praise opens our eyes to something that cannot be seen any other way but through suffering. A friend who has been a missionary in France for a long time told of extremely difficult circumstances that led her to inquire of a fellow worker, "How can you be so serene when everything has collapsed around you?"

"Well," the fellow missionary replied, "when I can't praise God for what he allows, I can always praise him for who he is in what he has allowed."

Praise God—and let him open your eyes to see who he is.

GOD WOULD SPARE US

*Have mercy on me, O God, because of your unfailing love. Because of your
great compassion, blot out the stain of my sins.*

PSALM 51:1

B eing sorry doesn't always change the thing you are sorry about.
David was sorry he had sinned with Bathsheba. But being sorry
didn't bring their baby or Uriah back from the dead. Being sorry didn't
mend Bathsheba's broken heart either.

"You may be sure that your sin will find you out" (Numbers 32:23).
This should caution us to watch our *P*s and *Q*s! God will forgive murder,
but the grave stands, a still and silent testimony to the act. God will
forgive the adulterer, but he may lose his wife to another man. God will
forgive the teenage drug addict, but the child's mind is destroyed and his
or her perception impaired. There *are* consequences to sin.

Absalom, David's favorite son, revolted against his father, raped
David's wives in public, and tried to kill him. Did Absalom's behavior
reflect his father's sexual license?

Joab, David's lifelong friend and trusted general, had received
David's message: "Station Uriah on the front lines where the battle is
fiercest. Then pull back so that he will be killed" (2 Samuel 11:15). Did
Joab's later decision to follow Absalom reflect his disillusionment with
King David?

You reap what you sow. God will forgive you, but the clock cannot
be turned back. The far-reaching results of sin are appalling, and God
would spare us.

TO READ: *Psalm 51:1-9*

FEELING FORGIVEN

Oh, give me back my joy again; you have broken me—now let me rejoice.

PSALM 51:8

David was feeling terribly guilty—and justifiably so. He had committed terrible sins and needed to be forgiven (2 Samuel 11). In this psalm David cries out to God, "Oh, give me back my joy again; you have broken me—now let me rejoice" (Psalm 51:8).

Guilt can be both good and bad. We can experience "false" guilt—guilty feelings when we are not guilty of anything. Sometimes feeling guilty is good, because we have done something wrong and it needs to be corrected. We may need to ask for forgiveness and make restitution to another person. Sometimes we need to run back to God. But even if we ask God to forgive us, sometimes we still don't *feel* forgiven. What do we do then?

Remember that if *God* has forgiven you, then *you* must be willing to forgive yourself. When you refuse to accept God's forgiveness, you are saying that Christ's sacrifice was not enough to handle *your* sin. Discipline your mind to stop thinking about whatever keeps making you feel guilty. Satan wants to keep you bound up in guilt so you will be ineffective for God. Remember also to pass along that forgiveness to others. Comforting others with the same comfort that you have received helps greatly in the healing process.

If you still don't feel forgiven, ask God to renew your spirit (Psalm 51:10) and restore the joy of your salvation (Psalm 51:12). Then stop waiting for the feelings to come—go teach others (Psalm 51:13) and praise God (Psalm 51:15). Move on!

APRIL

TO READ: *Psalm 51:10-19*

RENEWAL

Create in me a clean heart, O God. Renew a right spirit within me.
PSALM 51:10

The word *renew* conjures up the promise of a fresh start, a new day, daffodils, and spring. In this context, it also carries with it the sense of permanent renewal. David did not want God to renew him for a passing moment or a day. He wanted to know a steady spirit of commitment for the rest of his life. "Don't take your Holy Spirit from me," he pled (Psalm 51:11). David wanted desperately to experience a steady resolve to follow God's pathway.

God's Holy Spirit will lend our spirit his renewing, willing steadiness. David prayed that the Holy Spirit would not be removed from his heart. No believer of the present church age needs to pray that prayer. Christ promised that the Spirit would "never leave" (John 14:16).

But we, like David, need to constantly seek God's face, conscious of our need for a daily cleansing from sin and renewal of his power to continue. Are you tired of constantly coming short of his expectations, others' expectations, and even your own expectations? When you ask him to renew a right spirit within you, he will lend you his other self to help in renewing your resolve, restoring your joy, releasing your lips, and receiving your praise!

Mothers need renewal. Sometimes they give up believing their children will ever make it. They give up their hope of maintaining their own steady love, unbroken by temper or careless care. Mothers understand David's prayer. They echo it every day, and God hears and answers with an eternal *yes!*

TO READ: *Psalm 51:10-19*

A NEW MINISTRY

Then I will teach your ways to sinners, and they will return to you.

PSALM 51:13

A new ministry begins when we have a new sense of cleansing and renewal. After all, we have something new to share.

David knew that. Once God had forgiven him, he knew he could better teach repentance and renewal to other transgressors like himself.

Somehow someone on a platform is set apart from those in the audience. However, if the speaker is able to share the listeners' experiences, it helps the audience to identify. When I came out the other end of a long, dark tunnel of loneliness, experiencing depression and disgust with myself, I was ready to share my lessons with others still in the tunnel. As I began to speak, I hesitantly admitted my failures, and then discovered that many women identified with and responded to me. They felt I was just like they were—which of course I was!

When I shared the fact that I looked under the bed when I was alone at night, I found instant rapport! I was not proud of my lack of faith, simply truthful. The secret, of course, is not only to share one's shortcomings, but the answers! As we present the God of our salvation—from sin, failure, and fear—then sinners *will be* converted! It's neat to tell people that God can help them get into bed without looking under it! If God has cleansed you anew, he has a new ministry for you. Accept it.

TO READ: *Psalm 51:10-19*

GUILT DOESN'T KNOW ANY SONGS

Forgive me for shedding blood, O God who saves;
then I will joyfully sing of your forgiveness.

PSALM 51:14

When we are truly sorry, and truly forgiven, guilt cannot blanket our souls with depression anymore. Guilt smothers, whispering in our ears, "Don't try again; you'll fail." Or, "The thing you did is unforgivable; you'll never recover from it."

After you have been angry with yourself for hurting God and those you love, and he has forgiven you, you have to forgive yourself. After all, true repentance has led to true confession, which must lead to true freedom from guilt. "Forgive me for shedding blood, O God," cried David. David wanted his heart to sing again, but guilt doesn't know any songs! He longed to tell others that God was right and he was wrong, but guilt sealed his lips. Guilt wants you to go on being angry with yourself forever.

We may experience guilt because we *are* guilty. This helps us become angry with ourselves and confess our sin. When we hear God tell us he forgives us, we can stop being angry with ourselves. God can and will save us from the guilt and power of sin. Some people live all their lives forgiven, yet guilty. "I don't *feel* forgiven," said a despondent single. "How can I get out from under all this guilt?"

Ask God to forgive you for nursing guilt when he has dealt with it all. Dare to believe that the God of your salvation has saved you, not just from sin, but from guilt as well!

TO READ: *Psalm 51:10-19*

TRULY SORRY

The sacrifice you want is a broken spirit. A broken and repentant heart,
O God, you will not despise.

PSALM 51:17

G od sent Nathan to tell King David that he had seen what David had done to Uriah and was angry with him. David's repentance was immediate. "I have sinned against the LORD," he cried out (2 Samuel 12:13). He was not angry with Nathan, or with God, but at himself!

True repentance is being angry at yourself in the right way. Many of us are angry when we're found out—with the person who finds us out, or with the one with whom we sinned. When God sees us truly angry with ourselves for sinning, then he accepts our confession. A truly broken and repentant spirit he will *not* despise. As soon as David confessed his sin, Nathan discerned that the king was really sorry and said, "The LORD has forgiven you" (2 Samuel 12:13).

Being repentant means you allow God to speak to you about sin. You don't argue; you listen! God is our Judge. David acknowledged that fact: "You will be proved right in what you say, and your judgment against me is just" (Psalm 51:4).

Being repentant means you agree with your own conscience. "You desire honesty from the heart" (Psalm 51:6). Let's face it, we *know* when we have sinned. We can also know that he will forgive us if we want him to.

With whom are you angry? Why? Shouldn't you rather be angry with yourself for sinning? Wouldn't you like to hear God say to you, "The LORD has forgiven you"? You'll hear him say it, if you are truly sorry.

TO READ: *Psalm 56:1–13*

TRUSTING GOD

I trust in God, so why should I be afraid? What can mere mortals do to me?

PSALM 56:11

Are you good at taking risks, or are you frightened to trust God in case you are let down? The psalmist made it clear that because he trusted in God, he had no reason to be afraid: "I trust in God, so why should I be afraid? What can mere mortals do to me?" (Psalm 56:11).

God is trustworthy whether we trust him or not. But he would have us trust him so that we don't have to worry. Anxious Christians are not a good advertisement for their faith. In the end, it isn't the amount of trust we have, it's the object of our trust that matters.

All my life I have been afraid of speaking in front of people. What would happen if I forgot what I had to say? Would they listen to me? What if I said something wrong? Could I trust God to hold me safely and use me to help people? Over many years I have found the object of my faith totally reliable. In the measure that I have given myself to him, confident that he is worthy of carrying me through, I have found my fears groundless—and my faith well-grounded.

It is safe to trust God. God is not a frayed rope. He can always bear our weight—we can count on it.

A NEW SONG

Sing a new song to the LORD, for he has done wonderful deeds.
He has won a mighty victory by his power and holiness.

PSALM 98:1

Who needs a new song? Do you ever get tired of the old tune? I do! A new song! Spiritually, many of us need a new song to sing. Some of us are sung out, tired of singing solo or of being lost in a big choir where no one notices our contribution! God can give us a new song to sing. It will start when we meet with God and tune in to the vibrations of heaven. Songs you've never sung before have a fresh, sweet, winsome sound that alerts those around you to the state of your soul. God gave me a new song when my children got married, when my husband had to be away a lot, and when I got sick and had to have a scary operation. They were new songs because I'd never been in those situations, and new situations require new songs. They were not always happy songs, but who says all songs are happy ones? A minor key can be just as pretty as a major one.

The important thing is to sing a song—a new song of faith and hope, of self-discovery or God-discovery, at every turn of the road, every station, every resting place. Just today I asked him to help me find something to sing about as I washed up a pile of dirty dishes. He helped me compose a new song over the kitchen sink. God is never stuck for a tune. New songs are the Spirit's business—ask him to give you one.

TO READ: *Psalm 100:1–5*

KNOWING IS JOY

Acknowledge that the LORD is God! He made us, and we are his.
We are his people, the sheep of his pasture.

PSALM 100:3

J oy comes through obedience, separation, and knowledge. When you have to do something you are frightened of doing, then it's what you know that will determine how you feel!

The psalmist told us we can make a joyful noise to the Lord when we know the Lord is God (Psalm 100:1)! Do we believe that God holds the whole world in his hands? If so, then that knowledge can filter down through our brains to our emotions and gently untie the knots in our stomach.

When you are asked to stand up in front of a crowd of people (especially people you know well) and give a speech, it's what you know that will help you at that time. You know that "God, who calls you, is faithful; he will do this" (1 Thessalonians 5:24)! There is great joy in knowing that!

When you are having your in-laws stay for the weekend, it's what you know that will help you to look forward to the visit with gladness. You know that the Holy Spirit will shed his love abroad in your heart for your relatives. "Hallelujah; I need that," you mutter!

God is my Mighty Creator, Provider, Redeemer. Knowing that he *is* gives me a joyful expectation that he will be all that he is in my particular situation. There is great joy in knowing he will simply be himself and help me be myself, while others are busy being themselves! Knowing is joy!

TO READ: *Psalm 100:1-5*

THE ALTAR OF MY PRIDE

Enter his gates with thanksgiving; go into his courts with praise.
Give thanks to him and bless his name.

PSALM 100:4

O ur immediate family seems to be made up of individuals with extraordinary strength of character. Each person is a strong, independent creature with ideas all his own. As our family circle widens, it reveals more of the same! Grandmas and grandpas, aunts and uncles, and in-laws all seem incompatible, yet are called by God to love and understand each other. That annual family reunion can be quite a challenge, can't it?

In Old Testament times, thank offerings always were connected with communal affairs and usually were made at their culmination. Perhaps God knew the problems that would arise at Christmas, Thanksgiving, twenty-fifth wedding anniversaries, christenings, or graduations! Maybe he knew he would have to command us to be thankful if he ever was going to see us appreciate each other.

It really helps to face an ornery relative and have to search our minds for something to give thanks about! It helps to talk to a difficult cousin and have to apologize to her for some misunderstanding or another. I can always thank God for my growth in humility because of that!

Whenever you face a difficult relative, try a thank offering. Don't let anyone go home without knowing how thankful you are for them. And remember, thank offerings and peace offerings go together! Don't let the sun go down on your wrath without having made a peace offering on the altar of your pride. Such offerings bring to God the smell of a sweet savor.

TO READ: *Psalm 104:1-24*

SWIFT TO HEAR—
SURE TO BLESS

*You lay out the rafters of your home in the rain clouds. You make the clouds
your chariots; you ride upon the wings of the wind.*

PSALM 104:3

Wings occur frequently in the imagery of King David. If he wasn't
speaking of the warm wings of God's comforting and immediate
presence, he was writing of other sorts of wings. In Psalms 10 and 18, he
sings of deliverance, praising God not only for protection in the midst of
his internal troubles, but also for the intervention of God in his external
problems. He has been delivered from the hand of King Saul. He speaks
of the Lord God who flew "mounted on a mighty angel" (Psalm 18:10).

Again, in Psalm 104:3, he reminds himself of the God of creation who
can "ride upon the wings of the wind." I love the image of the Lord God
who made all things using the tempests as stepping stones. He strides across
our world watching out for us or riding the storm to fly to our aid. Such
poetry teaches me God's grand ability to be there wherever and whenever I
need help. I do not really believe he rides an angel like a horse or that the
winds truly have wings, but I *do* believe that he is swiftly able to control, not
only my troubled heart, but also my troubled world whenever and however
he wills. There are no winds that will blow upon me that are not the winds
of his will.

Next time you hear the wind rustling the leaves or whirling around
the eaves, listen awhile. God has come to remind you that he is present—
slow to anger, swift to hear, and sure to bless!

TO READ: *Psalm 119:1-24*

EVEN AT MIDNIGHT

Your decrees please me; they give me wise advice.

PSALM 119:24

⑨

"I don't have anyone to talk to," complained a middle-aged woman. "My husband watches football all the time, and my daughter has earphones so she can listen to her music without disturbing us all the time. I have many problems. I need to talk to somebody. That's why I came to you."

I asked her if she had ever turned to the Bible and let it be her counselor.

"Oh, I'm not good at understanding the Bible," she said. "I tried reading it once, but I didn't like it, so I gave up."

Opening the Word of God, I began to show her verses that matched her need. I turned to Psalm 119:103 and showed her the words: "How sweet are your words to my taste; they are sweeter than honey."

"That was a sweet time," she said after an hour's "discovery" session. She smiled and left with a small pamphlet to help her get started reading her Bible for herself.

After she had left, I found myself reflecting on all the times his Word has been my counselor and friend. Reading through Psalm 119 again, I borrowed the words and rejoiced: "I will quietly keep my mind on your decrees" (Psalm 119:95); "Your decrees are my treasure; they are truly my heart's delight" (Psalm 119:111); "I am overwhelmed continually with a desire for your laws" (Psalm 119:20); "At midnight I rise to thank you for your just laws" (Psalm 119:62).

TO READ: *Psalm 119:73-88*

THE RING OF TRUTH

I know, O LORD, that your decisions are fair;
you disciplined me because I needed it.
PSALM 119:75

O ur Bible is unique. It claims to be inspired by God (2 Timothy 3:16). Jesus endorsed it, saying, "People need more than bread for their life; they must feed on every word of God" (Matthew 4:4).

Its writers wrote history before the events they wrote about had ever happened. We call that prophecy.

Its stories tell us about real people who struggled as we struggle, and hurt as we hurt. It introduces us to people who lived and died, had children or couldn't, doubted God or displayed great faith in him.

But the Bible not only declares the events in God's plan for time and rings true, it also works in our lives when we put its wise advice into action, claim its promises, or heed its warnings.

For eighteen years my life was a bed of roses. Then I felt the thorns. I landed in a hospital where a fellow patient caused me to come face-to-face with the Christian gospel. I came to faith in Christ and knew the trust of the writer's words in Psalm 119:67, "I used to wander off until you disciplined me; but now I closely follow your word," and in Psalm 119:75, "You disciplined me because I needed it." I would say *Amen* to that.

Since that day I have seen other affliction, and I now fully understand that sentiment of Psalm 119:92, "If your law hadn't sustained me with joy, I would have died in my misery." My sheer delight in his law in those times of affliction has sustained me.

TO READ: *Psalm 119:89-104*

NATURE

Your faithfulness extends to every generation, as enduring as the earth you created. Your laws remain true today, for everything serves your plans.

PSALM 119:90-91

God has revealed himself in many ways. For example, he has shown himself to us in nature. For "from the time the world was created, people have seen the earth and sky and all that God made. They can clearly see his invisible qualities—his eternal power and divine nature. So they have no excuse whatsoever for not knowing God" (Romans 1:20).

As we were talking to some teenagers on the city streets, one said, "Just show me God and I'll believe." The city lay at the gateway to the beautiful English lake district, and I inquired if he ever took a country walk and appreciated the fabulous scenery.

"I know what you're going to say," he said. "You're going to tell me God made all of that! Well, I don't believe in God! I believe it all just happened!"

Taking my watch off my wrist, I opened the back of it and showed the kids the intricate workings. They were duly impressed. "It just happened," I said casually. "One day all the little pieces appeared from nowhere and fell into place inside this little gold case. Then it began to move at just the right pace and told the right time!"

"Do you think we're stupid?" exclaimed one of the boys. "That watch had to have had a maker."

"Right," I answered him. "And so did flowers and trees; and so did you and so did I." He got the point. God's attributes are displayed in his world. Nature is the servant that shows us the master!

TO READ: *Psalm 119:105-132*

LAMPLIGHT

Your word is a lamp for my feet and a light for my path.

PSALM 119:105

D o you find the Bible hard to understand? It will make it easier if you know the Author. He will explain his book to you. As you read, you'll discover that the Bible uses metaphors to describe itself. Psalm 119 is full of word pictures that describe God's Word. Psalm 119:105 says that the Bible is "a lamp for my feet and a light for my path."

Lamps and lights have many uses. A lamp carried in the hand shows the safe places for our immediate steps. A light held high illuminates the way ahead. Likewise, the Word of God shows us where to tread in a present dilemma and guides our feet in the right direction for our future. Perhaps we need some advice in a business relationship. Or maybe we suspect that our children are in trouble, and we need to know what to say to them. The Word of God is like a lamp, enlightening and inspiring us with principles to apply. As we read God's Word, his Spirit enlightens us, showing us that the Bible is always relevant and applicable to every situation we face.

God's lamp is always bright enough to illuminate the pitfalls. We need to be "bright" enough to avoid them! God will guide us and lead us, provoke us and poke us, through his Word, but only if we take the time to read it.

TO READ: *Psalm 137:1-9*

HANGING UP OUR HARPS

But how can we sing the songs of the LORD while in a foreign land?
PSALM 137:4

The children of israel were captives in the land of Babylon. The Babylonians had swept through their country, conquered the people, burned Jerusalem, torn down the holy temple, and taken the captives back with them.

By the rivers of Babylon, the captives sat down and wept and hung up their harps on the willow trees. The problem was aggravated by the Babylonians tormenting the children of Israel: "Sing us one of those songs of Jerusalem!" (Psalm 137:3). But the people sadly replied, "How can we sing the songs of the Lord while in a foreign land?" (Psalm 137:4). Somehow unbelievers expect those who claim a relationship with the Music Maker to make music at all times—even when they are in "a foreign land." Are you "captive" in a difficult situation? Have you hung up your harp?

I remember moving from the city to the country—a foreign land as far as I was concerned! I hung up my harp. But Jesus came along, reached up, and took it down again. "These people need to hear my music," he said quietly, giving me back my instrument. "You don't hang up your harp without permission, and I haven't given you permission."

So I began to play, in a minor key at first, but then in major chords of joy and triumph. I sang the familiar songs of my Lord. People listened, opened their lives, shared with me. Have you hung up your harp? Let Jesus get it down and tune it for you.

TO READ: *Psalm 143:1-12*

WHAT WOULD
DADDY DO?

*Teach me to do your will, for you are my God. May your gracious
Spirit lead me forward on a firm footing.*

PSALM 143:10

S o often we face difficult choices. We cannot learn God's will for us
unless the Holy Spirit helps us. As members of God's family, we have
the Holy Spirit. The psalmist prayed, "Teach me to do your will, for you
are my God. May your gracious Spirit lead me forward on a firm footing"
(Psalm 143:10). "Teach me" and "your gracious Spirit" go together. God's
gracious Spirit teaches us, guides us, and gives us the wisdom we need.

A father died and left his wife in charge of the family business. There
were many huge decisions to make. The wife had never been involved in
the day-to-day running of things and so was overwhelmed with the choices
set before her. "I'm trying to think of what Daddy would do," she would
say. Her daughter, who had run the business alongside her father and knew
his mind-set, used this knowledge to advise her mother. "This is what
Daddy would do," she would say confidently. What the daughter did for
the mother is what the Spirit of God does for us!

Who knows the mind of God better than the Spirit? The Bible says
that God's Spirit "searches out everything and shows us even God's deep
secrets" (1 Corinthians 2:10). The Spirit will advise us what is God's mind
on the matter. Then we will know which way to go, which choice to make,
which path to take. And God promises to lead us forward on "firm
footing."

TO READ: *Psalm 147:1-20*

THE BUSINESS OF BINDING OUR WOUNDS

He heals the brokenhearted, binding up their wounds.

PSALM 147:3

Are you brokenhearted? Have you been injured and feel there is no cure for your crushed spirit? God is ready to heal you.

God's promise to heal the brokenhearted is for all God's people everywhere. God does not heal from afar; he involves himself in the healing and the helping process. He binds up the wounds of all who fall and "lifts up those bent beneath their loads" (Psalm 145:14). We can be brokenhearted for all sorts of reasons. Life can beat us up. We can be wounded dreadfully by rejection or abuse. We may be crushed by a cruel remark or difficult circumstances.

Ezekiel 34 shows us God as a caring shepherd tending to his sheep. "I will search for my lost ones who strayed away, and I will bring them safely home again. I will bind up the injured and strengthen the weak" (Ezekiel 34:16). God speaks of his sheep being hurt by evil shepherds. Many people today have been injured by "bad shepherds," leaders who have deeply wounded them. Church splits and controversies can break your heart, but the Good Shepherd is near and will bind up your wounds.

If you are brokenhearted, call out to God. Remember that he is not a God who heals from a distance. "The Lord is close to all who call on him, yes, to all who call on him sincerely" (Psalm 145:18). Whatever the reason for our brokenness, God wants to mend us. He is in the business of binding up our wounds.

TO READ: *Proverbs 15:1–16*

GOD'S MEDICINE

A glad heart makes a happy face; a broken heart crushes the spirit.

PROVERBS 15:13

A smile in your heart means a smile on your face. When your heart has Jesus as its guest, it smiles. How can it do anything else? Even when you are called to suffer, you may be sad, but you needn't be sour, because you discover that you have been saved to sing!

"But," you may object, "how can I even smile when I'm suffering, much less sing about it?" Look at Jesus! Can you look at Jesus and remain sour? When I'm in trouble, I meet him in the secret place asking him for some medicine to mend my heart. And he gives me that medicine—his joy. Then I can help mend others. He sets my heart singing!

Guilt is another reason we need God's medicine. Guilt doesn't know any songs. It is very hard to crack a smile when we are beating ourselves over a bad mistake we've made. We can be so ashamed over sinful behavior that we dare not even look to Jesus because we know he won't be smiling about that particular sin. God offers forgiveness that mends our memories, and he smiles when he catches our whispered "sorrys" and turns them into joy. God's medicine is always available—just a prayer away. God's joy medicine cures the guilt so we can move on to share his medicine with others.

There is joy in serving Jesus, and when merry missionaries and contented Christians dispense God's joyous medicine to an unsmiling world, we are in business.

TO READ: *Proverbs 17:1-28*

A TRUE AND LOYAL FRIEND

A friend is always loyal, and a brother is born to help in time of need.

PROVERBS 17:17

Jesus is a perfect friend. We would do well to look at him as our model. First of all, Jesus is not a fair-weather friend. He is not in his friendships for what he can get out of them. Jesus always remains faithful, no matter how we treat him. Jesus washed the feet of his closest friends, the disciples, knowing that those very same feet would soon turn and run from him. He even washed the feet of Judas Iscariot, his betrayer (John 13:5, 10-11). Jesus, unlike the disciples, loved at all times. He truly fulfilled the proverb, "A friend is always loyal, and a brother is born to help in time of need" (Proverbs 17:17).

So what does that mean for me? It means listening to my friend patiently when she is struggling, instead of anxiously wanting to spend time on my own problems! It means looking after my friend's children one more time, even when it's inconvenient and I have a sneaking suspicion that she might be taking advantage of me. It means setting aside my plans for her plans. In other words, it means living a flexible life in order to allow God to plan my agenda on behalf of those who may need my time today. Proverbs 17:17 says, "A friend is always loyal." Christ loved his friends like this. I must love mine the same way. A true friend *stays* friends!

TO READ: *Ecclesiastes 3:1-2*

DEAD ON TIME!

A time to be born and a time to die.

ECCLESIASTES 3:2

As I grow older, I occasionally struggle with accepting wrinkles, double chins, a failing memory, and glasses! The day I got my first pair of bifocals a friend of mine (or so I thought!) left me a funny poem:

My glasses come in handy,
My hearing aid is fine,
My false teeth are just dandy,
But I sure do miss my mind!

That didn't help! My husband, seeing my struggle, usually tells me to get my theology straight—I was born at the right moment and will be "dead on time." Therefore, I must stop wanting to reverse the trend! Life has been so good to me, I cling to it. But I have a poor view of heaven if I want to stay on earth.

A friend of mine, my age and dying of cancer, told me people keep asking her if she is angry. "Why should I be angry?" she asked me. "I've had a marvelous life, and heaven will be even better. Sure, I'll miss everyone, and I hope they will miss me, but it's my time, and it's all right." What a contrast to the statement of a girl being interviewed on a TV show about her reaction when she discovered she had cancer. "I hit out at everyone in sight," she said. "It was so unfair! I hadn't had time to do everything I wanted to do. Mostly I was mad at God."

When you know Jesus, you let him wind your watch. When it stops, he gives you a new one with everlasting springs!

READ TIME
IS SEED TIME

A time to plant and a time to harvest.

ECCLESIASTES 3:2

Y ou don't plant seeds in frozen soil. You don't wait until autumn to prepare the ground. You plant seeds in the warm, moist springtime. That way you have a chance to pluck up that which you have planted.

I take every opportunity I am given to tell young mothers these things. It's hard to be a young mom these days. Many a single parent is left to cope with two or three toddlers. Trying to juggle a job and manage a home leaves little time to plant seed thoughts from God's Word in the moist soil of a child's springtime.

I am convinced the first five years of a child's life are vital. What they learn in these years shapes much of their future. This is the time to talk of Jesus and his friendship, and of God their Father and his care. This is the time to share picture books of their Savior and to tell stories that make Bible people walk off the pages and become their friends.

Read time is seed time! It will have to be a priority or it will never get done. The devil will see to that. He hates the little children and their springtimes. But if you would harvest a crop of Christian children who would minister to others, and perhaps to you in your old age, you will have to minister to them in their youth!

TO READ: *Ecclesiastes 3:1-3*

PRINCE

A time to kill and a time to heal.

ECCLESIASTES 3:3

W e bought a dog and named him Prince. By the time he had belonged to the family two weeks, the family belonged to him! He was a beautiful golden retriever and was supposed to be kept in the backyard. But he made himself at home wherever he would, and we settled down to sixteen marvelous "dog years." He was probably the most disobedient dog in the neighborhood and useless as a watchdog, but we loved him. He was something of a legend by the time we arrived in America. I could write a book about him! Then he got heartworm. I had never imagined there would be a time in my life when I must kill. Was this it?

Being a Christian makes a difference in attitude, even toward animals. After all, God made the animals and gave people dominion over them (Genesis 1:28). We should show respect to all of God's divine creation by the way we treat it—and that includes animals.

Prince survived his heartworm. It was a time to heal. Years later, when he was old and decrepit, our friends advised us to have him put to sleep. Was *this* the time to kill?

"We must make sure we don't just get rid of him because he's inconvenient," my husband said to me. "He's been a marvelous family friend."

In the end, we knew it was time—time to kill. It was very hard. Animal lovers will understand! But Jesus understood, too! "Nothing exists that he didn't make" (John 1:3), and that included Prince!

GOD'S WRECKING BALL

A time to tear down and a time to rebuild.

ECCLESIASTES 3:3

How can a Christian know what it is to rise triumphant unless she has first fallen down, defeated? "The way to *up* is *down,* and the way to *down* is *up*," someone has said. I do believe that the way to *up* is down. It's a matter of taking time to let the master builder demolish the old building so a new structure can rise on the old site!

Have you ever gazed in awe as a massive wrecking ball cracked the walls of a condemned apartment house and flung the bricks in the air, sending the structure to destruction in a cloud of choking dust? Have you ever wondered what could take the place of that familiar old building? Then you pass that way in a little time and see the modern replacement, which often makes the memory of the old distasteful.

It takes time to build the new in the place of the old. Therefore, "those who become Christians become new persons. They are not the same anymore, for the old life is gone. A new life has begun!" (2 Corinthians 5:17).

God can demolish the old life. Some of us need to be broken. He will have to use a very big wrecking ball on some of us! Not until that happens will there be the possibility of being built up again—a new house, a habitation fit for the Lord!

TO READ: *Ecclesiastes 3:1-4*

JOY AND TEARS

A time to cry and a time to laugh.
ECCLESIASTES 3:4

Listening to some people talk, you get the impression that tear ducts are supposed to dry up the moment you become a Christian. Looking at some people's faces, you get the impression that at the moment they are born again, Christians' mouths are frozen into a line of disapproval. But there is a time to laugh. We laugh when we celebrate life. I believe Jesus laughed, too.

There is a balance in life. The Bible says that there is a time for everything: "A time to cry and a time to laugh" (Ecclesiastes 3:4). There is a time when it is perfectly permissible for Christians to weep. There is far too much injustice in our world to stay a dry-eyed disciple. On the other hand, you love Jesus no less if you enjoy a season of celebration. There *is* a time to laugh; thank God for that!

As we build our bridges of friendship with unbelievers, we can build them under sunny skies. The time will come when the clouds gather and the rain falls. Then, after sharing laughter with them, we can also share their tears. Christian compassion doesn't begin only when tears fall; it begins as we laugh and rejoice when things are good. Then, when others face times of struggle, we weep as they weep. When we've shared both the joy and the tears with our unbelieving friends, we can introduce them to our friend, Jesus, who can give them the comfort they need.

TO READ: *Ecclesiastes 3:1-4*

TENDER TIME

A time to grieve and a time to dance.

ECCLESIASTES 3:4

J esus said that it's hard to mourn when the groom is with you. On the other hand, it's hard not to mourn when the groom is taken away (see Matthew 9:15)! When the wedding is in full swing, it is time to dance. If the groom were to die, it would be time to mourn.

I heard a true account of a wedding of two young Bible school students who really loved the Lord and were preparing to serve him together. On their way to their honeymoon hotel, the groom was killed in a car crash. How soon the dancing turned into mourning!

Sometimes the two things come so close to each other it shatters the soul. The parents of the young man who met such an untimely death did not believe their son's home call was some freakish accident. The Christian doesn't believe in accidents of that magnitude. Actually, there is no such thing as "untimely" death for the Christian, for we believe there is "a time to die" (Ecclesiastes 3:2).

Time is a kind cushion, separating the good days from the bad days, preparing us for change. Time heals. Time gives us perspective we've never had before. Time taken for grieving eventually helps us to dance. Time taken for dancing helps us to prepare ourselves to grieve. Time ripens us, like cheese, making us sharp. Time does not usually demand such instant adjustments as in this sad incident of such unexpected death. But when such things do happen, tender time takes care of the wounds.

TO READ: *Ecclesiastes 3:1–5*

THE DISAPPOINTMENT STONES

A time to scatter stones and a time to gather stones.

ECCLESIASTES 3:5

Perhaps the meaning of these phrases about stones refers to the way an Eastern gardener prepares to till his vineyard. These vineyards are often hacked out of the steep sides of the vales. The ground in Israel seems to be made of stones of every shape and size. There is a season when the owner of the vineyard has to clear the ground of stones, and other times when he needs to gather, for some useful purpose, the very stones he has thrown away.

A young missionary would travel many months on end teaching and preaching, so his time at home, though very important, was fleeting. His wife would make all sorts of plans, only to find her life littered with the stones of disappointments. There would always be some responsibility her husband had to fulfill, and her plans would be spoiled. Picking up her disappointments and throwing them at her mate solved nothing! It was time to cast the stones of disappointment into the corner of her life.

As time went on and the fruit of Christian perseverance began to grow in the cultivated ground, the young wife tentatively began to build a watchtower in her mind with the disappointment stones. From that tower she could watch for her husband to come home and prepare a suitable celebration.

There *is* a time to scatter stones, and there *is* a time to gather stones together. I know—I was that young wife!

TO READ: *Ecclesiastes 3:1-5*

A SPECIAL FAST

A time to embrace and a time to turn away.

ECCLESIASTES 3:5

O ur sexual appetites need to be under control. We do well to make our God the God of our loves. We cannot go around sleeping with whom we will and expect God to smile. The place for the full expression of the Christian's sexuality is within the boundaries of marriage—which are designed to nurture love to full maturity.

The Bible teaches us that fornication (sex before marriage) is sin. Adultery (extramarital sex) is also sin. Jesus, face-to-face with a woman taken in the very act of adultery, forgave her, but said, "Go and sin no more" (John 8:11). Once you have been face-to-face with Jesus, your sexuality must be subject to his commands.

The sexual act speaks of a commitment to a forever relationship with another human being and therein lies its wonder and enjoyment. How, then, can casual sex be part of a Christian lifestyle? For the couple who follows Christ, there is "a time to embrace and a time to turn away." We are not to withhold our bodies from our mates, using our sexuality as a weapon, but rather are to use our bodies to bless (1 Corinthians 7:3-5).

There are times, however, that God calls some of his children to a ministry that entails considerable separation for the kingdom's sake. Such has been our case. I would testify to the fact that as we have "fasted" in this area, God has given special grace for this special calling. But then he is a special God!

TO READ: *Ecclesiastes 3:1–6*

A TIME TO WORSHIP

A time to search and a time to lose.

ECCLESIASTES 3:6

D o you know how to live with little or much? Paul said he knew what it was "to live on almost nothing or with everything" (Philippians 4:12). Job knew, too. "Should we accept only good things from the hand of God and never anything bad?" (Job 2:10). When Job's world crashed around his ears, he "stood up and tore his robe in grief. Then he shaved his head and fell to the ground before God. He said, "I came naked from my mother's womb, and I will be stripped of everything when I die. The LORD gave me everything I had, and the LORD has taken it away. Praise the name of the LORD!" (Job 1:20-21)

The Bible goes on to say, "in all of this, Job did not sin by blaming God" (Job 1:22). When trouble comes our way, many of us collapse in a whimpering heap like Job, but few of us fall to the ground before God in worship. While sin stalks our earth, there will always be a time to lose. We shall lose our health and our friends. Some of us may lose a wife, a husband, or even a child. But there will be times to gain as well. Not only will we gain new spiritual insight through our trials as Job did, but some of us may well have years of blessing. God does give us all things richly to enjoy! Whether we have almost nothing, or whether we have everything, we must worship. Then all will be right.

TO READ: *Ecclesiastes 3:1–6*

THE GRATEFUL SHELF

A time to keep and a time to throw away.

ECCLESIASTES 3:6

I like to keep everything—tied up with pretty string, filed away in colored folders, or packed in boxes. I'm like my mother. When my mother died, I did not relish going through her house and disposing of her goods.

I was prepared for tears but not for the things that triggered them. I thought when I saw her favorite worn chair, or her beloved teakettle, or her walking cane, it would get to me. But it was the sight of dozens of little unimportant things wrapped up in plastic bags and sealed with rubber bands that finished me off. Even as I write this, I am crying. But that's all right—there's a time to remember!

My sister and I felt like reluctant thieves, rummaging through some-one's personal belongings. But it had to be done. There's a time to keep, but there's a time to throw away—and that time had come.

As we went about our necessary work, closed up in the silence of our deep sorrow, I realized how precious a time this was for both my sister and me. This was a time we could take "mother memories" and wrap them up more carefully than even the little plastic packets we found, tie them with the strings of love, and place them safely on the grateful shelf of our hearts. It was a time to throw away, but it was a time to keep as well, and we held each other, my sister and I, and thanked God for motherhood and daughterhood, sisterhood and family!

TO READ: *Ecclesiastes 3:1–7*

THE STITCHES OF FORGIVENESS

A time to tear and a time to mend.

ECCLESIASTES 3:7

"A time to tear" refers to the rending of garments in an outward show of distress or repentance. Reuben, returning to the pit where Joseph had been held, found him gone and tore his clothes in distress (Genesis 37:29).

Later, after God had miraculously preserved Joseph and he had become Pharaoh's right-hand man, his brothers, seeking food for the family, were tricked by Joseph, who had a cup put in Benjamin's sack. The brothers discovered this, "tore their clothing in despair, loaded the donkeys again, and returned to the city" (Genesis 44:13) to seek the mighty man's mercy.

This custom of tearing one's clothing dramatically demonstrated inward mourning and sorrow. But as is often the case with outward signs of inward things, the ritual eventually took the place of the reality.

Joel, the prophet, had to call Israel to true repentance. "That is why the Lord says, 'Turn to me now, while there is time! Give me your hearts. Come with fasting, weeping, and mourning. Don't tear your clothing in your grief; instead, tear your hearts.' Return to the LORD your God, for he is gracious and merciful. He is not easily angered. He is filled with kindness and is eager not to punish you" (Joel 2:12-13).

Joel knew that when we rend our hearts and not our clothing, God sews them up for us with the stitches of forgiveness.

TO READ: *Ecclesiastes 3:1–7*

TAMING MY TONGUE

A time to be quiet and a time to speak up.

ECCLESIASTES 3:7

I have a problem. I often open my mouth simply to change feet! I'm always saying the wrong thing!

I remember once going to hear a visiting preacher at our church. I was delighted to see two unfamiliar ladies in "my pew." Our church was small, and visitors were a rarity. I hoped the preacher would be good, and they would like the service and come again. The visiting preacher was not bad—he was terrible!

I watched the visitors carefully. The younger lady, looking embarrassed, glanced at the older one. As soon as the service was over, they rose to leave. I leaped around the pew, welcomed them profusely, and said I hoped they wouldn't judge the fellowship by this one visit.

"The preacher is usually very good," I said as quietly as I could. "I don't know where this man came from."

"I do," said the older lady icily. "He's my husband."

"And he's my dad," added the younger woman balefully.

This was definitely a time I should have kept quiet. Other times, I have kept quiet when I knew I should speak up!

"Who makes mouths?" God asked Moses (Exodus 4:11), when he was busy telling God he wouldn't be a good speaker. God told Moses to go, for God would help him speak.

My tongue needs teaching, too. I need the Lord God to instruct it when to speak and when to stay silent. I need to use it, to ask him to touch it, tame it, and turn it into an instrument of blessing!

MAY

TO READ: *Ecclesiastes 3:1-8*

THE SPOILER

A time to love and a time to hate.

ECCLESIASTES 3:8

W e know there is always a time to love, but is there ever a time to hate? I believe there is a legitimate case for hating whatever it is that spoils love.

What abusive man does not hate the temper that controls him? What alcoholic wife does not despise the addiction that is ruining her home and her relationships? There is definitely a time to hate that which destroys love. If we hate sin enough, we might be motivated to seek God's help to turn from it.

God hates sin. He hates it because he knows sin is a spoiler. Jesus showed us God's heart when he turned on the Pharisees, hating their hypocrisy and pride. "I hate pride" (Proverbs 8:13), said the Lord. God hates lying, divorce, and all sorts of abuses of human rights. He hates cheating and sexual perversion.

Yes, there is a time to hate. The problem comes when our love does not contain the element of hatred. False love allows anyone to do anything to anybody regardless of the consequences. False love even loves what God hates!

"God has given me this wonderful love for this married man," a woman told me.

"Nonsense," I replied. "He wouldn't. God hates adultery."

True love hates the thing that spoils it. True love has rules, and it confronts, disciplines, and shows itself strong in sticking to principles. True love is honest and open, willing to sacrifice itself, being first and foremost concerned with the loved one's highest good. There is a time to love. It's now!

TO READ: *Ecclesiastes 3:1–8*

AN ENEMY WORSE THAN HITLER

A time for war and a time for peace.

ECCLESIASTES 3:8

I t was a time of war. I was small, very insignificant, and extremely frightened. I sat on a little stool, looking up into the darkening sky at the searchlights seeking shapes—sinister shapes of war and hate and death. I didn't understand why the shapes might drop bombs.

My mother explained that an evil man called Hitler was trying to conquer the world, and someone had to try to stop his gobbling up all the nations on the globe. Then I dimly understood that sometimes there's a time for war.

After it was all over and I was grown and at college, I came across a book of photographs that had been taken in places called Belsen and Auschwitz. Then I understood more fully why I had had to run into the air-raid shelter, why my daddy had had to fight, and why my friend's uncle had been killed.

Now I am middle-aged, and it's a time of peace. My Bible instructs me to pray for peace in our time. If there is peace, we can attend to God's work and try to reach the half of our world that has never once heard about the Prince of Peace, Jesus Christ. When we live in a time of peace, we don't need to spend every waking moment in the business of survival. We can attend to those in the grip of an enemy worse than Hitler—Satan himself, who would gobble up people's souls. We can spend time caring for souls. We can fight the devil, for there is a time for war!

TIMING

*God has made everything beautiful for its own time. He has planted eternity
in the human heart, but even so, people cannot see the whole scope of
God's work from beginning to end.*

ECCLESIASTES 3:11

G od has painted time with changes. The kaleidoscopic movement of
innumerable processes will be seen in the end as "beautiful for its
own time." It may look a mess up close, just as putting your face too near
a big painting will distort your view of it. Stepping back puts it in better
perspective. One day, we will step back, look at the finished canvas of life
with the Artist by our side, and see it in all its beauty and completeness.

Ecclesiastes 3:11 goes on to say, "He has planted eternity in the
human heart." People who have a worldview from a worldly perspective
will fail to see beauty in black threads. All will be meaningless to them.

But for those of us who have eternity in our hearts, it is another
matter. We are given faith to believe that "people should eat and drink
and enjoy the fruits of their labor, for these are gifts from God"
(Ecclesiastes 3:13). And it is the grace of God that will enable us to leave
the explanations of the dark threads till heaven. This faith will help us to
rejoice and to enjoy our lives.

To everything there is a season: a time for this and a time for that.
There is a time to ask God to put eternity in your heart—now! Ask him.

TO READ: *Ecclesiastes 3:14-22*

A HYMN CALLED "FOREVER"

And I know that whatever God does is final. Nothing can be added to it or taken from it. God's purpose in this is that people should fear him.

ECCLESIASTES 3:14

God made man, and as Derek Kidner said in his book *A Time to Mourn and a Time to Dance*, "God has no abortive enterprises or forgotten men!"

God did not make the world, throw it into space, and then wonder where it went and what was happening to it. "Whatever God does is final"! What's more, "Nothing can be added to it."

People, however bright, cannot possibly create another world just like the present one. Whatever we can do—even of considerable value, wrought with incredible ingenuity—can never "be final" or eternal if we believe only in the now. If we are earthbound in mind and spirit, we cannot comprehend a God who foreknows all and overlooks nothing.

The frustration and emptiness of doing things that are only for now must lead some honest people to ask questions. What joy to tell the seeker that whatever God does is final and lasts forever.

He forgives me—that's final and it lasts forever. He will not suddenly change his mind. He loves me forever, and he changes me forever, refusing to let me jettison my preparation for life in another dimension. He gives me family who are forever: a forever husband, two forever sons, and a forever daughter. He sends me forever friends and helps me engage in forever pursuits.

Final and forever have already forgotten now. They linger for eternity; their joys expand, filling the universe, singing a hymn.

TO READ: *Ecclesiastes 6:1-9*

"IF ONLY" DREAMS

Enjoy what you have rather than desiring what you don't have. Just dreaming about nice things is meaningless; it is like chasing the wind.

ECCLESIASTES 6:9

Solomon, king of Israel and author of the book of Ecclesiastes, had a reputation for wisdom. He advised people to be content and to receive their daily life from God's hand. Complaining leads to frustration. In this book Solomon, the teacher, explains that although people cannot discover the whole plan of God for their life, they can still be obedient to what they already *know* is his will (Ecclesiastes 3:9-13). One part of God's will is that we live a lifestyle of contentment with what he has graciously given us—no matter how much or how little.

Being able to enjoy what you have involves thinking about how you can make the most of it. If we would put our time and energy into enjoying what we have instead of dreaming "if only" dreams, we would find the potential for laughter, social interaction, and happiness right under our nose.

I have seen people all over the world playing games with their children with sticks, stones, plants and flowers, sand and rocks, food and drink, and simple cardboard boxes. In our Western culture, parents have an uphill battle to focus on the present realities, to creatively explore their children's potential, and to refuse to join the world in "keeping up with the Joneses." This is not an easy task, but the Lord wants to help us. So take the Teacher's advice: "Enjoy what you have rather than desiring what you don't have. Just dreaming about nice things is meaningless; it is like chasing the wind" (Ecclesiastes 6:9).

TO READ: *Song of Songs 2:8–17*

LITTLE FOXES

*"Quick! Catch all the little foxes before they ruin the vineyard of your love,
for the grapevines are all in blossom."*

SONG OF SONGS 2:15

This picture describes the love of the couple as a "vineyard." It also describes the "little foxes" that would come in and "ruin the vineyard" of their love.

Our life is like a vineyard, of which God is the caretaker. Within the heart of repentant men and women, the Caretaker plants his choicest vine, Jesus. But the devil, God's enemy, sends his little foxes into the vineyard to spoil the fruit of the vine. In my experience, it has usually been the "little foxes" that have caused the most damage to my Christian testimony. Big adversaries like a bear are easy to see, but little foxes are harder to find! There are the little foxes of lying, slander, laziness, and selfishness. When the foxes get in, they spoil the fruit that God is trying to grow in our life. We need to "catch all the little foxes before they ruin the vineyard" (Song of Songs 2:15).

So what are some of these little foxes in the vineyard in our life? We must ask God to help us live in reality, willing to admit that the little foxes ruin our love for God and for other people.

We must remember that the Caretaker is in his tower, helping watch out for the foxes. Ask him to help you catch the little foxes that threaten your vineyard. When the fruit of the vine is preserved, the Owner of the vineyard is glorified!

TO READ: *Isaiah 1:1–19*

DOUBLE-DYED

"Come now, let us argue this out," says the LORD. *"No matter how deep the stain of your sins, I can remove it. I can make you as clean as freshly fallen snow. Even if you are stained as red as crimson, I can make you as white as wool."*

ISAIAH 1:18

I saiah was a great prophet. His messages brought comfort to the few among God's people who were true believers. He constantly reminded them of the "covenant of grace." At the same time, he brought a message of severe warning to those who refused to listen to the doctrine of life. When the Lord called his rebellious people to "argue this out," he did not call them to debate, but rather to agree with his verdict. He wanted them to acknowledge that their actions had not been in accordance with reason.

All sin is unreasonable. The people's sin is described as a deep stain (other versions say "scarlet," a red stain that we know is difficult to remove). This contrasts to the stark whiteness of snow. When yarns were dyed scarlet (or crimson) in biblical times, the process required two baths or double-dyeing. When Christ forgave my sin, I was very conscious that grace invited not a dialogue but a reasonable confession of the "double-dyed" mess I had made of my life. God wanted me to agree with his verdict and submit to his decision concerning my sin. I felt like a small sheep whose wool had been dyed crimson by wrongdoing, and I was pretty red-faced about it all.

What joy to enter the "covenant of grace" and experience the whiteness of the soul that coming to God brings! Have you come to the point of accepting God's verdict of your life, or are you still arguing your case?

TO READ: *Isaiah 5:1-7*

SOUR GRAPES

"What more could I have done to cultivate a rich harvest?
Why did my vineyard give me wild grapes when I expected sweet ones?"

ISAIAH 5:4

In this poem, Israel is likened to a vineyard—a metaphor frequently used by the prophets. The song reminded God's people of the love and benefits bestowed upon them.

Israel had the favorable position on a "rich and fertile hill" (Isaiah 5:1) and a watchtower for protection. Despite God's careful tending, however, the vineyard produced sour grapes. "What more could I have done?" Yahweh cried.

Our life is like a vineyard. Believers in the Western world have been hedged about; we live in the most fruitful hills. What is more, we have the presence of the Holy Spirit protecting us, like the tower in the vineyard. God is carefully tending us. He rightly expects sweet fruit from our life, so why do we so often produce sour grapes?

Do you have an acid spirit? Perhaps you have been soured by the broken promises of a friend. Maybe someone has been promoted over your head who, in your opinion, can't do the job as well as you can. Maybe things have happened in your life that make you feel justified in being sour. You would be wrong.

Why do you imagine the Gardener came into your life—to attend to your whims and caprices or to prune your life for spiritual fruitfulness? When God asks, "Why the sour grapes?" he expects an answer, but you probably won't have a good one. Let God prune what he needs to prune in order to help your character "sweeten up" for him.

TO READ: *Isaiah 6:1-13*

HAPPINESS IN HOLINESS

*In the year King Uzziah died, I saw the Lord. He was sitting on a
lofty throne, and the train of his robe filled the Temple.*

ISAIAH 6:1

G od told Moses, "You may not look directly at my face, for no one may
see me and live" (Exodus 33:20). No one can look at God and live
because God is so holy and we are so unholy. Yet Jesus said that "God
blesses those whose hearts are pure, for they will see God" (Matthew 5:8).
We will "see" God when our hearts are pure, but how does that happen?

In a vision, Isaiah saw the holiness of God. Such a realization of the
Lord's holiness brought about a searing awareness of his own sinfulness.

Whenever we see God's holiness with the eyes of faith, we will find
ourselves reacting as the prophet Isaiah did. Yet as soon as we verbalize
this sense of our own sinfulness, God will move in to clean us up.

The very "holiest" of Christian people sin. It will be so until we get to
heaven. The woman who is ready for God to cleanse her, however, is the
woman God can use (Isaiah 6:8).

Even though the great prophet Isaiah was a holy man, he needed
God's cleansing in order to see God aright and see what God wanted him
to do. There is happiness in holiness. Cleansing and contentment go
together.

The only way to keep our heart pure is to constantly turn to God for
forgiveness and cleansing. That makes us "holy" in his eyes. Being holy
brings a holy happiness only God can offer. We need to take him up on it.

TO READ: *Isaiah 6:1-13*

WORSHIP

In a great chorus they sang, "Holy, holy, holy is the LORD Almighty! The whole earth is filled with his glory!" The glorious singing shook the Temple to its foundations, and the entire sanctuary was filled with smoke.

ISAIAH 6:3-4

T he temple shook at the voice of him who cried. I used to think that this verse referred to God, but then I realized the text reveals it is the voice of the angel that shakes heaven. If such a tumult occurs at the voice of an angel, whatever will happen when God himself speaks?

We take the privilege of worship far too lightly. We get too chummy with God, or try to bring him down to our level. A friend he is—but an almighty Friend, a holy Friend. As we come to understand his ineffable nature, we shall be saved from irreverent attitudes in prayer. And yet he encourages us to "come boldly to the throne of our gracious God. There we will receive his mercy, and we will find grace to help us when we need it" (Hebrews 4:16). It is because Jesus our Advocate is at the right hand of God that we dare to come boldly before his throne.

When God's angels acknowledged God's Person and attributed worth to him, "the entire sanctuary was filled with smoke." This undoubtedly refers to the *shekinah* glory—the presence of God made manifest. So when you and I attribute worth to God in worship, heaven is moved and God will show himself—if not to the world, certainly to the worshiper. The awesome reality of God may cause us fear, as it did Isaiah, but it hopefully will lead us to submission and a deep desire to serve our lost world.

TO READ: *Isaiah 6:1-13*

LIPS OF TRUTH

*Then one of the seraphim flew over to the altar, and he picked up a burning
coal with a pair of tongs. He touched my lips with it and said,
"See, this coal has touched your lips. Now your guilt is removed,
and your sins are forgiven."*

ISAIAH 6:6-7

When we have a vision of God, we get a true look at ourselves. "My
destruction is sealed!" we say. Seeing him looking at me makes me
aware of the blemishes in my character. When I see the Lord, I see the
world, too. I stop saying, "Here am I, send somebody else," and I start
saying, "Lord, I'll go! Send me." He then equips me by cleansing me for
service. What I say will burn its way into people's thoughts and bring
them to the point of deciding for or against God.

"But whom do I talk to?" you may ask. "How am I expected to know
who needs God's message?" God told Isaiah what to tell "these people."
"These people" were the same people Isaiah had been preaching to for a
long, long time. He had been getting discouraged because they hadn't
responded, but God sent his prophet right back to tell them all over again.
What was more, the Lord told Isaiah that they still wouldn't listen! But
that was not to be his concern.

How do you keep going when all your effort seems futile? You'll
need time to get a fresh vision of God—which will give you a fresh vision
of yourself, a new look at your world, and a new concern in your heart.
Then you'll be able to go back to rebellious people and see a difference.
Not in them, perhaps, but certainly in you! You'll find you have the
capacity to be faithful without having to see the results.

TO READ: *Isaiah 9:1-7*

LIGHT AT THE END
OF THE TUNNEL

*The people who walk in darkness will see a great light—a light that will
shine on all who live in the land where death casts its shadow.*

ISAIAH 9:2

A re you in need of a glimmer of light at the end of the tunnel? Isaiah
promises that even in darkness, even in death itself, there is good
ground for hope. The power of God is able to restore life to his people
even when they appear already dead!

What is that great light? It is the Savior, Jesus Christ. This prediction
was fulfilled by Christ's coming (Matthew 4:16). The light of Christ
brought the promise of deliverance for Israel. A new day had come!

The Savior is a great light in the darkness to us as well. Maybe you live
in the darkness of divorce or in the shadow of death. Some of you may be
watching a loved one slowly disintegrate before your eyes. Perhaps you have
given up seeing any light in a dark family or church situation. Others, in
seemingly perfect circumstances, live in the deepest darkness of all—
depression that nothing seems to penetrate! Listen to the Good News!
There's light at the end of the tunnel—look up and see Jesus standing there!
Hear what he says: "I am the light of the world. If you follow me, you won't
be stumbling through the darkness, because you will have the light that
leads to life" (John 8:12).

The Word of God penetrates the darkness of our soul. It's as if God
penetrates the darkness with his inescapable light. Ask God to penetrate
your tunnel of darkness with his glorious light.

THE KEY TO BLESSING

For a child is born to us, a son is given to us. And the government will rest on his shoulders. These will be his royal titles: Wonderful Counselor, Mighty God, Everlasting Father, Prince of Peace.

ISAIAH 9:6

T he image in this verse reflects the custom of carrying long, heavy, frequently used keys over the shoulder. The symbolism is extensive. The very act says "authority"! The priest who exercised such authority had command of the royal chambers and a right to admit or refuse people to the royal presence. John, in Revelation 3:7, describes the risen, ascended, glorified Lord Jesus as our High Priest: "He is the one who has the key of David. He opens doors, and no one can shut them; he shuts doors, and no one can open them."

God invested all priestly authority in Jesus Christ, his Son. It is Jesus who has the keys! The government is upon his shoulders!

And what does all this mean to you and me? It means Jesus Christ has command of God's royal chambers—and the right to admit us into God's presence. That is why Hebrews 4:16 says, "So let us come boldly to the throne of our gracious God. There we will receive his mercy, and we will find grace to help us when we need it."

The Scriptures say we have a high priest (Hebrews 4:14). You can know you have such a high priest if he "has" you! Has he forgiven your sin? If not, he has the right to refuse your entrance to the King's chambers; but if so, then you can be assured that when you draw near to the throne, there will be grace to help.

TO READ: *Isaiah 27:2-13*

FRESH FRUIT

The time is coming when my people will take root. Israel will
bud and blossom and fill the whole earth with her fruit!

ISAIAH 27:6

After fencing his vineyard, Yahweh did everything necessary to ensure good fruit, including planting the fertile soil with "choice vines" (Isaiah 5:2). But God's chosen ones became a wild vine; because Israel did not obey (Isaiah 5:5-6). But God also promised that he would preserve the few who believed. From the remnant of faithful people would come the choicest of vines—Jesus Christ. The Savior used this vineyard metaphor in the Gospels, saying, "I am the true vine, and my Father is the gardener" (John 15:1).

Do you realize you have been grafted into the choicest vine? Jesus is the Vine, and you are a cherished branch. His Father is your Father and mine—the Gardener. The fruit of his Spirit (Galatians 5:22-23) will grow within us as we let Christ fill us. When we abide in the Vine, God develops his character in us by pruning, tending, feeding, watering, and nurturing us so that we, in turn, may care for others. It is not always pleasant to be pruned, but it is necessary. Sometimes God prunes our life by cutting "deadwood" out of us—the deadwood of wrong relationships, an evil habit, or even sheer laziness. Once he is finished with his pruning, the buds and blossoms can flourish and bear fruit. Fruit hangs on the outside of the tree—displaying the tree's nature, enhancing the tree's beauty, and refreshing those who partake of it. When we are inwardly submissive, we are outwardly obedient—and a hungry world is glad!

TO READ: *Isaiah 29:1-24*

THE POTTER
AND THE CLAY

How stupid can you be? He is the potter, and he is certainly greater
than you. You are only the jars he makes! Should the thing that was created
say to the one who made it, "He didn't make us"? Does a jar ever say,
"The potter who made me is stupid"?

ISAIAH 29:16

The disciples had turned the world "upside down" (Acts 17:6). Yet,
they actually had turned it right side up! People who know Jesus do
that. People who don't know Jesus, however, may be described as pots
that turn themselves upside down on the potter's wheel and tell the potter
to take his hands off their lives.

A disciple personally knows the potter who molds marred lives over
again, keeping one hand inside the pot and the other outside. A disciple
knows that a pot is only as good outside as it is inside. A disciple knows
that to function she will have to be fired in the kiln. The number of firings
depends on how the pot will be used, but the good potter watches the
clay carefully. When the color comes up, the potter removes the pot from
the fire. He will not leave it in the heat to be cracked and ruined.

Disciples have a wonderful relationship with God through Christ, a
relationship as close as an earthly potter has to his clay. Don't turn yourself
upside down on the wheel; let him turn you right side up. Once we allow
the potter to mold us as he desires, we will begin to have a sense of destiny
about our life. He takes his time making a work of art. Our part is to be still
and let him finish his work. We let him turn us right side up so we can go
out and turn our world upside down for him!

TO READ: Isaiah 32:1-8

A SHELTER
AGAINST THE STORM

Look, a righteous king is coming! And honest princes will rule
under him. He will shelter Israel from the storm and the wind.
He will refresh her as a river in the desert and as
the cool shadow of a large rock in a hot and weary land.

ISAIAH 32:1-2

This passage is an oracle about the coming King. It speaks of his own
qualities given by the Spirit of the Lord, but also speaks of the same
Spirit in the character of the King's subjects.

If the King be king of my life, then I shall be a shelter from the wind.
In his strength, I can stand in the middle and be a shelter for those who
need to get out of the storm for a while.

Do you know anybody against whom the stormy gales of adversity
are raging? Do you have a friend who needs you to be her shelter for
awhile against the howling winds that rage around her? I think of a friend
whose husband will not speak to her. Her children are hostile. She knows
and loves the Lord, but she lives alone in a house full of strangers who
have but one thing in common—their name.

Since no one speaks to her, she desperately needs someone to talk
to. When we meet each other, we stop to chat or take time out for a cup
of coffee. Occasionally, I meet her husband, and he talks to me. More
accurately, he talks *at* me. Somehow he feels better once he's unloaded,
and he goes home to his wife and asks her to pass the sugar at breakfast!
Now, that's progress, and she calls me to rejoice. I have been a shelter, a
windbreak, and I am glad!

TO READ: *Isaiah 32:1-8*

A REFRESHING RIVER IN THE DESERT

He will shelter Israel from the storm and the wind.
He will refresh her as a river in the desert and as the cool shadow
of a large rock in a hot and weary land.

ISAIAH 32:2

A river in the desert. What could be more desirable?
When we think of water, we think of the Holy Spirit. Jesus said
that "the water I give them takes away thirst altogether. It becomes a
perpetual spring within them, giving them eternal life" (John 4:14). He
also said, "If you are thirsty, come to me! If you believe in me, come and
drink! For the Scriptures declare that rivers of living water will flow out
from within" (John 7:37-38). By this, he meant the Spirit.

In myself, if Christ by his Spirit does not live in me, I have no power
to refresh people who thirst inwardly for eternal things. But if he does
indeed live within my heart, I can become a river in the desert, bringing
the water of life to those who are thirsty.

When I first came to Christ and had my own needs met and my
inner thirst satisfied, I realized my friends were thirsty too. I prayed I
would become a river.

One of my best friends asked me to play tennis. She knew something
had happened to me and was curious. In between "love-fifteen" and
"love-thirty," she asked me to explain my new satisfaction. I had the great
joy of diverting some of the living water over her! Before we got to game
point, Jesus had won, and she was as drenched with delight as I was. She
was well on the way to becoming a refreshing river too!

TO READ: *Isaiah 32:1-8*

A COOL SHADOW
IN A HOT LAND

He will shelter Israel from the storm and the wind.
He will refresh her as a river in the desert and as the
cool shadow of a large rock in a hot and weary land.

ISAIAH 32:2

Not only can I be a shelter and a river, I can be like a large rock casting a cool shadow—a solid piece of permanence rising up out of a weary land. Notice I said "like" a large rock. God is the Rock. David told the Lord he loved him for his rocklike qualities (Psalm 18:1-2). He knew he could rely on God's rocklike permanence, eternal strength, and stability as a refuge for his frail human nature.

This was a favorite theme of the king. David lived much of his life in the rocks of the Holy Land. When he was chased by his enemies, he knew what it was to run into the crevasses and caves and find shelter there. He could always rely on the caves being in exactly the same place he had left them! They seemed to be eternally reliable.

"I love you, LORD; you are my strength," sang David. "The LORD is my rock, my fortress, and my savior; my God is my rock, in whom I find protection" (Psalm 18:1-2). We all need such a wall of permanence in our lives. We need to lean back and find the granite firm against our backs. Sometimes we need to find a crevasse in the rock and hide ourselves from our enemies.

The prophet Isaiah tells us when our Rock is King, we become like a shadow of the Rock to others. Do others look at you and me and see us as shadows of our Rock within the weary land?

TO READ: *Isaiah 35:1-10*

DO AS I DO

With this news, strengthen those who have tired hands,
and encourage those who have weak knees. Say to those who are afraid,
"Be strong, and do not fear, for your God is coming to destroy your enemies.
He is coming to save you."
ISAIAH 35:3-4

We have great news to share, but we can't do it well if we have tired hands and weak knees. If we are to be strong as we share with others, we must daily be allowing God to strengthen us. It's the easiest thing in the world to say, "Do as I say, and not as I do!"

My schedule of speaking engagements is full. I spend much time preparing my messages. It's hard sometimes to make sure it is my own before it becomes anyone else's. If the water has not flowed over me, I will not see it flow over others.

I had been preparing a message on prayer. I had a good outline: three points—all beginning with the same letter so that people could remember them; some excellent illustrations to let some light into the structure of the talk; and, of course, lots of Scripture passages. I wanted very much for the ladies to get the point.

As I put the finishing touches on my talk, I glanced at the clock. It was very late, and my family was long since in bed and asleep. I tumbled into bed, and then tumbled out again! I had almost forgotten the water needed to flow over me before I could be a watershed for others! I needed to pray! Are you telling people to do as you say, or to do as you do?

TO READ: *Isaiah 40:18–31*

THE DISCIPLINE
OF DROPPING THINGS

But those who wait on the LORD *will find new strength.*
They will fly high on wings like eagles. They will run and not grow weary.
They will walk and not faint.

ISAIAH 40:31

When I begin to "wait" on the Lord, the difference will be felt deep down within me. He will do "a new thing" inside, while the old things outside remain the same. There *will* be a difference! But I shall need to learn the discipline of dropping things from my busy schedule. I will not get all accomplished in a day. Some *important* tasks will not get done, because the *all-important* must.

But I *will* meet with you, my God! You and I shall talk together. Then you will tell me not to dwell upon the past—to forget the former things. You will make a way in the desert and pour streams into the wasteland. You will give my thirsty soul a drink! As I learn to listen to the heartbeat of your soul, you will help me to rejoice. We will talk about our children, and I shall draw courage from your promises to Israel. I will hear you say, "I will pour out my Spirit and my blessings on your children" (Isaiah 44:3).

Yes, there will be a difference when I wait—not a change of circumstance without, but certainly a change of attitude within. Dropping the lesser to pick up the greater must become a daily habit, a question of necessity, not choice. A life like the one awaiting us in heaven. If I will but wait upon the Lord, then other things will have to wait. My schedule will not be my master, but my slave. Time is for choosing to take time—to make time—for eternal things.

TO READ: *Isaiah 40:18-31*

WEARY WOMEN

But those who wait on the LORD will find new strength.
They will fly high on wings like eagles. They will run and not grow weary.
They will walk and not faint.

ISAIAH 40:31

Weary women everywhere! I see them, I listen to them, I look into their tired eyes and wonder how they became so "wearied out" in the first place. Life has surely pounded some of them right into the ground! To others life has apparently been good, but still a weariness invades their personalities.

In the Bible the unweary God speaks to the point, telling us that "even youths will become exhausted" (Isaiah 40:30). The Creator, who is never weary, invites the wearied ones to spend time in his presence; to bathe in the atmosphere of eternal strength; to drink in the air of his power-giving presence—to "wait" long enough to renew their lives. God will mend our raw nerve endings with the stitches of his peace. God's promise to those who look to him for such renewal is that they will not be shamed (Isaiah 49:23).

Are you weary of your weariness? Wouldn't you like to rise above it? Have confidence in the Lord, who can help you soar on wings like the eagle! Start "waiting" today. You can wait on the Lord anytime, anywhere. You can stop internally even as you are busy externally. You can wait on the Lord in a car, in the supermarket, at the playground, or in a meeting. When you feel almost too weary to flap your wings one more time, try "waiting." Soon you'll be competing with the eagle—and soaring high.

TO READ: *Isaiah 42:1–17*

CHOSEN AND PRECIOUS

"Look at my servant, whom I strengthen. He is my chosen one,
and I am pleased with him. I have put my Spirit upon him.
He will reveal justice to the nations."

ISAIAH 42:1

I saiah may have wondered about the identity of this servant. Some say
Isaiah was writing of the Jewish people in exile; some say the prophets.
Others say the servant was Cyrus, king of Persia, whom the Scriptures
acknowledge as an instrument used by God on Israel's behalf (Isaiah 45:1).

However, most commentators agree that the role of the servant in this
verse is fulfilled in Jesus Christ. The servant is described as upheld by God
even while God lays a charge upon him, as masters do with faithful
servants. Christ is elected for the service to which he came, and he dwells
deeply in God's love. Peter describes Christ Jesus as a chosen cornerstone of
God's building (1 Peter 2:6-7). "This is my beloved Son," God announced
at Jesus' baptism (Matthew 3:17). "He is precious to God who chose him,"
Peter wrote (1 Peter 2:4).

Is God's servant, Jesus Christ, precious to you? Or is he merely a
name in a book, a founder of a church, a historical character, or a nice
idea? If Jesus is chosen and precious to God, then it follows that he
should be chosen and precious to you.

How personal is your relationship with Jesus Christ? You can't have
a relationship with God without first loving Jesus, who is "the way"
(John 14:6). Once you begin such a relationship, you will spend the rest
of your life realizing that you too are chosen and precious to God. What
a wonderful way to live!

TO READ: *Isaiah 42:1-17*

BRUISED BUT
NEVER BROKEN

"He will not crush those who are weak or quench the smallest hope.
He will bring full justice to all who have been wronged."

ISAIAH 42:3

Y ou would think that the bruises that the Savior endured on earth
would have crushed the spirit right out of him. But God helped him.
"Look at my servant, whom I strengthen," he said (Isaiah 42:1). The Lord
will not allow the weak to be crushed or the smallest hope to be quenched.

There is no question about it. On the cross, our Savior was bruised
and battered beyond measure, and his light was almost extinguished by
the deluge of our sin, but he was never broken beyond mending. What a
tender word this is!

One version translates this verse, "A bruised reed he will not break"
(42:3, NIV). The reed or dalamus plant has a hollow stem and grows by the
sides of lakes and rivers. It was used for making music or fashioned into
pens for writing. It is weak, fragile, and brittle. It is easily snapped by the
foot of a wild beast, by the wind, or even by a bird that lights upon it.
Once it is broken it is of no use whatsoever. Other stems can be mended,
but not the reed. Jesus was bruised but never broken. God looked at his
precious, bruised One and said, "I must mend this reed. It was meant for
music!"

Are you bruised? Do you feel like your hope has been quenched?
Listen to the promise of God: "Never crushed or quenched." Dare to
believe it!

TO READ: *Isaiah 42:1–17*

THE DEATH OF DISCOURAGEMENT

"I, the LORD, have called you to demonstrate my righteousness.
I will guard and support you, for I have given you to my people
as the personal confirmation of my covenant with them.
And you will be a light to guide all nations to me."

ISAIAH 42:6

The Lord promises to direct his servant, to be his protector and keeper, sharing his presence in all things. "I will guard and support you," God promises.

There must have been many wearisome days when Jesus of Nazareth, the servant of the Lord, thought of those words. Did he recite: "He will not stop until truth and righteousness prevail throughout the earth" (Isaiah 42:4), as he wrestled with ornery disciples, rebuked pious Pharisees, or dealt with the rank unbelief of the people? When the process was slow and the days were long, Jesus Christ experienced the immediate assistance of God. And so may we!

We, too, are his servants. If we have been born from above, we are dressed in his Spirit. We, too, must bring a right answer to a wrong world, and we, too, can know he will guard and support us, and give us his immediate assistance in the face of frustration and persecution.

If Christ is not discouraged, knowing his kingdom has come in the hearts of people and will one day come universally, then we need not be discouraged either. God gave Jesus his "personal confirmation of [his] covenant with them. And you will be a light to guide all nations to me" (Isaiah 42:6). The word *covenant* means "promise." God promised us light in place of darkness. He promised that prisoners would be set free (Isaiah 42:7). The death of discouragement and true spiritual freedom begin here and now for the Lord's servants!

WINGED WORDS

The Sovereign LORD *has given me his words of wisdom, so that I know what to say to all these weary ones. Morning by morning he wakens me and opens my understanding to his will.*

ISAIAH 50:4

Isaiah spoke of the Christ who would come to earth with the "know-how" to wing his words into the hearts of the weary. As his Father had taught him, so would he speak.

When Christ was about to leave this world, he promised to send the same Spirit of truth that indwelt him to indwell us. This way we, too, could have the "know-how" to speak a word to the weary at the right time and in the right way. Our part would be to waken morning by morning "to hear" what he has to say and to "be open" to understanding his will! Then we would be ready for anything and anybody.

You and I are promised the "know-how" to answer a hostile teenager, even if we haven't had time to read a book on child rearing or pick up the phone to ask a friend's advice! We will discover that we can cope with an unbeliever's questions, however young we may be as Christians. We will find that the Christ within us will make our tongue know what to say to the weary ones around us, seasoned words that will help to ease their sufferings. In Christ we are promised both the "know-how" and the "know-when" that we cannot possibly know without him!

TO READ: *Isaiah 53:1–12*

SATISFACTION

When he sees all that is accomplished by his anguish, he will be satisfied.
And because of what he has experienced, my righteous servant will make it
possible for many to be counted righteous, for he will bear all their sins.

ISAIAH 53:11

The scriptures tell us that Jesus found satisfaction *after* his sufferings. For some of us it will be the same. Death, which has been described as the last step of faith, will see us through the door to daylight's delight. Satisfaction, as the world understands it, may never come to some of us in this life. But one day *after* it is over, we will be met with the Savior's "Well done," and we will be satisfied.

What is satisfaction? Hollywood insists that it includes "beauty" and must be pursued by all means and to all ends. We are asked to believe that to be truly satisfied with ourselves we must be truly beautiful. Yet in Isaiah 53, we read about Jesus: "There was nothing beautiful or majestic about his appearance, nothing to attract us to him" (Isaiah 53:2). Apparently, in God's value system, appearance is not all that important! It's what people *do* because of who they *are* that matters in the highest place, not how they dress it up or paint it on. Jesus, contrary to popular opinion in his day, was a divine success and gained satisfaction from knowing that "the LORD's plan will prosper in his hands" (Isaiah 53:10).

The one who concentrates on pleasing him *before* death discovers that after the crushing and the cross there will be the crown! *So be it.*

TO READ: *Isaiah 55:1-13*

HEART HUNGER

"Why spend your money on food that does not give you strength?
Why pay for food that does you no good? Listen, and I will tell you
where to get food that is good for the soul!"

ISAIAH 55:2

Isaiah echoes an invitation repeated often by God's messengers throughout the Bible. The nation of Israel had been wandering from the Lord.
But God, in his mercy, called the people back to him. God continues to call
us, offering "soul food"—food that nourishes us spiritually. But notice the
words in these verses: *come, listen, seek,* and *call* on him. God will not force-
feed us, but he gladly provides what we need when we come to him.

Jesus said, "God blesses you who are hungry now, for you will be
satisfied" (Luke 6:21). A true disciple of Jesus Christ experiences a gnawing
hunger to know him better and a spiritual thirst that can only be quenched
by staying close to him. Those who never need him will never truly know
him. But those who humbly come, hungry to know him better, will be
satisfied.

In the last invitation to humankind in the Scriptures, the same
invitation is given. "The Spirit and the bride say, 'Come.' Let each one who
hears them say, 'Come.' Let the thirsty ones come—anyone who wants to.
Let them come and drink the water of life without charge" (Revelation
22:17). The invitation is offered to everyone—it is open to all.

If you do not yet know the Lord, but you are hungry and thirsty, you
have come to the right place—his Word. Where is your hunger fed and
your thirst assuaged? At Jesus' feet! Come, eat and drink.

TO READ: *Isaiah 61:1–11*

NEW CLOTHES

*To all who mourn in Israel, he will give beauty for ashes, joy instead of
mourning, praise instead of despair. For the LORD has planted them
like strong and graceful oaks for his own glory.*

ISAIAH 61:3

Acertain situation arose in my life that caused me to go to bed in
"despair" and to awaken feeling as if I had not slept at all. I can only
describe the experience as a "spirit of heaviness." I walked bowed down
under the weight of my problem.

Then I came upon Isaiah 61:3. What a promise! He would give me
"joy instead of mourning" and "praise instead of despair"! But how? A
change of attitude was surely necessary, but the heaviness I felt had
seemingly robbed me of the strength to even try!

Examining the burden I was carrying, I recognized that *I* had picked
it up and put it on myself. The burden was weighing me down, binding
up my movements, making me unable to function, keeping me from
reaching out and touching people.

The problem had to do with a fellow Christian—someone I had
loved, but now had almost come to hate! Victory gained on my knees
would dissipate immediately upon sight of this person! The enemy would
come in like a flood and almost drop the burden back on me, weighing
me down once again. Praise to God for coming along and trading the
burden for a load of joy.

If we will allow God to place on us a load of joy and praise, we will
begin to sing again; and others, who are also carrying burdens, will listen
to our song!

TO READ: *Isaiah 40:11; 46:4; 53:4; 63:9*

CARRIED

In all their suffering he also suffered, and he personally rescued them.
In his love and mercy he redeemed them. He lifted them up
and carried them through all the years.

ISAIAH 63:9

Our compassionate God carries those for whom he cares. He is a
"carrying" God.

At times, we all need to be carried. We may fall behind like little
children whose legs are too weak to keep walking through sand. Other
times, we might be more like lambs that persist in straying from the
shepherd and risk falling prey to enemies.

God always promises to carry us—even until our old age (Isaiah
46:4). But it costs to carry. In order for Jesus to carry our sins, he first had
to carry his cross (John 19:17). Jesus carried that cross for us.

Perhaps you can be Jesus' arms for someone else today—someone
who needs to be carried. Conversion to Christ puts us into a carrying
mode. We can reflect his likeness by carrying one another's burdens. It
will cost to carry, but think of Jesus' example and thank him for never
getting tired of carrying mine.

Not too long ago one of my friends called me to tell me that her
husband had left her. Having just walked through that particular situation
with a close relative, I reacted quite wrongly, thinking, *Not again, Lord—
it's unfair to expect me to do this again!* At once I knew this was one more
personal task he wanted me to pick up. Others could have done it, but
then I would have missed his will for my life in this respect. *You carry me,
Lord,* I prayed, *as I carry her.*

I will, he promised.

TO READ: *Isaiah 64:1–9*

ACCEPTING YOURSELF IS THE KEY TO USEFULNESS

And yet, LORD, you are our Father. We are the clay, and you are the potter.
We are all formed by your hand.

ISAIAH 64:8

Do you want to be useful to God? Maybe you feel that some of your personality characteristics get in the way. However, to serve God you need not change your entire personality. God made you just the way you are and wants you to serve him with who you are.

God wants us to understand that he lovingly made us, and he wants us to accept how he made us. When you become a disciple, God the potter doesn't change *who* you are; instead, he changes *what* you are *without Christ*. The potter won't change your personality—he simply will use who you are to better effect.

Self-acceptance is a key to usefulness for God. When I was eighteen, I became ill and was taken to a hospital. Maureen, the nurse assigned to me, immediately made me worse! She was impatient, rude, and very brusque. Then she became a Christian. God tempered her impatience into swift efficiency and transformed her brusqueness into briskness. She would come back in her spare time and give herself to her patients. All things had become new, although Maureen's basic personality was the same. God did not change who she was but what she had been without Christ.

We can ask the potter who formed us what he has in mind for us. Accept how he made you, and then step back and let him transform you!

THE LONG ROAD
OF OBEDIENCE

*"For my people have done two evil things: They have forsaken me—
the fountain of living water. And they have dug for themselves
cracked cisterns that can hold no water at all!"*
JEREMIAH 2:13

J eremiah spoke the words of the Lord, telling Israel that they were like
cracked cisterns. The water collected in cracked cisterns is often foul
tasting and full of worms. This pictures the people's disobedience and
idolatry. Instead of loving and worshiping their God—their "fountain of
living water"—they turned to worthless idols, in effect digging their own
leaky cisterns.

How do we know if we, like the people of Israel, are guilty of
preferring the cracked cistern over the fountain? It all begins when we
deliberately ignore the word of God in order to do what we want to do.
When what we want to do becomes more important to us than what God
wants us to do, we'll end up with a foul taste in our mouth. D. L. Moody
said about the Bible: "This book will keep you from sin, or sin will keep
you from this book."

To forsake and forget the Lord and his word is an "evil, bitter thing"
(Jeremiah 2:19)—as bitter as the foul waters of so-called satisfaction from
the cisterns we have dug for ourselves. Are you disobeying God—drinking
out of a cracked cistern? Turn back to God and his fountain of living
water; you'll find it on the long road of obedience. Start by responding to
God's invitation to heal your wayward heart (Jeremiah 3:22), and admit
that disobedience is a sin, not just a shortcoming (Jeremiah 3:25). It's a
long road, but God gives refreshment along the way. It's worth the
journey.

JUNE

TO READ: *Jeremiah 11:18-23*

EVEN IN ANATHOTH

The men of Anathoth wanted me dead. They said they would kill me
if I did not stop speaking in the LORD's name.

JEREMIAH 11:21

One of the worst kinds of loneliness is spiritual loneliness. Jeremiah experienced this in his own hometown, Anathoth (Jeremiah 1:1). No one wanted to hear his message. The townsfolk—his neighbors, friends, and even his own family—hated him. He was crushed when he realized that the people closest to him were not about to follow King Josiah's reforms and return to the Lord.

What did Jeremiah do? First, he complained bitterly to God. "Now let me bring you this complaint," he lamented (Jeremiah 12:1). We are allowed to do that, you know. We can tell God what it feels like to be spiritually alone among the people who matter most to us. He understands when we gripe about the wicked getting away without punishment—and even prospering (Jeremiah 12:2-4).

After making his complaint, Jeremiah listened to God—but it wasn't easy! Jeremiah would continue to be an object of scorn and revenge (Jeremiah 12:5-6), but God promised, "I will restore you so you can continue to serve me. . . . I will protect and deliver you" (Jeremiah 15:19-20).

Loneliness can draw us into a deeper commitment to God. There comes a time when the words of the hymn "I Have Decided to Follow Jesus" become our own. We need to say, "Though none go with me, still I will follow. No turning back, no turning back." May we learn that loneliness sometimes is the price we must pay for our faith—even in "Anathoth," our home.

TO READ: *Jeremiah 17:7–10*

THE DECEITFUL HEART

"The human heart is most deceitful and desperately wicked.
Who really knows how bad it is?"

JEREMIAH 17:9

D id you know that we are responsible for our response to temptation? If we believe that, we may not yield quite so quickly, and
certainly we would not want to be a temptation to anyone else. If I sin
in response to someone's tempting me, that's bad; but if I initiate a
temptation and cause both of us to sin, that's even worse!

In the story of David and Bathsheba (2 Samuel 11), David led
Bathsheba into sin. However, when she realized David's intentions, she
might have refused his advances, but she apparently acquiesced. Both
David and Bathsheba were in a tempting situation. There was a chance to
stop, but they did not. It might have helped them to realize what Jeremiah
explained, "The human heart is most deceitful and desperately wicked.
Who really knows how bad it is?" (Jeremiah 17:9).

We women need to be very careful not to get ourselves into such
tempting situations. We also need to be sure not to *be* temptations. Do
we consciously or unconsciously send tempting signals? What messages
do we send with our eyes, our words, our clothing? Those who meet the
opportunity for unfaithfulness know the battle that ensues. They know
they are capable of sin. The marvelous thing about being a Christian is
that at such a time, God says he'll give us the power to say no. Say no to
sending the wrong signals; say no to inappropriate desires; say no to
temptation. You'll never be sorry.

JEHOVAH-TSIDKENU

"For the time is coming," says the LORD, *"when I will place a righteous*
Branch on King David's throne. He will be a King who rules with wisdom.
He will do what is just and right throughout the land. And this is his name:
'The LORD *Is Our Righteousness.' In that day Judah will be saved,*
and Israel will live in safety."

JEREMIAH 23:5-6

Many of us look back to the good old days. But Israel was told by
Jeremiah to look forward to the good new days that lay ahead.
Jehovah himself would provide not only a lamb for an atoning sacrifice,
but a hope for the future. Psychologists tell us people cannot function
without hope. Yet many people today feel a hopelessness that never seems
to go away.

Without Christ there is no hope for the future because he is the future.
God holds the future as surely as he holds the past and the present. He is
working his purposes out. He knows the plans that he has for us: plans of
good and not of disaster. Without God, without Christ, without hope, we
are lost people groping in the dark for some meaning to life.

"The time is coming," says the Lord, when he will provide one who
will put all things in their proper place. Rights will be respected and wrongs
redressed. There will be salvation and security for God's people. This is our
hope. There's a new day coming for the believer.

Jehovah-Tsidkenu gives us that new day, that hope, that future. Do you
feel hopeless? "Hope in God" (Psalm 42:5).

TO READ: *Jeremiah 36:1–32; 45:1–5*

TELLING THE TRUTH TO THOSE WHO LOVE THE LIE

"Are you seeking great things for yourself? Don't do it! But don't be discouraged. I will bring great disaster upon all these people, but I will protect you wherever you go. I, the LORD, have spoken!"

JEREMIAH 45:5

B aruch was a respected scribe (a person who read, wrote, and taught). It may have been tempting to seek great things for himself, since scribes were highly honored in those days. Instead of playing it safe, Baruch continued to bring Jeremiah's words to a nation intent on rejecting the God of those words.

After Baruch recorded God's message, he was sent to read it to the people (Jeremiah 36:5). Baruch bravely read aloud to the public and the officials (Jeremiah 36:10, 13-20). Eventually King Jehoiakim heard the message. As each page was read to him he cut it up with a knife and burned it (Jeremiah 36:23). He wanted to arrest Jeremiah and Baruch, but the Lord hid them (Jeremiah 36:26).

There is a price to pay if we, like Jeremiah and Baruch, want to tell the truth to those who love the lie! The devil will try to distract us, tempting us to seek the world's honor and praise. Perhaps skeptics or persecutors will try to destroy God's word, or maybe a religious scholar's knife will cut it to pieces. But as in Jeremiah's and Baruch's case, God preserved his word (Jeremiah 36:32). Jeremiah and Baruch simply wrote it all over again.

At times we may have to stand and defend God's word and principles to those who do not want to hear it. May we be found in the faithful company of Jeremiah and Baruch, reporting the Lord's words faithfully, whatever the price or people's reactions.

TO READ: *Ezekiel 2:1–10*

BEING AFRAID
OF THEIR ANGRY LOOKS

"Son of man, do not fear them. Don't be afraid even though their threats
are sharp as thorns and barbed like briers, and they sting like scorpions.
Do not be dismayed by their dark scowls. For remember, they are rebels!
You must give them my messages whether they listen or not.
But they won't listen, for they are completely rebellious!"
EZEKIEL 2:6-7

E zekiel was called to an incredibly difficult task. God was sending
Ezekiel "to the nation of Israel, a nation that is rebelling against me.
. . . They are a hard-hearted and stubborn people" (Ezekiel 2:3-4). The
task would be difficult, but Ezekiel served an efficient, able God who
promised to equip him.

Ezekiel faced a dilemma many of us face. He could easily have allowed
the response of people to determine his words and actions. But God clearly
warned him that the recipients' response to Ezekiel's message was not to
govern the nature or manner of his ministry. God told Ezekiel to be strong
and not react in fear and discouragement. Ezekiel knew that no one would
listen, but he kept on speaking, leaving the outcome to God.

To whom do you need to speak a message of truth? A spouse, friend,
or relative whom you know will be less than receptive to your words?
What's stopping you? The thought of their "dark scowls," their angry faces?
It's not easy to say what must be said when you are risking alienation or
hostility. It's so much easier to follow a course of "peace at any price."

We need not be dismayed by people's angry looks. God promises to
strengthen us. Obedience to God is the key, not only to overcoming our
fear of people's angry faces but to doing and saying the right thing in the
right way at the right time to the right people!

TO READ: *Ezekiel 8:17-18; 9:1-4; 10:18-19; 11:22-25*

THE FULLNESS OF HIS GLORY

Then the glory of the God of Israel rose up from between the cherubim,
where it had rested, and moved to the entrance of the Temple.

EZEKIEL 9:3

I n the old testament the presence of God was manifested by a cloud that symbolized the fullness of his glory. The cloud of glory—the *Shekinah* of God—had come to live among his people in the Tabernacle (Exodus 40:34) and later in the temple (1 Kings 8:10-11). In Ezekiel, however, there is a graphic warning. In a vision Ezekiel saw God's glory departing from Israel because of the nation's sin (Ezekiel 9:3).

While here on earth Christ showed Peter, James, and John a little glimpse of his glory when he was transfigured before them (Matthew 17:1-6). God's glory becomes part of our life through the Holy Spirit, who takes up residence in us when we accept Christ as our Savior. The Holy Spirit is our assurance that we will share in Christ's glory. But we need to "let the Holy Spirit fill and control" us (Ephesians 5:18). This command is in the present tense, indicating our need to constantly be filled and controlled by the Spirit. Far from being a once-and-for-all act, being filled with the Spirit is an ongoing experience for the believer. As his children, we ought to reflect his glory as we allow God to transform us into his image.

You may be a believer, but are you filled with the fullness of God's glory? Do you even know whether God's glory is present in your life? May the blessing of the fullness of the glory of the Lord be ours! May the fullness of his glory shine out and draw others to him!

TO READ: *Ezekiel 11:14–21*

THE HEART TRANSPLANT

"And I will give them singleness of heart and put a new spirit within them.
I will take away their hearts of stone and give them tender hearts instead."

EZEKIEL 11:19

H ave you ever heard of a person needing a heart transplant and someone still alive saying, "Take mine"? It happened. At the cross, God the Father accepted the heart of his only Son, Jesus Christ, and offered it to a dying world.

The Bible says that we each need a new heart because our human heart is stubborn and rebellious (Jeremiah 5:23), deceitful and wicked (Jeremiah 17:9), and able to turn us away from God (Hebrews 3:12). But God promises "a new heart." God made a promise about this divine transplant. To the believers in Corinth Paul wrote that they were "a letter from Christ . . . written not with pen and ink, but with the Spirit of the living God. It is carved not on stone, but on human hearts" (2 Corinthians 3:3).

If you desire this heart transplant, God promises to give you his heart as your own. Only then can you begin to develop God-honoring character. As we come to him for forgiveness, he has promised to help us live in "moral excellence" (2 Peter 1:5). Such character is impossible apart from the Holy Spirit's work in our new heart. By accepting this new heart, we can "share in his divine nature" (2 Peter 1:4). The heart transplant is only the beginning, but you do need to begin. Do you want godly character? Let God give you a new heart.

TO READ: *Ezekiel 24:15-27*

SURRENDERING TO OBEDIENCE

"Son of man, I am going to take away your dearest treasure.
Suddenly she will die. Yet you must not show any sorrow.
Do not weep; let there be no tears."

EZEKIEL 24:16

E zekiel was ever conscious that his people were caught up in a tragedy of their own making and that he had been called to warn them of the coming consequences of their sin.

Chapter 24 describes the death of Ezekiel's beloved wife. Those whom God calls are often asked to surrender their personal life to obey the call of their public responsibility. So it was for Ezekiel. He was told in advance of his wife's death, but to the rest of the people, her death was sudden and unexpected. God commanded Ezekiel not to weep or mourn out loud in the accustomed way. The day after his wife was taken from him, Ezekiel simply records, "The next morning I did everything I had been told to do" (Ezekiel 24:18). What a night of private anguish he must have suffered! Yet the whole tragedy was an opportunity for God to drive home a startling warning about the lack of grief Israel must soon exhibit when faced with the destruction of their beloved temple and a bleak future. Just as Ezekiel's beloved wife had died suddenly and Ezekiel could not express grief, so the temple—the Jews' dearest possession—would shortly be destroyed, and they would not be able to mourn or weep (Ezekiel 24:20-22).

Personal grief and sorrow in God's hands can result in powerful ministry! We must so surrender to obedience that whatever happens to us, those who are watching us will hear the voice of God speaking to them through us.

THE WEALTH OF FAITH

"Yes, your wisdom has made you very rich,
and your riches have made you very proud."
EZEKIEL 28:5

God addressed the king of Tyre through the prophet Ezekiel. God would bring an army against this king that would bring him "down to the pit" (Ezekiel 28:8). The king of Tyre had wisdom and understanding but had used them for evil and personal gain. Thus God would bring judgment and destruction (Ezekiel 28:4-10).

People tend to attribute all they accumulate and achieve to their own prowess. Rarely do they realize that riches and honor come from God alone, that power and might are in his hand, and that people only become great and strong at his discretion (1 Chronicles 29:12). The problem today is that being very rich and very proud is considered very good, while being very poor and very humble is considered unfortunate. The king of Tyre had "amassed great wealth" (Ezekiel 28:4), but his great wealth filled him with violence (Ezekiel 28:16). In contrast, Jesus, "though he was very rich, yet for your sakes he became poor, so that by his poverty he could make you rich" (2 Corinthians 8:9).

We need to watch carefully how we use the gifts God has given us. He has bestowed them on us in free grace for our good and for eternal, not earthly, gain! "Hasn't God chosen the poor in this world to be rich in faith?" (James 2:5). The wealth of faith is the only wealth that lasts for eternity.

WHEN YOU DON'T WANT TO LISTEN

"Son of man, describe to the people of Israel the Temple I have shown you.
Tell them its appearance and its plan so they
will be ashamed of all their sins."
EZEKIEL 43:10

God's voice can humble us, stand us up, and strengthen us to hear more. A glimpse of his glory puts us on our face; a touch of his Spirit sets us on our feet. Only then are we ready to hear his voice. We must be prepared to hear his voice because what we hear when the voice speaks may not always be what we expect or want to hear!

Ezekiel was told that his life would be hard and his ministry unappreciated (Ezekiel 2:6-7). God made him a watchman over people who didn't want watching! Over and over, God told Ezekiel to deliver laments and dire messages of doom: "Sing this funeral song for the princes of Israel" (Ezekiel 19:1), and "Prophesy against the shepherds, the leaders of Israel" (Ezekiel 34:2). These strong words were for leaders and kings as well as Ezekiel's peers. Then Ezekiel was told to speak to the people about the temple "so they will be ashamed of all their sins" (Ezekiel 43:10). Why? Because God required "absolute holiness" in his temple (Ezekiel 43:12). God's words were meant to shame the people. The people didn't want to hear what God had to say, but they surely needed to.

Are you sure you want to hear God's voice? Are you willing to face what God may say to you? God wants you to listen to his words.

TO READ: *Ezekiel 47:1-12*

THE WATER OF LIFE

"Everything that touches the water of this river will live.
Fish will abound in the Dead Sea, for its waters will be healed.
Wherever this water flows, everything will live."
EZEKIEL 47:9

The prophet Ezekiel pictures the nation of Israel not only receiving the spiritual blessings God would bring them in the future but also passing on those blessings to the whole world. God is the source of this plenteous river of blessing. The stream of life flows out from the heavenly sanctuary, and God promises that "everything that touches the water of this river will live" (Ezekiel 47:9). John recorded the same vision in Revelation 22:1-2: "The angel showed me a pure river with the water of life, clear as crystal, flowing from the throne of God and of the Lamb."

Jesus also spoke of rivers of living water that flow out of our heart when he, the source of that "water," lives in us (John 7:37-39). Jesus is the source of our life! When I realize that the river of God flows in and through me, and that "wherever this water flows, everything will live" (Ezekiel 47:9), I want to make sure no sin dams up the flow, no worldliness pollutes the life-giving water, and no selfishness diverts the water for my own personal use! I could divert that water by worrying instead of trusting, losing my temper instead of being more patient, or straying instead of praying. Instead, I desire to be a channel of God's refreshment wherever I go.

God's power transforms us, and through us, he can bless others. Are you a life-giving stream, bringing joy to all who know you? Once you've been refreshed by God, let him refresh others through you!

TO READ: *Daniel 1:1–21*

MAKING UP YOUR MIND

*But Daniel made up his mind not to defile himself by eating the food
and wine given to them by the king. He asked the chief official
for permission to eat other things instead.*

DANIEL 1:8

D aniel had been taken captive to Babylon. He was chosen among other strong and healthy young Israelite men to serve in the royal palace and to be prepared for leadership in Nebuchadnezzar's kingdom. What an opportunity for Daniel to take advantage of his position and comply with all the orders he was given. After all, he was being groomed for greatness. Daniel and the other trainees were given "a daily ration of the best food and wine" from the king's kitchens (Daniel 1:5). So why would Daniel jeopardize his career by refusing to eat the food offered by the king? Daniel took this extraordinary action because he had "made up his mind not to defile himself by eating the food and wine given to them by the king" (Daniel 1:8). Daniel's reasoning is unknown, but the food may have contained items prohibited to a Jew.

Daniel made it one of his top priorities not to defile himself. Can you and I say the same? If we claim that King Jesus has our heart allegiance before any other allegiance on earth, can we say that we've made up our mind not to defile ourselves—by marrying someone who isn't a believer, or by illicit sex, or by sloppy work habits, or by telling lies and half-truths?

Daniel stuck to his priorities, and God stuck to Daniel, making him an indispensable servant to the king and a model for us all.

TO READ: *Daniel 6:1–28*

PRAYING IN DIFFICULT CIMCUMSTANCES

But when Daniel learned that the law had been signed, he went home
and knelt down as usual in his upstairs room, with its windows open
toward Jerusalem. He prayed three times a day, just as he had always done,
giving thanks to his God.

DANIEL 6:10

W e need to ask ourselves, "How important is prayer in my life? If praying to God were suddenly outlawed, would I be a Daniel and pray as he did? Is my prayer life worth being thrown into a den of lions?"

Daniel's time with God was apparently worth losing his life (Daniel 6:7-10). It must have been tempting to pray only *once*, don't you think? But Daniel, a man greatly esteemed and beloved by God, never missed a beat. His daily habit was to pray three times a day, and that's what he continued to do, even when threatened with death. It was the Jews' habit during their days in exile to open their windows toward Jerusalem when they prayed. I must admit that if I had been Daniel, I would have been tempted to *close* the window while I had my devotions! But Daniel didn't care who saw him or what the repercussions would be.

What can we learn from Daniel? We must pray regularly—no matter what. Prayer links us to God, who can keep us safe both in and out of the lions' den. Prayer not only helps us grow in our trust in God (Daniel 6:23), it also helps others grow (Daniel 6:25-27). The end result of Daniel's daily prayers was testimony to Daniel's God by King Darius himself.

Can we be like Daniel? Do we pray heartily in the difficult circumstances of life? We could start even now! Who knows who will be touched by our prayers?

TO READ: *Daniel 6:16–28*

MOUTH TRAPS

*"My God sent his angel to shut the lions' mouths so that they would
not hurt me, for I have been found innocent in his sight.
And I have not wronged you, Your Majesty."*

DANIEL 6:22

W e were enjoying a prayer meeting. Fifteen women had gathered to
talk to God. To encourage our hearts, we were reading together
from the Word. We marveled at Daniel, noting that something wonderful
happened every time he prayed.

"How brave and courageous he was," said one.

"How close he kept to the Father," exclaimed another.

"How special his gifts—and how faithful a servant!" added a third.
There was silence. . . .

"What I like best about this story," said one of my friends, "is the bit
about the lions. Daniel said in 6:22, 'My God sent his angel to shut the
lions' mouths so that they would not hurt me.' If God shut the lions'
mouths, I know he can surely shut mine!"

We prayed about that—all of us.

As a young man and a slave under a foreign king, Daniel had relied
on his God and learned when to open and when to close his mouth, so
Daniel's wisdom was esteemed by four great rulers—Nebuchadnezzar,
Belshazzar, Darius, and Cyrus. Even Belshazzar's mother recommended
listening to Daniel's words of wisdom: "There is a man in your kingdom
who has within him the spirit of the holy gods. During Nebuchadnezzar's
reign, this man was found to have insight, understanding, and wisdom as
though he himself were a god" (Daniel 5:11). Daniel was wise—and his
words reflected it.

When you can control your tongue, God gets the glory and people
are amazed.

TO READ: *Daniel 10:1-19*

DEEPLY LOVED

"Don't be afraid," he said, "for you are deeply loved by God.
Be at peace; take heart and be strong!" As he spoke these words,
I suddenly felt stronger and said to him, "Now you may speak,
my lord, for you have strengthened me."
DANIEL 10:19

God is the refuge for his people and the conqueror of nations. God commands a heavenly host—spirits that battle the abounding evil that threatens us. But many people wonder if angels really exist. What does the Bible say about them?

God shows us his power not only through his personal intervention but also by sending individual members of his host to empower, console, or encourage us in our earthly pilgrimage. People do not always recognize angels because these heavenly visitors have the ability to appear as humans. Some of us have perhaps "entertained angels without realizing it!" (Hebrews 13:2). In this passage, an angel strengthened Daniel after he recognized his heavenly visitor.

The hosts of the Lord are marvelous—but not nearly as marvelous as the Lord of hosts. "But angels are only servants. They are spirits sent from God to care for those who will receive salvation" (Hebrews 1:14). God may choose to visit our discouraged heart by sending us angelic help or by touching us personally with his Spirit. However he deems suitable will be just what we need when we need it! One way or another he will make his love real to our heart. "For we know how dearly God loves us, because he has given us the Holy Spirit to fill our hearts with his love" (Romans 5:5). It is that grand knowledge—his love for us—that will set us on our feet and strengthen us.

TO READ: *Hosea 6:1–11*

PRESSING ON

"Oh, that we might know the LORD! Let us press on to know him!
Then he will respond to us as surely as the arrival of dawn or
the coming of rains in early spring."

HOSEA 6:3

The people of Israel were not committed to God. They did not repent of their sins. The prophet Hosea pled with the people: "Oh, that we might know the Lord! Let us press on to know him! Then he will respond to us as surely as the arrival of dawn or the coming of rains in early spring" (Hosea 6:3). The people thought they knew God, but they had not "pressed on" to know him.

Whether you can recall that first invitation to Christ or not, it is more important to answer the question, "Am I a Christian now?" Then you must think about whether you know him better now than you did when you first met him; in other words, have you grown, "pressed on"?

When we look at the call of the disciples to follow Jesus, we see three things—an introduction to Jesus, an investigation of Jesus, and ongoing instruction by Jesus. Are you getting to know Jesus rather than just knowing facts about him? Have you investigated and understood the Christianity you have embraced? Are you being instructed by him now? Being a disciple means pressing on to know the Lord. Are you pressing on, or have you gotten stuck somewhere along the way? "Return to the Lord," as Hosea calls you to do (Hosea 6:1). Then you will find God's sweet response as sure as the coming of the dawn.

TO READ: *Joel 2:12-32*

OUT OF BROKENNESS COMES BLESSING

That is why the LORD says, "Turn to me now, while there is time! Give me
your hearts. Come with fasting, weeping, and mourning. Don't tear your
clothing in your grief; instead, tear your hearts." Return to the LORD your
God, for he is gracious and merciful. He is not easily angered. He is filled
with kindness and is eager not to punish you.

JOEL 2:12-13

To give God our heart may mean a tearing within, a brokenness of
spirit, a horrified realization that our sins have grieved the very heart
of God. This *should* tear us up inside. Yet our loving God *wants* to forgive
us. Out of our brokenness, he wants to give blessing. For a revival of our
relationship with God, we will need, first and foremost, to give our heart
into his hand. No business is more important or urgent than doing
business with God.

It's essential business—this tearing of the heart. Perhaps there has
been too much preaching and posturing and not enough praying! Real
praying—prayer that allows God to get his hands on our heart—brings
results. Turning back to God, however, requires discipline like that of
an athlete, disregarding the inevitable pain involved. The discipline of
devotion includes the willingness to be broken in order to be restored.

This message to Israel to turn back to God carried a promise of
restoration and revival (Joel 2:18-32). The promise pertains today—no
restoration without returning, no revival without repentance! It's all a
matter of the heart. Does our heart break because of the sin that breaks
the heart of God? Do we give God permission to break our heart for him?
Such spiritual sensitivity is a daily discipline, a moment-by-moment
exercise of realizing the pain that unholiness causes him! When we give
God our heart, we must expect that it will be broken. But out of the
brokenness comes blessing!

TO READ: *Amos 1:1-15*

THE ROAR OF THE LION

"The LORD's voice roars from his Temple on Mount Zion; he thunders from Jerusalem! Suddenly, the lush pastures of the shepherds dry up. All the grass on Mount Carmel withers and dies."

AMOS 1:2

Have you ever wondered what God's voice sounds like? Amos said, "The Lord's voice roars from his Temple on Mount Zion; he thunders from Jerusalem!" (Amos 1:2). When God speaks, he means business. God had a message for his people, Israel, who were trying their best *not* to listen to him! When that is the case, God finds someone like Amos, who first listens to God's voice and then makes sure he does his share of roaring as he passes God's message along!

God's voice is the roar of a lion. Have you ever heard the Lion roar? Listen the next time you read the Scriptures. You won't be disappointed. It isn't hard to hear the Lord, for his roar demands our attention. It isn't hard to understand his voice, for he makes sure we hear what he wants us to hear. It is wise to listen when the Lion roars!

Do you face a problem and need a solution? Are you in the middle of a dilemma? Are you in danger of compromising your high standards and don't know where to look for guidance? Listen for the roar of the Lion in his Word. God is so much more eager to let us know what he thinks than we are to hear it! Make no mistake about it. God has spoken clearly in his Word. When his answer is clear, it will speak as loudly as the roar of a lion. If you're open to it, he will make sure you hear him.

THE MUSIC
OF OUR LIVES

"Away with your hymns of praise! They are only noise to my ears. I will not listen to your music, no matter how lovely it is. Instead, I want to see a mighty flood of justice, a river of righteous living that will never run dry."

AMOS 5:23-24

H ave you ever wondered what God thinks of your singing? Next Sunday, while everyone is singing, look around you. People may all look perfectly respectable and worshipful, even be singing in harmony, but remember that God is listening to the music of the heart. I need to be honest about my heart attitude as I worship God. Am I just performing for others? Is my worship no more than show and pretense? Have I become so good at putting on a show that nobody knows but God? God may be saying to me, "Don't think you are fooling me. You might be singing in harmony, but I know you're out of tune with me and with others in the fellowship."

People make judgments based on outward appearances, but God "looks at a person's thoughts and intentions" (1 Samuel 16:7). He warns his people to stop being hypocritical and come back to him. If we need to do some business with God, it's a good idea to do it before next Sunday. Make sure the Lord has no reason to say to the angels that your singing is "only noise" (Amos 5:23).

What God desires from his people are actions that grow out of their relationship with him—"a mighty flood of justice, a river of righteous living" (Amos 5:24). God wants people to worship him not only on Sunday with the music of their mouths but on every day of the week with the music of their lives.

TO READ: *Jonah 1:1-17*

GOING UP A DOWN STREET

*But Jonah got up and went in the opposite direction in order to get away
from the LORD. He went down to the seacoast, to the port of Joppa, where he
found a ship leaving for Tarshish. He bought a ticket and went on board,
hoping that by going away to the west he could escape from the LORD.*

JONAH 1:3

Y ou can be a believer and still find yourself running away from the
Lord. The problem is, when you run in the wrong direction, others
often get drawn into the repercussions of your disobedience. In Jonah's
case, the sailors got caught up in the drama. As Jonah tried to escape God,
God sent a storm to stop him. The storm was so severe that the ship's crew
lost all of their cargo and feared for their lives (Jonah 1:5). Jonah understood that he had put them in danger because he was running away from
the Lord (Jonah 1:10). You never live or die only to yourself; your actions
always affect others.

Just as the sailors watched Jonah, people watch us and don't
appreciate it when we let them down. Years ago I had a boyfriend who
didn't know Christ. I ran in the opposite direction. I stopped going to
church for a time and avoided my Christian friends. But I found, like
Jonah, that I could escape my friends but I couldn't escape God. It didn't
do me a bit of good boarding the ship of escapism, for it foundered in the
waves of God's Word! I had to live a life of obedience again—which for
me included giving up the boyfriend. Then I offered songs of praise and
vowed to go the right direction—God's way. Perhaps God has given you a
clear assignment, but you are running in the opposite direction. Don't do
it! God desires only your good. Just follow his direction.

A FEW WARM COALS

*"Your leader will break out and lead you out of exile. He will bring you
through the gates of your cities of captivity, back to your own land.
Your king will lead you; the LORD himself will guide you."*

MICAH 2:13

G od loves to do significant things through the insignificant. The
remnant, the few Israelites who were left, was a small group. But
God called this group of people to make a significant difference in their
world.

Some of the Lord's people are willing to make a difference. Micah
prophesied: "Your leader will break out and lead you out of exile. He will
bring you through the gates of your cities of captivity, back to your own
land. Your king will lead you; the Lord himself will guide you" (Micah
2:13). As the sheep will follow the ram who can break through the
enclosure with his horns, so God's people will follow their leader, who
will bring the remnant of faithful people out of captivity. Through that
small but faithful remnant, God would do great things.

Vance Havner once said, "The way to start a fire isn't to first try and
light a log, but rather to blow on a few warm coals." The small, insignificant
remnant can start the fire! In every church there are a few "warm coals."
They may not be the wisest, richest, or most gifted people in the congregation, but they are warm toward God and open to his word. They want to
follow God and make a difference. The seemingly insignificant can became
great and do great things for God. Even a few warm coals can start a fire.
How warm are you?

TO READ: *Micah 6:1–8*

PUTTING PEOPLE FIRST

*No, O people, the LORD has already told you what is good,
and this is what he requires: to do what is right, to love mercy,
and to walk humbly with your God.*

MICAH 6:8

P eople matter more than schedules. People matter more than programs. Making people a priority means putting people first. This is the way Jesus lived. This is the way God wants us to live. After all—it is *people* who receive salvation. Micah tells the people, "The Lord has already told you what is good, and this is what he requires: to do what is right, to love mercy, and to walk humbly with your God" (Micah 6:8).

Doing what is right means living rightly as a parent, a wife, or a single person in my home or workplace. It means responding rightly to wrong behavior and judging rightly when conflicts arise.

Having mercy means I have a passionate concern that those who cannot speak up for themselves receive justice. This concern may lead me to get involved in prison ministry, PTA meetings, refugee resettlement, or practical concern for unborn children or unwed mothers. Such activities sometimes have to come before my own career advancement or ambition.

Walking humbly with my God will manifest itself in my esteeming others as better than myself. It will mean not pushing my own agenda or trampling over others' efforts. Living up to these requirements will result in my treating people as Christ would treat them, looking out for others' interests before my own, and generally putting people first day by day. Putting people first will make you more like Jesus, who always made sure his relationships, first with God and then with people, were top priorities.

HOME IS THE WILL OF GOD

*"On that day I will gather you together and bring you home again.
I will give you a good name, a name of distinction among all the nations
of the earth. They will praise you as I restore your fortunes before
their very eyes. I, the LORD, have spoken!"*

ZEPHANIAH 3:20

God promised his people, "I will gather you together and bring you home again" (Zephaniah 3:20). There is a longing for that "coming home" feeling in most of our hearts.

My husband, Stuart, and I were halfway through a two-month tour of ministry in Africa. Every four days or so, we set off for the next conference, traveling by small plane, car, truck, or even bush taxi, arriving at new compounds and having every meal with a new family. We slept in different beds, met different bugs, ate different food, and drank different water. After this experience, we felt a little different! This did not make for a particularly settled feeling.

Being an outside ear meant that we were there to do a lot of loving listening to the missionaries. They so enjoyed having someone to talk to, encouragement, new ideas from home, and often a good laugh to help them relax!

Watching and listening to those missionaries, I learned that *home* isn't a little box in a safe subdivision. Being settled isn't a car in the garage, membership in a club, or even model children making model grades. Being fulfilled does not consist of a husband's climb up the corporate ladder or paid vacations to Hawaii.

Home is the will of God, and if you are settled into his will, you will be settled into whatever way-out situation you find yourself. The God of peace will see to that!

OBSTACLES

"Nothing, not even a mighty mountain, will stand in Zerubbabel's way;
it will flatten out before him! Then Zerubbabel will set the final stone
of the Temple in place, and the people will shout:
'May God bless it! May God bless it!'"

ZECHARIAH 4:7

God promised through the prophet Zechariah that the obstacles to Zerubbabel's task of rebuilding the temple would be removed. God himself would intervene, so the temple would be finished. No mountain, however high, could stand in Zerubbabel's way. God himself would flatten it out before him.

But what about *my* mountains? Sometimes it's not just a case of moving the mountains. Sometimes they just need to be turned into molehills or flattened out so we can walk right over them. God can turn difficult mountain passes into roadways of redemption. As we all face and overcome obstacles through faith in God's power, we will find ourselves traveling along a spiritual highway into new dimensions of growth that can help others. When we face roadblocks along the path of life, it's good to stop and realize that our human ingenuity or sheer willpower may not be enough to resolve the problem.

Jesus told us to have faith in him, and mountains will be removed (Matthew 17:20). Maybe you are facing a personal mountain that blocks you from the blessings God would give you. There is not a mountain God cannot make into a road. He who made the mountains can demolish them. To believe that is to see the entrance ramp on the road out of your dilemma. It may take time—God knows that. But he says, "Do not despise these small beginnings, for the Lord rejoices to see the work begin" (Zechariah 4:10). Keep walking step by step, and let God take care of the mountains.

WATCHING
FOR HIS COMING

Watch, for the day of the LORD *is coming when your possessions*
will be plundered right in front of you!

ZECHARIAH 14:1

G et real," shouted a young man. "There's no way you can get me to
believe Jesus is coming again!" Yet Christians believe that he is!
Zechariah spoke of such a day. Jesus describes the same event: "Everyone
will see the Son of Man arrive on the clouds with power and great glory"
(Luke 21:27).

After Jesus' ascension into heaven, angels appeared and assured the
disciples that Jesus would physically return just as he had physically left
(Acts 1:11). So someday, sometime, it *will* happen. We cannot know the
exact time (Matthew 24:36), but Jesus has told us to be ready (Luke 12:40).
So how are we to prepare for that momentous moment?

First, we can avoid the scoffer's error: "Jesus promised to come back,
did he? Then where is he?" (2 Peter 3:4). If we know that his return is a
reality, then we can be patient. Second, we can ask God to create a sense
of urgency within us for those who are not yet saved. Third, we can heed
James's advice: "Don't grumble about each other, my brothers and sisters,
or God will judge you. For look! The great Judge is coming. He is standing
at the door!" (James 5:9). Fourth, we can let the reality of Christ's return
govern our behavior. The prophet Zechariah, hundreds of years before
Christ, knew of a coming day of the Lord and looked forward to it with
hope and expectation. Let's check out the reality of our faith—and be
found watching.

TO READ: *Malachi 4:1–6*

HEALING IN HIS WINGS

"But for you who fear my name, the Sun of Righteousness will rise
with healing in his wings. And you will go free,
leaping with joy like calves let out to pasture."

MALACHI 4:2

The prophet Malachi closes the door of the Old Testament with a stern message concerning the corruption of the priests of Israel, the sins of the people against their families, and their miserly conduct toward God. Malachi speaks of judgment and retribution upon "the arrogant and the wicked," warning that they "will be burned up like straw . . . [and] consumed like a tree" (Malachi 4:1). God was rebuking the leaders of Israel. Their job was to bring comfort, help, and healing to the flock, but they had forsaken their God and their people.

Despite the failure of Israel's leaders, God closes the Old Testament with the promise of a new day that's about to dawn. The two beautiful metaphors in this text—the sunrise of righteousness and the wings of help and healing—paint the portrait of the mending of people's hearts and minds. Bethlehem saw the sunrise when Christ was born to dissipate the darkness of people's souls. Jesus came to save us from corruption, heartache, and all manner of sinful ambitions. He came to lift us above all our pain on the wings of his healing atonement. He came to open the door of our heart.

Do you know anyone whose heart needs opening—who needs the comfort and healing that only God can give? Healing flies from Calvary, swiftly down the troubled tunnels of time to those who fear his name. He promises comfort. The Son of God has risen—with healing in his wings!

TO READ: *Matthew 4:18-25*

A RADICAL CHANGE

Jesus called out to them, "Come, be my disciples,
and I will show you how to fish for people!"

MATTHEW 4:19

Jesus always managed to communicate to people where they were. He did not come to Peter and Andrew and say, "Follow me, and I will make you astronauts, or computer experts, or preachers!" He used terms that would be most familiar to them. He wanted them to know there was a cost involved. Commitment meant a radical change. "If you follow me, you will catch people instead of fish," he said. Now *that* was a change!

Peter and Andrew were casting their nets into the sea at the time Jesus called them. The Bible says that "they left their nets at once and went with him" (Matthew 4:20). It must have been difficult for them to drop their heavy involvement with their daily tasks and leave just at that moment. But catching people, in all probability, always will be very inconvenient. Jesus did not tell them to finish the job at hand and come along when they felt more inclined. He called them, and they left their nets and came.

James and John were also busy when Jesus came by. They were not actually casting their nets into the sea, but were mending them (see Matthew 4:21). They "immediately" left their aging father, their nets and boats—all that they loved—and followed him.

What are your "nets"? Jesus is asking you to catch men and women for his kingdom. This will involve commitment and a radical change in your life. Will you obey—immediately—like the early disciples?

TO READ: *Matthew 5:1-16*

THE LAMPSTAND OF LOVE

"You are the light of the world—like a city on a mountain, glowing in the night for all to see."

MATTHEW 5:14

When Jesus said, "You are the light of the world," he meant just that. He didn't say, "Would you like to be the light of the world?" or "I would be so pleased if you got around to being the light of the world before you die." He said, "You *are* the light of the world." If Jesus, the Light, lives within, he lives to shine without. He wants us to shine first into the dark world; second, into the lives of other Christians; and third, into our homes.

We must let our light shine into the world. Jesus told us that we are to be as bright as "a city on a mountain, glowing in the night for all to see" (Matthew 5:14). Such a light cannot be hidden, and neither can the light of the world. The surrounding darkness will only enhance its shining.

We must also shine in the church. "But if we are living in the light of God's presence . . . then we have fellowship with each other" (1 John 1:7). As we let the light search our hearts and as we obey its revelations, we will keep our relationships light and right.

We must be light in our homes. "Don't hide your light under a basket! Instead, put it on a stand and let it shine for all," said Jesus (Matthew 5:15). We shine when we serve and love our families. We shine most of all when we live our lives on the lampstand of love.

TO READ: *Matthew 7:21-29*

THE STORM

"Though the rain comes in torrents and the floodwaters rise and the winds beat against that house, it won't collapse, because it is built on rock."

MATTHEW 7:25

W e live in a society where the concept of Christian marriage—of marriage itself—is under incredible attack. The problem could well be described as a rising flood of divorce statistics. We feel that we are indeed going against the stream of general opinion if we hold to a marriage ethic as taught in the Scriptures.

Some friends of mine were introduced at a neighborhood party as the only couple in the room still on their first marriage. "How cute!" commented one of their new friends. It's now "cute" to be married more than five years!

Hundreds of people busily construct their homes on the sand of secularism and allow themselves and their marriages to be engulfed in the mainstream of public opinion. When their tottering house collapses around their ears, they make little effort to save it. The Bible says that fools build their houses on the sand.

The world may consider it wise to opt out of a marriage at the slightest hint of a storm, but that is being worldly wise. When we build our individual lives and our marriages upon the Rock, they will not be shaken by the floods of opposition. God's wisdom teaches us that there is another way. Notice the text says that the floods came and the winds blew; it doesn't say *if*. Difficulties and trial will inevitably come. But we can weather the storms if our marriage is built on solid rock!

TO READ: *Matthew 8:23-27*

IS GOD SLEEPING ON THE JOB?

Suddenly, a terrible storm came up, with waves breaking into the boat.
But Jesus was sleeping.

MATTHEW 8:24

J esus and the disciples got into a boat and "started across the lake"—referring to the Sea of Galilee. "Suddenly, a terrible storm came up, with waves breaking into the boat" (Matthew 8:23-24). While not unusual, storms on the Sea of Galilee would come up suddenly and could be very violent. The disciples were frightened, but Jesus "was sleeping" (Matthew 8:24). The disciples must have felt like Jesus was sleeping on the job. They were hurt at his apparent indifference to their plight: "Teacher, don't you even care that we are going to drown?" they asked him (Mark 4:38).

Who of us has not experienced a sudden squall in life's placid waters and suddenly been nearly swamped? Maybe we have been healthy one day and facing a terrible prognosis the next. Maybe the storm has taken the form of a divorce, sudden unemployment, or a house fire. Maybe it's just the little stresses building up in our too-busy lives that suddenly threaten to sink us. Christ may well be "on board," but that doesn't stop us from feeling frightened, bewildered, and hurt that he is apparently sleeping on the job.

The disciples' fear was addressed when Christ woke up, rebuked the men and the storm (in that order), and asked the men what had happened to their faith (Matthew 8:26-27). Fear and faith are antithetical—Jesus expects us to trust him in the storms of life. Why should we? Because he controls all nature and can control our stormy human situations, as well as give us peace.

JULY

TO READ: *Matthew 11:1–19*

HUMILITY IS GROWN IN THE DESERT

"Are you really the Messiah we've been waiting for, or should we keep looking for someone else?" Jesus told them, "Go back to John and tell him about what you have heard and seen."

MATTHEW 11:3-4

Humility is grown in the desert. John the Baptist cultivated a wilderness lifestyle. He would rather have done without "things" than without God. Humility is modeled after other godly people.

John's model was Elijah. John came in the spirit and power of the great Old Testament prophet! Elijah lived in the desert, too. He was conscious of his own shortcomings. When his faith faltered, he cried out to God, "I am no better than my ancestors" (1 Kings 19:4).

John had his shortcomings as well. At one point in his life, when he had been put in prison, he had horrible doubts about Jesus. He was tortured with thoughts that perhaps he had made a terrible mistake. Maybe Jesus was not the Messiah after all. Had he baptized the wrong person? Perhaps he had said all the wrong things in his sermons!

Humility can ask questions; humility is not afraid to send a message to Jesus and ask him to help with doubts. That's what John did, and Jesus gave him assurance and encouragement at once.

If we have humility, we know we can tell Jesus when we're weak. Humility helps us to be strong, even when we are in a prison of death, doubt, or despair.

Prideful people won't ask. They try to figure it all out for themselves. But then, pride doesn't live in the desert with God. Do you have questions, doubts, fears? Take them to Jesus.

TO READ: *Matthew 11:20-30*

"I CAN'T CARRY MORE, LORD"

Then Jesus said, "Come to me, all of you who are weary and carry heavy burdens, and I will give you rest."

MATTHEW 11:28

J esus calls us to carry the burdens he has especially prepared for us. If we stay close to him, he will help us carry the load however weary we are. "But I'm sinking," you say. "I can't carry any more." Yet the burdens he asks you to bear will never sink you! How could they? He made you able to bear them. If we are experiencing that sinking feeling, it may be because we have taken on a load that has no resemblance to the load he specifically planned for us. Jesus promises that the load he asks us to bear for him will be light (Matthew 11:30). This is because his big shoulder is shouldering the main weight of it already. If we stay close to him, we will find that our load is not only light, but even a delight.

We don't have to carry everything alone, you know. Sometimes when we are groaning under all the responsibilities we have taken on ourselves, someone else comes along and shoves his or her own problems on us. This can happen on the home front or the church front! The secret of discerning which particular burdens God wants us to bear lies in Matthew 11:29: "Take my yoke upon you. Let me teach you, because I am humble and gentle, and you will find rest for your souls." When we are yoked to Jesus, he will teach us what to take on and what to leave for someone else to carry.

TO READ: *Matthew 14:1–14*

GOD-FOCUSED

As soon as Jesus heard the news, he went off by himself in a boat to a remote area to be alone. But the crowds heard where he was headed and followed by land from many villages.

MATTHEW 14:13

E ven if we try not to overload the boat of our life, chances are we still are carrying a load. Troubles, burdens, and stresses are a part of life.

Jesus experienced all sorts of burdens and stresses, several of which are recorded in Matthew 14. First, he received news of John the Baptist's murder. So he withdrew to a quiet place, but the crowds followed. He then fed those people, persuaded his disciples to go ahead of him in the boat, walked on the water, and then healed many people. Now I would say that's a whole lot of pressure in a very short time!

So how did Jesus handle his pressures? He was not resentful of interruptions. When faced with others' pain, he healed it. When encountering his disciples' lack of faith, he pushed them to grow. Jesus was God-focused rather than self-focused. His heavenly Father promised him power to do all he had planned for him to do.

How Jesus responded to the pressure of accomplishing his Father's will shows us how Jesus turned to God as his source of power (Matthew 14:23). Jesus said, "I live by the power of the living Father who sent me" (John 6:57). We should take heart and allow our daily burdens to make us like Jesus: God-focused. That mind-set helped him focus on others and serve them. Pressures give us a grand opportunity to see God do what seems impossible.

TO READ: *Matthew 14:1–14*

UPSET PLANS

A vast crowd was there as he stepped from the boat,
and he had compassion on them and healed their sick.

MATTHEW 14:14

How do you react when somebody upsets your plans? Perhaps you have planned a lovely day at the zoo with the children, when, at the last minute, you get a phone call from work. Or perhaps you have dreamed of a special vacation. The plans are in place, but a distant relative dies and you have to go to the funeral. You get as upset as your upset plans!

Something like that happened to the disciples. They had planned a lovely vacation with Jesus. They had the place all picked out—a resort area on beautiful Lake Galilee.

They needed a vacation! They had just received the terrible news that their dear colleague and friend, John the Baptist, had been cruelly murdered. They had been terribly busy for days—keeping the crowds of people who came to see Jesus in order, helping take the sick to the master, and controlling the children who got under everyone's feet. Feeding and housing their party and making endless travel arrangements was hard work. How relieved they must have been when they were actually on their way away from it all!

But "it all" met them as soon as they stepped out of the boat on the other side of the lake. Jesus was moved as he looked at the multitude of need. The disciples looked at the multitude and needed to have them *re*-moved! How would you have reacted? Take a hint from Jesus. Sometimes an upset means a special appointment made by God himself.

TO READ: *Matthew 14:22-33*

FACING UP TO THE SUPERNATURAL

When the disciples saw him, they screamed in terror,
thinking he was a ghost.

MATTHEW 14:26

The disciples "screamed in terror." Even Peter was frightened. We need to take note of the fact that Peter was not afraid of the *storm.* Peter, the intrepid fisherman, knew the Sea of Galilee like the back of his hand. He respected her moods and knew she could be very dangerous at times, but he had experienced storms before. He didn't know, however, if he could handle a ghost!

Have you ever noticed how many folks are totally self-confident until faced with the supernatural? Sometimes we meet people who are not one whit frightened by the storms of life (they've been around) but are petrified when presented with the claims of Jesus Christ!

Are you frightened by things you don't understand? Has someone "put you off" Christianity because they made it sound a bit "spooky"?

Jesus Christ told the disciples not to be afraid of him. He wasn't a ghost. He was and is God, and you don't ever need to be afraid of God—unless, of course, you have never asked him to forgive your sins! Then, you have good reason to cry out for fear.

Perhaps it's time you invited Christ into the boat of your life to handle the storm of your fears about himself. He will forgive your sins. He will bring peace and purpose to your life. You'll be glad that you met him!

TO READ: *Matthew 14:22-33*

KEEPING YOUR EYES ON JESUS

*But when he looked around at the high waves, he was terrified and
began to sink. "Save me, Lord!" he shouted.*

MATTHEW 14:30

Peter, having overcome his fear of Jesus, decided to walk on the water,
too! He was wise enough to wait until Jesus told him it was all right
to try. Then he clambered over the side of his boat to go to him.

As soon as we get over our fear of the supernatural by recognizing
and acknowledging God's lordship over everything in heaven and on
earth, we will want to experience that power for ourselves. I believe, for
example, that Jesus could do extraordinary things. Not only could he heal
sick people, he could keep his temper, be unselfish, and always say the
right thing.

Can I do what Jesus did? Can I stride over the circumstances of my
life in triumph? Can I walk over the waters of worries and fears? Yes, if I
keep my eyes on him.

Peter unfortunately forgot who was keeping him afloat and started
to look at the reasons he should be sinking. As soon as we do that, we are
sunk! Peter had been afraid to face the supernatural. Having overcome
that fear, he then became afraid he couldn't depend on God to see him
through.

It's a matter of keeping our eyes on Jesus, not on the storm. And
remember, if we begin to sink, we can cry out to him. He will put out his
hand and save us. It's important to him that we continue on in faith and
succeed in the tasks to which he has called us!

TO READ: *Matthew 16:13-19*

WHO DO YOU SAY HE IS?

Simon Peter answered, "You are the Messiah, the Son of the living God."

MATTHEW 16:16

At the age of twelve Jesus clearly stated that he knew his identity as the Son of God (Luke 2:49), yet he went back to Nazareth and subjected himself to Mary's and Joseph's authority and waited another eighteen years to begin his ministry.

How did Jesus know his identity? That Jesus was both fully God and fully man is a tenet of our Christian faith. Only God could effect the redemption of the human race.

Being perfect God yet perfect man does not mean that Jesus was born a superbaby! He was a human baby with a human nature, yet perfect God with God's nature. The mystery of Jesus' divine and human nature is impossible for finite minds to grasp—it must be accepted by faith.

We may not be able to understand it all, but we can accept the truth by faith. The Bible is a reliable record of truth, and God intends us to trust the information we read there. Jesus Christ was a historical figure. He was not merely a good man who came to an untimely end or a deluded person with grandiose ideas about himself. Jesus was God, and he was also human. Peter had that "big moment" when he said to Jesus, "You are the Messiah, the Son of the living God" (Matthew 16:16). When you believe that, it will be a big moment for you because it will change your life! Thank Jesus Christ for becoming human so that he could bring you to God.

TO READ: *Matthew 17:14-20*

COMING DOWN FROM THE MOUNTAIN

Jesus replied, "You stubborn, faithless people! How long must I be with you until you believe? How long must I put up with you? Bring the boy to me."

MATTHEW 17:17

Have you ever been to a wonderful retreat and had a "mountaintop" experience? But the time then came to return to earth! It's different in the valley, isn't it? We often meet weak Christians who are waiting for us to be strong. They want us to fix all the problems they should be able to handle themselves (Matthew 17:16). Jesus had been on the mountain with his heavenly Father, having literally a "glorious time." But at the foot of the mountain was a demon-possessed boy, and Jesus' own followers "couldn't heal him" (Matthew 17:16). Hence his frustration. The disciples couldn't help a parent in pain, and they couldn't rescue a child being torn apart by destructive forces. Surely they were as frustrated as Jesus was!

But notice that Jesus didn't let frustration keep him from meeting needs. He helped the distraught father and he healed the demon-possessed boy (Matthew 17:18). Then he began, again, to patiently train his twelve disciples (Matthew 17:20). Jesus explained that "this kind can be cast out only by prayer" (Mark 9:29). Somehow the disciples had lost their focus. They were spiritually unprepared for the work that Jesus had called them to do.

What will it take for us to please Jesus instead of frustrating him? We should spend time in prayer (Mark 9:29)—in other words, focusing on Christ. Then we'll be prepared for all that he has called us to do, and the people waiting for us in the valley will not be disappointed.

TO READ: *Matthew 20:17-28*

THERE'S A NEW WORLD COMING

"When we get to Jerusalem," he said, "the Son of Man will be betrayed to the leading priests and the teachers of religious law. They will sentence him to die. Then they will hand him over to the Romans to be mocked, whipped, and crucified. But on the third day he will be raised from the dead."

MATTHEW 20:18-19

With the benefit of two thousand years of hindsight, we understand there could be no Easter morning without a Good Friday. However, as far as the disciples of Jesus were concerned, on that Friday after the crucifixion, the Cross was the end of all their highest hopes and most daring dreams.

Jesus had certainly done his best to prepare his followers for the Cross, for on three occasions he had told them that he would die, but also that he would rise again. The first occasion was after Peter's confession of faith (Matthew 16:21). The second was after Jesus was transfigured (Matthew 17:22-23). The third was as he and his disciples were going to Jerusalem for the last time. Jesus spoke of himself, saying, "They will hand him over to the Romans to be mocked, whipped, and crucified. But on the third day he will be raised from the dead" (Matthew 20:19). It seems strange that not one of the disciples remembered the momentous promise that Jesus would rise again.

Why is it so important to believe in Jesus' resurrection? Because we who believe it and confess him as Lord will be raised too! By far the biggest problem in life is death. But for the believer, the stone has been rolled away from the tomb of death. It's empty! Death for the Christian is the gateway into life. Christ has gone before to tell us there is a new world ahead of us, and those of us who believe can face the grave with utmost confidence in that promise.

TO READ: *Matthew 23:37-39*

WEIRD BIRDS

"O Jerusalem, Jerusalem, the city that kills the prophets and stones God's messengers! How often I have wanted to gather your children together as a hen protects her chicks beneath her wings, but you wouldn't let me."

MATTHEW 23:37

D avid prayed, "Guard me as the apple of your eye. Hide me in the shadow of your wings. Protect me from wicked people who attack me, from murderous enemies who surround me" (Psalm 17:8-9).

David looked for a secret place of security and found a ready refuge in God. David cried, "I will hide beneath the shadow of your wings until this violent storm is past" (Psalm 57:1). The "violent storm" was the result of David's disastrous relationship with King Saul, who had forced David to run for his life and hide in the caves of the rock.

Do you know where to go in the midst of your storms? Is there a familiar saving shadow known to your spirit? When Jesus walked our earth, he described people as "baby chicks" running around in circles, scattering in every direction. He longed to gather men and women under his wonderful wings of love—but they wouldn't let him. It's a silly chicken who would rather be in the middle of the storm than be sheltered by Christ. It is my sad conclusion that our world is populated with such weird birds! Are you "under his wings" or "out in the storm"? The choice is yours.

We need to pray, "Lord Jesus, shelter me in your shadow, welcome me under your wings—till these storms have passed."

TO READ: *Matthew 26:31–56*

MAKING THE TEAM

He went on a little farther and fell face down on the ground, praying,
"My Father! If it is possible, let this cup of suffering be taken away from me.
Yet I want your will, not mine."

MATTHEW 26:39

O ur son Peter was trying out for the basketball team and asked me
to pray that he would make it.

"I'll ask that the right thing will happen for you," I told him.

Pete shot me a somewhat apprehensive glance. "Don't do that,
Mom," he pleaded. "Just pray that I make the team!"

How often do I pray like that! So often I don't want the *right* thing
to happen; I just want to make the team. I can remember praying "Pete
prayers" when I was very young. "O God," I would say, "I want a pretty
day on Saturday," or "Please help me to pass the examination without
having to do any studying!" Children make such elementary requests.
But when we become adults, we are supposed to put away childish
things (1 Corinthians 13:11). God intends us to learn how to praise
him for Saturday's rain and to ask him for help as we do our homework.

Peter grew up to play basketball for his college. Once when he was
trying hard to qualify for a place, he again said, "Pray for me, Mom."

"What for, Pete?" I asked.

"Pray I will make the team only if I'm the best man for the job," he
said quietly. Pete has come a long way.

Have I? Have you? Prayer after all is the means by which we sense
God's desires, and they become our own. We might even begin to care
more about the team than we care about the team's caring for us!

TO READ: *Matthew 26:31-56*

THE CUP

Again he left them and prayed, "My Father! If this cup cannot be taken away until I drink it, your will be done."

MATTHEW 26:42

I n the garden of Gethsemane, Jesus was in agony. Not physical agony—that would come later—but spiritual agony, knowing what it would mean to bear the sin of the whole world for us. Jesus knew that God's will must be done and that it must be done by him alone. There was no one else good enough or powerful enough to deal with sin. Only God could do that. Jesus also understood that his cup would be filled with intense suffering. It would not be a pleasant drink, but he would drink it because it was the Father's will.

There will be times in our life when, like Jesus, we will have a "Gethsemane experience." Perhaps with pain and tears, we too may wrestle with a cup of suffering that we know God is asking us to drink. But also, after asking him if there is any other way we can go and receiving a heavenly negative answer, if we say, "Your will be done," we can know plainly that God will assist us in doing whatever we need to do.

When we have the cup in our hand, it helps to think about Gethsemane. Whatever cup of suffering God asks us to drink, it could never be a cup like his, and it will never need to be drunk alone. It can be a comfort to remember Jesus in Gethsemane, preparing to drink the cup for us.

THE GREATEST HOPE

Then Jesus said to them, "Don't be afraid! Go tell my brothers to
leave for Galilee, and they will see me there."

MATTHEW 28:10

We must make it our highest priority to know Christ as our Savior. We need to become his disciples. But how can we know that Christ has come into our life? Will we feel different? Not immediately. But we should feel different in a week, a month, or a year. As we realize our wealth in him, we will understand and value promises like, "Those the Father has given me will come to me, and I will never reject them" (John 6:37). When we make Jesus our highest priority, we will find that he gives us our greatest hope.

Jesus has promised to keep us throughout life and to save us in the end. He will pray for us now, and he will present us before his Father and his angels with exceeding joy. He will introduce us to God in the courts of heaven as those who have trusted him to save us.

If you found a doctor who cured you of an incurable illness, you would surely share all the details with others who have that illness. Well, if you have found Christ, who has cured you of the deadly disease of sin, you ought to share your greatest priority and greatest hope with others! Why don't you tell someone about this confidence you have in Christ? God makes us his priority, and we should make him ours.

TO READ: *Matthew 28:1-20*

WHAT NEXT?

"Therefore, go and make disciples of all the nations, baptizing them in the
name of the Father and the Son and the Holy Spirit. Teach these new
disciples to obey all the commands I have given you. And be sure of this:
I am with you always, even to the end of the age."

MATTHEW 28:19-20

When we ask Christ to come into our lives, does he change us immediately? Do we become immediately all that we were meant to be? Does he make us act perfect right away?

Yes, and no. He does make an immediate change, for he makes us his own and he sees us as righteous. However, it will take some time for us to see changes in our lives. After all, if we make a deposit in an interest-bearing account, we won't see the growth of our money right away. It takes time. But the more time passes, the more we see the value of our investment.

We can trust God's Word. He has promised to keep us to the end—and beyond. He has changed us forever, and he will continue to change us day by day. He will guide us now, and he will one day present us before his Father and his angels with exceeding joy. He will introduce us to God in the courts of heaven as those who have trusted him to save us.

After accepting Christ, we need to tell others what we have done. Sharing with others is not only good for our souls, it is good for other souls, too! They may hear and believe as we have.

We also need to join a church that teaches the Bible as the inspired Word of God. As we serve Jesus day by day, he will make us more like himself—then we will really feel at home when we get to heaven!

TO READ: *Mark 4:30–41*

BEST REST

Jesus was sleeping at the back of the boat with his head on a cushion.
Frantically they woke him up, shouting,
"Teacher, don't you even care that we are going to drown?"

MARK 4:38

S tress and pressure that come from the storms of life have an uncanny ability to keep us awake at night and sometimes even make us unable to function during the day. How can we rest while our "vessel" is being battered by a gale-force wind? Yet Jesus could *sleep* under such circumstances! When a storm arose while he was on board a boat, "Jesus was sleeping at the back of the boat with his head on a cushion" (Mark 4:38). Jesus knew what it was to rest in the middle of the storm. He knew he was safe in his Father's arms.

The pressure may not be removed, but God is able to give us such an attitude toward it that we are as content with the pressure as without it! Seem impossible? It's not. This kind of rest is a release from mental and spiritual weariness, not a release from the work or labor of bearing the burden. We can handle the gale-force winds that assail us; we can let our little "boat" be rocked, and we can labor with intensity without wearing ourselves out. It is rest, not leisure! It is rest from self-consciousness, and it is rest from fear. Jesus asked his terrified disciples, "Why are you so afraid? Do you still not have faith in me?" (Mark 4:40). As Jesus rested in the Father during the storm, he expected his friends to rest in him. This is the best rest.

TO READ: *Mark 6:30-56*

IN THE MIDDLE
OF THE MUDDLE

Afterward he went up into the hills by himself to pray.

MARK 6:46

A s a young mother with three preschool children, a husband who traveled, and responsibilities outside the home, I found an unlikely oasis. My children's playpen stood "in the middle of the muddle." So I put the kids out, climbed in, and spent fifteen blissful minutes a day talking with God. I used that time alone with him to sort out the muddle and ask him to help me as a wife and mother be of maximum worth to him.

After our eldest son was grown, he told me that he and his sister had learned to leave me alone when they saw me in their playpen with my Bible on my lap and a cup of English tea in my hand. "Why was that?" I asked him.

"Because we came to appreciate the fact that you were a whole lot nicer mother when you got out than when you got in," he replied.

On one occasion, after teaching and feeding five thousand men and their families, Jesus sent the people home, and "afterward he went up into the hills by himself to pray" (Mark 6:46). Jesus always made time to be with his Father.

If we would make sure our life is of maximum worth to our family, we can start by giving the maximum time possible to develop our relationship with God. By all means, make a habit of going "into the hills by yourself" to pray, but also take time out somehow, somewhere, in the middle of the muddle. You'll be a whole lot better because of it!

TO READ: *Mark 8:1–10*

YOUR HURT
IN MY HEART

*"I feel sorry for these people. They have been here with me for three days,
and they have nothing left to eat."*

MARK 8:2

I t's easy to grow so self-centered that we don't look past our own problems or pain. Do we respond like Jesus did when faced with people in obvious distress and confusion? Jesus had been teaching and healing in the towns and villages of Galilee. At this time, a huge crowd had been with Jesus for three days, and they ran out of food. "I feel sorry for these people," the Lord said. "They have been here with me for three days, and they have nothing left to eat" (Mark 8:2).

Jesus felt sorry—he felt what we would call "pity" or "compassion." Jesus had a shepherd's heart that was moved as he observed the crowds of people around him who needed a "shepherd" to lead and guide them "because their problems were so great and they didn't know where to go for help" (Matthew 9:36). Someone has defined compassion as "your hurt in my heart." Jesus definitely took the hurt of people into his heart.

Perhaps you object to this challenge to care compassionately for others. Maybe you think you have too many hurts of your own. Yet the Lord heals our own hurts as we reach out to attend to the hurts of others.

Jesus feels people's hurt in his heart, and he is in my heart—so guess what happens: Their hurt is in my heart! Once we feel great compassion for others, we will discover a great motivating force that will move us to compassionate action.

TO READ: *Mark 10:35-45*

ASKING JESUS THE RIGHT THINGS

"In your glorious Kingdom, we want to sit in places of honor next to you,"
they said, "one at your right and the other at your left."

MARK 10:37

Isn't it surprising that James and John had just had a mountaintop experience, yet they hit rock bottom in the valley only a few days later? They had seen Jesus transfigured before them, then they had come down into the valley and heard the Lord rebuke their brother disciples for their lack of faith. Perhaps they despised their friends.

After all, James and John believed that Jesus could do anything. Hadn't they themselves just heard the voice of God affirming him? How strange, then, to find the brothers behaving in such a childish way. A little while later, believing themselves to be Jesus' favorites, they requested that he keep a chair just for them on each side of his heavenly throne. The Bible says that "When the ten other disciples discovered what James and John had asked, they were indignant" (Mark 10:41).

Oh, be assured, the ten will *always* hear it! Competitive spirits don't ever whisper; they shout! They are bound to be heard! Jesus must have been frustrated all over again; this time, with James and John! He reminded them that unbelievers compete with each other, but disciples must not (see Mark 10:42-43).

We must be careful to ask Jesus the right things. If we watch how he lived in the Gospels, we will begin to know instinctively which prayers are out of order. There is so much we need to ask of Jesus every day; let's not ask him for the wrong things!

TO READ: *Mark 12:41-44*

GULLIBLE GIVING

"For they gave a tiny part of their surplus, but she,
poor as she is, has given everything she has."

MARK 12:44

A mericans are so gullible," a rescue mission supervisor told me. "Did you hear about the man who went out and raised two hundred dollars in half an hour from people on the street by telling them he was collecting for 'The Unknown Soldier's Widow'?" I confessed I hadn't heard about it, but I wondered if it were true.

I thought about the money that I gave away to charity. Gullible giving is not God's way. Guidelines have been given to us. Tithes first—10 percent of all our income. This is his. We touch it not, lest we be guilty of thievery—robbing divinity is a heinous crime! Offerings next. David said, "I cannot present burnt offerings to the LORD my God that have cost me nothing" (2 Samuel 24:24). What say you? Think of the widow. She only had two pennies. She could have thought that two pennies were too little to give. But Jesus didn't think so. He knew that generous giving from what God has given us will make us richer than the richest king.

Spastic generosity, triggered by nerves, touched off by impassioned pleas of poverty, or doled out to starving unfortunates pictured in scraggy photographs, is not the best help we can give. Careful accounting of our budget—as if we were handling someone else's funds—is the way to go. After all, we are merely stewards, and as the Bible reminds us, "A person who is put in charge as a manager must be faithful" (1 Corinthians 4:2).

GOD'S ARSENAL

"Keep alert and pray. Otherwise temptation will overpower you.
For though the spirit is willing enough, the body is weak."

MARK 14:38

J esus knows us humans very well, doesn't he? After all, he came to live in our world, in part so that he might experience what it's like to be human—faced with pain, difficulty, and, yes, even temptations. "This High Priest of ours understands our weaknesses, for he faced all of the same temptations we do, yet he did not sin" (Hebrews 4:15). Jesus knows that no matter how willing we may be to walk with him, serve him, and obey him, at times our "body" doesn't want to.

So how do we strengthen ourselves? Our best defense is to be prepared spiritually—we need to keep alert and pray, as Jesus said. The best weapon of defense in our arsenal is the word of God. When Jesus was tempted by Satan (and Satan even used Scripture that he twisted to his own purpose), Jesus saw through Satan's lies and quoted Scripture, used correctly, back at him. We learn from the Bible what is right and what is wrong. If we are daily in God's word, we will become familiar with it and will be able to use it when we face temptation. This is part of what it means to "keep alert" (Mark 14:38).

A second weapon of defense is prayer. Jesus told his disciples to pray, so that when temptation would strike, they could be in tune with God and do his will. We must do the same.

TO READ: *Mark 15:21-41*

ACCEPT THE CROSS

When the Roman officer who stood facing him saw how he had died,
he exclaimed, "Truly, this was the Son of God!"

MARK 15:39

We cannot be Christians without the Cross. The Cross tells us sin has been "crossed out" and dealt with. The Cross tells us what a holy God thinks about our sinful nature—it had to be judged. Someone had to be punished for our sin. It was either going to be us or a substitute. The Cross gave us our substitute: Jesus Christ, who died in our place.

Most of the world doesn't even know what it is doing to Jesus Christ. To count him of no worth, to misunderstand his work at the Cross, to live as if he had never lived or died, to reject his claims to be master of our lives, or to relegate him to a brief hour on Easter or Christmas is to despise him as surely as the soldiers crucified him on that hill far away. To reject Jesus is to throw away the only chance for forgiveness.

Jesus died in our place on a wooden cross two thousand years ago so we could be forgiven. We only have to accept that forgiveness. We have to accept the Cross. The Roman army officer realized that something extraordinary had happened and said, "Truly, this was the Son of God!" (Mark 15:39).

We can attend church regularly, teach Sunday school, and sing in the choir, yet if we refuse to accept the Cross, we will be shut out of heaven. You and I cannot get to heaven except through the door shaped like a cross.

DOING THINGS THAT HAVE BEEN DONE BEFORE

Having carefully investigated all of these accounts from the beginning,
I have decided to write a careful summary for you.

LUKE 1:3

The fact that others had written the story of Jesus and the Good News did not hinder Luke from taking up the pen. He acknowledged the fact that "many people have written accounts about the events that took place among us" (Luke 1:1), but Luke also decided to write.

Sometimes we become stagnant because others seem to be doing all the work. Why offer to teach Sunday school if there are plenty of teachers? Why join the choir when it has a full contingent of sopranos? Why write a book when others have written before us? Why visit the sick when there's a committee appointed to do all that?

The answer to the "why" is found here. Luke knew others had written, but he decided to also do so. What others do is their business; what I do is mine. We need to find the goodwill of God for our lives and to do it cheerfully. Jesus said to God, "I brought glory to you here on earth by doing everything you told me to do" (John 17:4), and then he went home to heaven. We must do the same; whether others have taught, sung, written, or visited the sick before us is really quite irrelevant. We must seek God's face, discover our gifts, and do his will with all our might. When it seems good to me, and I sense his direction, I go ahead and leave the rest to him.

TO READ: *Luke 1:5-25*

PRAYER IS A PLACE

*As was the custom of the priests, he was chosen by lot to enter
the sanctuary and burn incense in the LORD's presence.*

LUKE 1:9

P rayer has been described in many ways—intercession, praise, the
debating chamber of the soul. Prayer is all these things and more. But
prayer, first and foremost, is a place to meet. In the Old Testament, God
invited his people to meet him at the altar of incense in the tabernacle:
"This is to be a daily burnt offering given from generation to generation.
Offer it in the LORD's presence at the Tabernacle entrance, where I will
meet you and speak with you" (Exodus 29:42).

In the New Testament, Jesus spoke of finding a private place where
you can shut the door behind you and pray (Matthew 6:6)—and he
served as an example for us by going frequently to a solitary place. "But,"
wails a young mother, "what can I do? I have forty kids under three years
of age!"

Now, I know *that* is not really true! You only have four—it just
feels like forty! I managed to find a place once when I was in a similar
predicament. I climbed into the children's playpen and put the toddlers
out! Five minutes with God by my "altar of incense" made all the
difference in the world—my world!

Yes, prayer is a place to meet; this is God's design. We need to pray
about finding that personal place of prayer.

"Lord, help me to find my solitary place; and whether it be in
church, in a closet, or even in a playpen, meet me there—even as you
promised. Amen."

TO READ: *Luke 1:5-25*

PRAYER IS A TIME

While the incense was being burned, a great crowd stood outside, praying.

LUKE 1:10

For the Old Testament priest Aaron, his sons, and indeed, for all people, God designed a specific time for prayer. Every morning and evening the priest burned holy incense upon the altar in the tabernacle. This was to be done not only when the people were faced with trials, fears, or death; it was to be offered perpetually—"from generation to generation" (Exodus 30:8). Often, however, we rush to that altar only in times of extremity, anxiety, or perplexity. We don't practice perpetual praise, and therefore we are not in the habit of giving thanks in all things when trouble comes (Ephesians 5:20). But our text from Luke reminds us that the people were praying regularly "while the incense was being burned"—not just in the hour of need!

Jesus told us that his people should pray constantly and never give up (Luke 18:1). "Keep on praying," echoed the apostle Paul (1 Thessalonians 5:17).

God designed the altar of incense so that it could be carried by the children of Israel in their desert pilgrimage—a perpetual reminder of their perpetual privilege (Exodus 30:1-10). However, it is worth noting that such prayer was to be a privilege of obedience. God's rules are rules. He didn't say, "I'll meet you there if you like, if you remember, or if you're desperate!" God told Aaron that "he *must* burn fragrant incense on the altar" (Exodus 30:7, italics mine). Such perpetual praise is not merely an option for the child of God. It is a simple, sweet necessity, for it glorifies the Lord.

TO READ: *Luke 1:26-38*

GRAVE DOUBTS

*"You will become pregnant and have a son, and you are to name him
Jesus."... Mary asked the angel, "But how can I have a baby?
I am a virgin."*

LUKE 1:31, 34

M ary had grave doubts about the grave risks of being highly favored
of God. She must have been tempted to think about other godly
men and women who had been specially chosen, too.

There was Daniel, who was described by another great angel as a
man "greatly loved" (Daniel 10:11) of his God. Yet Daniel had ended up
in a lions' den!

Then there was David—he had been hounded from pillar to post by
the king's army and had lived in the dens of the earth. God seemed to ask
such hard things of his favored ones!

How was Mary going to be able to cope with the privilege of being
highly favored of God? She had no problems believing God could do
what he had promised he would do. Her fears were rather within herself.
Would she be able to do what she had promised? How could she have a
baby when she wasn't even married? It seemed impossible—harder than
facing Daniel's lions or David's Goliath and Saul's army combined! In
other words, Mary surely had grave doubts concerning her own abilities.

Have you ever doubted your own ability to obey God? Oh, you know
what God wants you to do. He has made that abundantly obvious, but
just how, you wonder, are you going to accomplish it? God supplies the
answer to our grave doubts about the grave risks of obedience. He offers
us the promise of his power—the overshadowing of his Holy Spirit.

TO READ: *Luke 1:26-38*

OBEDIENCE IS
A LONELY PLACE

*Mary responded, "I am the Lord's servant, and I am willing to accept
whatever he wants. May everything you have said come true."
And then the angel left.*

LUKE 1:38

N ow why ever did the angel just leave Mary? Wouldn't you have
thought the angel would have stayed? After telling her what was
going to happen to her, the very least he could have done was to stick
around and see her through.

Mary must have wondered how she was ever going to manage. But
the fact of the matter was that the angel departed and left her to face the
grave consequences of her submission. Where was the angel when she had
to try to explain the situation to Joseph? If only the angel had appeared by
her side as she struggled to relate her incredible experience, Joseph might
have believed her! She had to explain herself to her parents. Where was
the angel then?

Mary discovered that obedience can be a lonely place. To say yes to
God when an angel is talking to you is one thing, but to go on saying yes
when the angel has left is another thing altogether! But God wants to see
if we will walk on in the dark.

If we can come to that point, we may have the privilege of having the
angel slip back and whisper in our ear, "God has decided to bless you"
(Luke 1:30), and that should be enough! What is God asking you to do?
Will you do it? More importantly, will you do it without the angel?

TO READ: *Luke 1:39-56*

THANK GOD
FOR ELIZABETH

*Elizabeth gave a glad cry and exclaimed to Mary, "You are blessed by
God above all other women, and your child is blessed."*

LUKE 1:42

If obedience is doing without the angel, how am I going to get through?
The answer, of course, is faith for the times I don't *feel* like doing the
right thing. The first step to faith is saying yes. Mary said yes to the angel.
After the angel left her, she followed through. She stuck to her word.

I have noticed that women are quite easily moved to say yes to God
at a conference or praise gathering, responding readily and sincerely at
such times. But what happens when they walk through their own front
doors and are confronted by harassed husbands who've been left to
baby-sit lively toddlers while they've been away getting their inspiration?
Perhaps they don't understand their wives' delight and dedication.

Mary did a very wise thing. She sought out one person whom she
knew would understand, and went to her for encouragement and support.
Thank God for our Elizabeths—those women who recognize our dilemmas
and join us in prayer and praise, who have also known what it means to
utter the yes of relinquishment!

When I first became a Christian at the age of eighteen, and my own
dear family did not quite understand me, God provided an Elizabeth—a
sweet, older lady at my church who took me under her wing. Remembering
her encouragement makes me want to be that sort of help to others.

Look around and ask God for your Elizabeth. Or perhaps you can be
an Elizabeth to someone else.

TO READ: *Luke 2:39-52*

THE FATHER'S BUSINESS

"But why did you need to search?" he asked. "You should have known that I would be in my Father's house."

LUKE 2:49

I cannot help but wonder what Jesus was like as a child. Yet Scripture closes the curtains firmly on us, having allowed only a few people to witness the little boy's growth from babyhood.

When Jesus was around six, he would have started school. For five years, along with his friends from the village, he would have memorized the Pentateuch—the first five books of the Bible. Then, at age twelve, he was presented to the learned scholars in the temple at Jerusalem and tested with questions arising from his training. Needless to say, he passed with flying colors!

Then Jesus' parents lost track of him in the big city of Jerusalem! When his parents asked him why he had treated them this way, he answered, "You should have known that I would be in my Father's house" (Luke 2:49).

This was the God-man coming of age and telling his world that first and foremost he must be about his Father's heavenly business. Although he loved his parents dearly, there was a relationship that superseded even the most important earthly tie. This is what I must be about, he was saying.

Can we honestly say our relationship with God and doing his business come first, that our Father's interests supersede our own interests?

What are the *musts* in our life? Does God truly come first in our decisions, plans, goals, and daily walk? Jesus put his Father's business first, and we should do no less.

TO READ: *Luke 2:39-52*

A GREAT PLACE
TO GROW

So Jesus grew both in height and in wisdom,
and he was loved by God and by all who knew him.

LUKE 2:52

Home is a great place to grow. Jesus grew at home in four different ways. First of all, he grew in height. Home is a great place to play, to eat, to sleep, to develop a healthy physique. This is all preparation for God's plan for your life.

Second, Jesus grew in wisdom. You gain wisdom and insight for yourself at home. You watch your mother and your father parenting, whether they do it right or do it wrong!

Third, Jesus was loved by God. The family is intended to be the place you learn the fundamental tenets of your faith, but the church is intended to supplement and deepen that knowledge. Jesus and his family always went to the synagogue (Luke 4:16).

Fourth, Jesus was also loved by all who knew him. We grow in favor with people when we live at home in a manner that honors him. If I am an angel in church, but a devil at home, what is the use of that? Home is an ideal place for the sort of growth that shows us how to get along with people. What better people than my brothers and sisters can teach me that! Home is a great place for breeding character—either good or bad.

Jesus increased in four ways—intellectually, physically, spiritually, and socially. Yes, home is a great place to grow!

TO READ: *Luke 4:14-30*

YOUR OWN HOMETOWN

Then Jesus returned to Galilee, filled with the Holy Spirit's power.
Soon he became well known throughout the surrounding country.
He taught in their synagogues and was praised by everyone.

LUKE 4:14-15

Jesus started where he was. He began in Galilee. He did not start in Rome, or even in Jerusalem. He came out of the desert and began his ministry in the "surrounding country."

Many of us come to Jesus wanting to serve in Rome, or at least expecting to do something big in Jerusalem. But if we follow his example, we must do what he did—start in the "surrounding country." Start in church. Join a fellowship of believers and take the opportunities it offers. Jesus "taught in their synagogues."

"Well, now," I seem to hear you say, "I'm not Jesus! If I could preach like him or even like John the Baptist, I'd offer my services to my local congregation!" But even though Jesus was the best preacher in the world, people didn't always appreciate his sermons!

The Bible says he was "praised by everyone," but a day or so later when he preached in his own home church, he ran into trouble. "No prophet is accepted in his own hometown" (Luke 4:24). All who heard that particular message were so angry with him, they tried to throw him over a cliff (see Luke 4:29)! You don't learn to minister by finding ready-made situations with no opposition. You learn as Jesus learned, by starting in the surrounding region, even in your own hometown!

TO READ: *Luke 5:1-11*

GETTING IN DEEP

When he had finished speaking, he said to Simon, "Now go out where
it is deeper and let down your nets, and you will catch many fish."
LUKE 5:4

⑥

J esus had already called the disciples to himself. At this point in the
Gospel story, they were working with Jesus in their spare time while
trying to keep up with their fishing business. Then one day, Jesus used
Peter's boat as a pulpit and "sat in the boat and taught the crowds from
there" (Luke 5:3).

I wonder what the sermon was? Maybe it was about forsaking
everything and following him.

After the sermon, the Lord told Peter to launch out into the deep.
Peter did what he was told, even though he was somewhat skeptical. After
all, as he told the master, "We worked hard all last night and didn't catch
a thing" (Luke 5:5).

But because Jesus, the maker of fishes, told them where to fish, they
caught many. More importantly, Jesus caught a lot of committed men!
Simon Peter was astonished, afraid, and ashamed of his confusion. All who
were with him, including James and John, felt the same way. "And as soon
as they landed, they left everything and followed Jesus" (Luke 5:11).

There comes a time when you have to launch out into the deep.
Some of us paddle around the shallows all our lives. It's time we took a
risk and began to do what Jesus tells us to do. Once we are out of our
depth, we will be astonished too. We will want to forsake all—even our
boats, our beloved ones, and our most familiar things—and follow him
to the ends of the earth.

AUGUST

TO READ: *Luke 5:1-11*

THIRTY YEARS LATER

His partners, James and John, the sons of Zebedee, were also amazed.
Jesus replied to Simon, "Don't be afraid!
From now on you'll be fishing for people!"

LUKE 5:10

For many people, a call to follow Jesus is all they ever hear. They never hear his Spirit say that it's time to launch out into the deep. One reason they do not hear is that they make sure they are not listening! Jesus will not use a megaphone. You will be safe if you stay out of earshot. But if you stay close to him, you will be bound to hear the commissioning call of the Lord.

Very soon after I accepted Christ, he asked me to let him preach from the boat of my life. This necessitated my moving out a safe distance from the shore. After catching some fish (what a thrill!), I was hooked myself! Once you have caught men and women for Christ and his kingdom, there appears no sane alternative under heaven. You have to forsake all and follow him!

The first time I led someone to Christ, the joy and astonishment was enough to make me decide there was nothing in life I would rather do. Whether I continued to teach to support myself or depended on the church for my full salary appeared a minor consideration. The most important decision was full commitment to the art and technique of fishing for people for the rest of my days. I couldn't wait to start and, thirty years later, I have absolutely no plans to stop! It's marvelous, fishing with Jesus!

TO READ: *Luke 5:1-11*

WHAT IS A "CALL" OF GOD?

And as soon as they landed, they left everything and followed Jesus.

LUKE 5:11

What is a "call" of God? Jesus calls in different ways in different situations.

There is a call to discipleship. Whether we serve Christ at home, in the marketplace, or in a faraway country, all of us are to put him and his call as our first priority.

There is also a call to special service that might lead us in another direction in life. When Jesus called these four fishermen to full-time service, they were already his disciples but were still involved in their business. Jesus came where they were washing their nets and called them to lay down their life's work to do his. So Peter, Andrew, James, and John "left everything and followed Jesus" (Luke 5:11). This kind of call may mean leaving our home or job.

A third type of call is illustrated in the life of Peter. This is the call to recommitment after failure. After Jesus' resurrection, he met Peter on a sandy beach and said, "Follow me" (John 21:19), letting Peter know that he was forgiven and still needed for the work of the kingdom. We, too, can still be used by God, even after we have failed him.

Wherever we are in our spiritual journey, we need to listen to and obey God's voice. He may be calling us to put the interests and plans of God before our own whatever the cost or to come back to God even after we've failed him. Be listening so that when God calls, in whatever way God calls, you'll be ready to answer.

TO READ: *Luke 7:36-50*

LOVING GOD

*"I tell you, her sins—and they are many—have been forgiven,
so she has shown me much love. But a person who is
forgiven little shows only little love."*

LUKE 7:47

Have you ever wanted to love God more and wondered how to do it?
In Luke 7 we are introduced to a woman who had been forgiven
much.

Her action of kneeling behind Jesus, and anointing and kissing his
feet, took much courage for this "immoral" woman (Luke 7:37). Her need
and desire for forgiveness gave her the courage. Her outpouring of love was
an expression of profound sorrow for her sin and perhaps gratefulness that
she could be forgiven. Jesus made the point that because her many sins had
been forgiven, she was showing "much love" (Luke 7:47). Jesus publicly
affirmed her forgiveness, then added, "Your faith has saved you; go in
peace" (Luke 7:50).

When we experience God's forgiveness for the many sins we have
committed, our love response will depend on our realization of the
seriousness of sin and what it cost the Lord Jesus to put it right. When
I was a new convert to Christianity, I looked at my life through God's
eyes. As I read the Scriptures and thought about the Cross, I began to be
thoroughly upset by the fact that my sins were the reason for his death.
Yes, I had been forgiven much, and the more I recognized my need of a
Savior and his willingness to forgive me, the more my love for him grew.

Ask the Lord to show you the depths of your sin and what it cost the
Lord Jesus to forgive you. The depths of his redeeming love will deepen
your own love response to him.

TO READ: Luke 8:1-18

THE SEED

"A farmer went out to plant some seed. As he scattered it across his field,
some seed fell on a footpath, where it was stepped on,
and the birds came and ate it."

LUKE 8:5

"Anyone who is willing to hear should listen and understand!" said Jesus (Luke 8:8). He was telling a story about a farmer sowing seed. "The seed is God's message," he said (Luke 8:11). The speaker can control the message, but cannot control the hearers. The hearers evaluate the word of God as they receive it from the preacher.

All too often, the personality of the preacher gets in the way, and the hearers end up evaluating the preacher, not what he said. If you dislike the man, you probably will have little respect for his message. Yet Jesus said when his farmers—or preachers—scatter the seed, we should receive it.

In a little English churchyard, there stands a tall, beautiful oak tree. There is nothing strange about that, until you realize it is growing right through the middle of a gravestone! The force of life has been so strong that it has split the stones in two as the tree has pushed upward toward the light. What dynamic power in a tiny acorn!

There is similar power in the seed of God. When sown in good soil, though buried underneath concrete, it will break through. The first thing we need to do is receive the seed sown by the preachers God has given us. We must listen to God's message and then go to God's Word and discover it for ourselves. The more we study and read, the more that tiny acorn from God's Word can grow into a strong oak in our lives!

TO READ: *Luke 8:1–18*

PATHWAY THINKING

*"The seed that fell on the hard path represents those who hear the message,
but then the Devil comes and steals it away and prevents them
from believing and being saved."*

LUKE 8:12

As the farmer sowed his seed, he inadvertently dropped some on the hard path that wound through the cultivated areas. Jesus compared this picture to the minds of "pathway people" who receive the Word of God without understanding (Matthew 13:19).

The mind is the avenue through which truth travels to our hearts to give us spiritual experience. If the soil of our minds is like pathway soil, nothing will take root, and the seeds of the fruit of truth will not be carried along into our understanding. The wind of other concerns will blow it away before it has time to be translated into sense.

Satan stands by the pathway person's mind. He watches the seed fall and snatches it away like a ravenous bird. He doesn't want that person to believe the message and be saved, so he will distract in any way he can (Mark 4:15).

Pathway people do not believe they need Jesus Christ. They may not accept the fact that he is divine, or relate him to themselves or their dilemma. In fact, pathway people do not even believe they are in a dilemma. They never listen in church. They fill their minds with thistle fluff that will not trouble them. They believe anything that is comfortable, acceptable, and even respectable.

Is your mind like pathway soil? Or is it a fertile field where the seed can grow?

TO READ: *Luke 8:1-18*

ROOTED AND GROUNDED

*"The rocky soil represents those who hear the message with joy.
But like young plants in such soil, their roots don't go very deep.
They believe for a while, but they wilt when the hot winds of testing blow."*

LUKE 8:13

W hen the going gets tough, the tough get going," so they say. Yet those who do not let the seed of the Word of God take root in their lives, will *get* going, but not be able to *keep* going when the tough times come!

"Nobody told me my Christianity would cause such trouble at home," complained a teenager accusingly. But Jesus was always warning people about the costliness of being his disciples (Luke 14:26-33).

It's all very well to get worked up at a meeting or a conference and to go home on a spiritual high. But ahead is Monday morning, or a husband who doesn't want anything to do with your Christ, or maybe a hostile teenager who will laugh at you. What happens when you offend your friends with the great glad news of your conversion? If your life is filled with rocks, and there has been little attempt to cultivate and pull out the weeds and the stones, your profession of faith will never stand up to opposition.

Jesus says his seed will test us and find us wanting if we are all noise and no fruit. When a rootless believer feels the hot sun and burning winds of rejection, he will soon wither away. Let us grow roots downward, so we can bear fruit upward!

TO READ: *Luke 8:1–18*

PLEASURE'S PRETTY FLOWERS

"The thorny ground represents those who hear and accept the message,
but all too quickly the message is crowded out by the cares and riches
and pleasures of this life. And so they never grow into maturity."

LUKE 8:14

Weeds are awful things. Who has ever kept a garden and has not wanted to have a word with Adam about being the cause of all these choking growths? "Cares and riches and pleasures of this life" can very easily choke the spiritual seed God wishes to cultivate. But it doesn't have to be so. God has given us all things richly to enjoy, and it is the love of money—not money itself—that can become an obsession. But there is no doubt about it—there are many beautiful weeds!

My husband's favorite color is yellow. Every spring he smiles with satisfaction at our yellow lawn—a sea of golden dandelions, stretching from boundary to boundary. Our neighbors do not share his joy. In fact, spring is a time I try to leave and return to the house in the dark to avoid a confrontation! Dandelions are pretty, but if not dealt with, they will choke the grass and spread to other lawns, causing consternation everywhere.

Pleasures are pretty, too. We need the Sower to test the soil of our lives and make sure the seed of truth is growing strongly and is not being choked by pleasure's pretty flowers. A garden is intended to produce fruit. We need to give our heavenly Gardener permission to till the garden of our lives and rid our souls of weeds.

TO READ: *Luke 8:1–18*

GOOD SOIL

*"But the good soil represents honest, good-hearted people who hear
God's message, cling to it, and steadily produce a huge harvest."*

LUKE 8:15

The Bible says, "The way to identify a tree or a person is by the kind of fruit that is produced" (Matthew 7:20). The authentic Christian hears and receives the Word of God, makes sure the roots of that seed go deep into her thinking, weathers the storms of opposition, and does not allow worry weeds or pleasure's pretty flowers to choke the fruit that is inevitable if the conditions are right.

When the Bible talks about fruit, it is referring to character (Galatians 5:22-23). If we fill our lives with good soil, we will need to bring forth his fruit "with patience." Character is not grown in a single night. It takes a long time to learn self-control and love, to live peaceably with all people, or to suffer long and patiently.

Finally, a word of caution: It is the Sower who will judge and test the soil. That is not our job. The fruit should give us a hint as to where people stand. But in the last analysis, the Savior will decide.

I dreamt death came the other night
  and Heaven's gates swung wide.
An angel with a halo bright
  ushered me inside.
And there to my astonishment stood folks
  I'd judged and labeled
As "quite unfit," "of little worth,"
  and "spiritually disabled."
Indignant words rose to my lips, but
  never were set free,
For every face showed stunned surprise;
  No one expected me!

TO READ: *Luke 9:49-50*

COPING WITH PRIVILEGE

John said to Jesus, "Master, we saw someone using your name to cast out
demons. We tried to stop him because he isn't in our group."

LUKE 9:49

We are supposed to learn humility on the mountain! Jesus took his three special friends up the Mount of Transfiguration to teach them humility. They were supposed to see how great Jesus was and how small they were. Visions of God should do that to us, and not result in a sense of our own importance!

The nine disciples at the foot of the mountain could not help a family in trouble. James and John could not cope with privilege. It went to their heads. It wasn't long before they were telling the master to forbid "outsiders" a ministry. When we begin to think that we are the only ones who have a corner on the truth, we are in trouble. Jesus said, "Don't stop him! Anyone who is not against you is for you" (Luke 9:50).

Some of us have been blessed beyond measure. We come from Christian homes and have been taught the Bible from our youth. We have listened to God's best on radio and TV. We have bookcases full of excellent Christian literature. We have peace in our country and may worship freely. Much has indeed been given to us and much will indeed be required!

God requires our toleration of those less privileged. We are to support the weak, encourage the ignorant, disciple the undisciplined, and discern gifts in others. We are not to forbid a ministry! We are to use our privilege to the advantage of others!

TO READ: *Luke 10:1–16*

THE NEW RECRUITS

*The Lord now chose seventy-two other disciples and sent them on ahead in
pairs to all the towns and villages he planned to visit.*

LUKE 10:1

J esus had spent a very frustrating time with his twelve specially chosen
men. If I had been Jesus, I would not have felt like choosing another
seventy-two! If the twelve represented the best, Jesus must have worried
about the new recruits! But the Lord worked with raw material, and he
never gave up!

When I am training others to go out and serve God, I gain help from
the Lord's example. He went right ahead choosing people to do his work,
trusting them with ministry, and dealing with their failures. After the
twelve had failed, disappointed, and frustrated him, the seventy-two
returned rejoicing! "Lord," they said, "even the demons obey us when
we use your name!" (Luke 10:17).

Fancy the seventy-two doing better than the twelve! That must have
been a humbling experience for Jesus' closest disciples. I wonder how they
handled that! Can you handle someone else's success? When a younger
Christian succeeds where you have failed, can you rejoice?

Jesus was delighted! He said, "O Father, Lord of heaven and earth,
thank you for hiding the truth from those who think themselves so wise
and clever, and for revealing it to the childlike. Yes, Father, it pleased you
to do it this way" (Luke 10:21). New recruits should delight us. It's the old
recruits that can give us a hard time. Old or young, we need to remember
we are part of Jesus' army. If we would only stop fighting each other, we
may get around to winning the war!

TO READ: *Luke 15:11-32*

THE LONG WALK HOME

*"We had to celebrate this happy day. For your brother was dead and
has come back to life! He was lost, but now he is found!"*

LUKE 15:32

God is like the father in this story. We are like the Prodigal Son.
When we sin and turn away from the Father, he doesn't stop us
or run after us. He gives us the dignity of choice, but he also gives us the
freedom to live with the consequences of our choices!

Like the Prodigal Son, sinful humanity "lives it up," wasting life in
rebellious living (Luke 15:13). After a while, the "pigsty" in which humanity
finds itself doesn't seem such a good idea after all. So some of us prodigals
come to our senses and return to our offended and grieving Father (Luke
15:17). And, like the prodigal son, we find our Father waiting and watching
for our return. True repentance leads to forgiveness. God forgives us and
brings us back to himself.

The grace of God is clear in this parable. The son wasted his
inheritance, hurt his father deeply, and brought dishonor to the family
name. But when he came to his senses, the son realized that the only
thing to do was to take that long walk home and beg for forgiveness.

The human race is composed of prodigals. All of us have been on the
road of rebellion, seeking to find our own way. Each individual needs to
make that long walk home! Have you returned to God? Have you
renewed that broken relationship with your Father? He is watching and
waiting for your return. And he has a party planned!

THE SEEKING GOD

*"And I, the Son of Man, have come to seek and
save those like him who are lost."*

LUKE 19:10

G od is a bridge builder. When humanity's relationship with God was
spoiled, God began to build a bridge—a bridge he could walk over
to seek lost humanity. That bridge was Jesus Christ. Why did God bother
with sinful humanity? Because he loves us. John 3:16 says, "For God so
loved the world that he gave his only Son." Not only did he give, but he
seeks. God is a seeking God. He came in Christ Jesus "to seek and save
those . . . who are lost" (Luke 19:10).

Jesus told some stories to illustrate how God seeks people and wants
to save them. In the first story, a shepherd realized that he had lost a
precious sheep, and so went and searched diligently until he found the
straying animal. He was so happy when he found the sheep that he had a
party (Luke 15:6). In the same way, there is joy in heaven every time the
heavenly Father finds a straying human being, for he came to "save those
. . . who are lost" (Luke 19:10).

God wants to save you! He wants you to come to him through faith
in his Son. The Bible says that the angels rejoice when even one sinner
comes to Christ (Luke 15:10). There's a party being planned in heaven,
and you're the guest of honor! Respond to God, for he is seeking you.
What joy—for you and for all of heaven—when he finds you!

TO READ: *Luke 22:1-30*

WASHING THE FEET OF JUDAS

"For I, the Son of Man, must die since it is part of God's plan.
But how terrible it will be for my betrayer!"

LUKE 22:22

J esus provided an unforgettable example of serving others when he washed his disciples' dusty feet. Luke 22 and John 13 are parallel passages describing the same event—the last supper Jesus had with his disciples. The passage in John shows us that Jesus lovingly washed the feet of all his disciples, including Judas Iscariot, for he had not yet left to do his evil deed (John 13:30). Not only did Jesus show his disciples how to serve one another, but he also showed them, as they might later understand, that such service would always be appropriate no matter how their audience responded.

What a great gesture! I can see Jesus lovingly handling the traitor's feet, well aware that those same feet would shortly lead Jesus' enemies to the Garden of Gethsemane to arrest him! I can see him looking into Judas's eyes, while Judas tried to avert his own.

So often we want to be appreciated for our gracious acts of service. We look for something in return, but a servant spirit is a giving-with-no-strings-attached spirit. In this case washing the traitor's feet did not turn the man's heart back to God. But Jesus, knowing it wouldn't change Judas's mind, washed his feet anyway. That's grace. Grace gives without expecting a return.

By loving and serving our enemies, we may reconcile them to the Lord and to us—or we may not. But whether or not there is repentance and reconciliation is not the point. He who washed feet calls us to do the same, whatever the results may be!

TO READ: *Luke 23:1-12*

WHAT WAS JESUS DOING?

He asked Jesus question after question, but Jesus refused to answer.
LUKE 23:9

P erhaps you would never play such cruel word games with Jesus as Herod did, but there are other games just as hurtful to the Savior. Human beings can play the games of indifference, of rejection, or of willful ignorance. Modern people have grown "tolerant"—they simply walk over their Savior's sorrows and go on their way untouched, unreached, and unregenerate.

"Here is the man!" cried Pilate, displaying the tortured Christ, sure his sufferings would engender pity. Instead, the chief priests and officers cried out, "Crucify! Crucify!" (John 19:6). And what was Jesus doing while all this was going on? Nothing! He who had the power to summon ten thousand angels to his help chose to stand helplessly, resigned to die because there was no other way to reconcile the world to God! He who had the power to consume his enemies with the breath of his mouth refused to answer, though every effort was employed to make him talk. Jesus didn't play games with his enemies; he was tall and straight and true. He told us he was the truth, the way, and eternal life—and then rested his case. He neither teased us with the unattainable nor taunted us with the irresistible, but simply offered us salvation. Here is the man! The Man of men—God himself in human form!

Then dare to play your games if you will! As for me, I am sold—devastated by the story of the God-man subjected to humiliation that defies description. I am captured, reduced to tears—I worship!

TO READ: *Luke 23:26-38*

WHAT WAS
JESUS THINKING?

*Finally, they came to a place called The Skull. All three were crucified
there—Jesus on the center cross, and the two criminals on either side. Jesus
said, "Father, forgive these people, because they don't know what they are
doing." And the soldiers gambled for his clothes by throwing dice.*

LUKE 23:33-34

W hat does a person think about when he is being crucified? When
you are the Son of God dying for a lost world, you think of
forgiveness. Jesus showed us how to react to the ones responsible for our
agony! We are to pardon them for it! But how on earth do we do that? We
pray about it! What a part prayer played in the life of our Lord—Jesus,
hanging on the cross, was in prayer! He was in prayer for his tormentors.
Whom did Jesus need to pardon? The disciples who forsook him and fled,
the soldiers who played dice for his clothes, the Pharisees who railed at
him, and the people who simply stood watching!

Who is causing your suffering? Have friends seen your misfortune
and forsaken you? Have people railed at you in the heat of an argument?
Have others simply stood seeing your pain and doing nothing to help?
Whom do you need to forgive?

We are commanded to forgive by the one who forgave us. "Pray for
those who despitefully use you, and forgive as you have been forgiven,"
Jesus said. When we understand the breadth of Christ's forgiveness,
perhaps we will not find it impossible to pardon our own persecutors!
Then we will need to tell those who have hurt us that we have forgiven
them. Jesus prayed aloud, so everyone could hear: "Father, forgive these
people, because they don't know what they are doing."

TO READ: *Luke 23:39-43*

WHAT WAS JESUS SAYING?

And Jesus replied, "I assure you, today you will be with me in paradise."

LUKE 23:43

Jesus talked to the repentant thief on the cross and promised him paradise. When you are by the side of a dying person, paradise is a great topic of conversation. Even if you, too, are suffering, thinking of paradise can help. Jesus cared about thieves, robbers, and scoundrels. He took a cross from a murderer and chose to die among thieves! He forgave torturers and blessed the disciples that had abandoned him to his fate. He met treachery with the promises of God.

Are you sitting by the bedside of a dying friend? Think on paradise. Are you parting with a loved one? Listen to what Jesus is saying! "Today you will be with me in paradise." He will keep them safely for you, and he will keep you safely for them! He will reunite you in heaven—till then, abide in his love and care.

> *In heavenly love abiding,*
> *No change my heart shall fear;*
> *And safe is such confiding,*
> *For nothing changes here.*
> *The storm may roar without me,*
> *My heart may low be laid;*
> *But God is round about me,*
> *And can I be dismayed?*
> *Wherever He may guide me,*
> *No want shall turn me back;*
> *My Shepherd is beside me,*
> *And nothing can I lack.*
> *His wisdom ever waketh,*
> *His sight is never dim;*
> *He knows the way He taketh,*
> *And I will walk with Him.*
> —ANNA L. WARING, 1850

TO READ: *Luke 24:13-34*

THE BIG, DARK HOUSE

Then Jesus quoted passages from the writings of Moses and all the prophets,
explaining what all the Scriptures said about himself.

LUKE 24:27

"The Old Testament is like a big, dark house. I'm afraid to go inside,"
a teenager once told me. What a joy to take her hand, step inside the
Scriptures, and see the Holy Spirit switch the light on, banishing her grim
forebodings! In the Old Testament there are so many wonderful stories
about real people with whom we can identify. There is adventure, history,
poetry, and lots of good advice as well.

But perhaps you feel like my friend did about the Old Testament.
The Bible says, "All Scripture is inspired by God and is useful to teach us
what is true" (2 Timothy 3:16). *All* means the Old Testament as well as
the New Testament. God breathed into the spirits of holy men of the past,
inspiring and moving them to write down the rich record that became the
Bible. We need to read the entire Bible. The Old Testament prepares for
the New, and the New helps to explain the Old. A good reference Bible
will help to link the Old and New Testaments together and explain some
of the basics you may need to know.

Don't be afraid of the Old Testament. It may seem like a big, dark
house, but the Holy Spirit can turn on the lights. The Old Testament
wasn't done away with when the New Testament was written. The Old
Testament is also Christ's home, for he lives in all Scripture, walking its
grand corridors, hoping to meet us there.

TO READ: *John 1:1-18*

WE HAVE TO BE FAMILY

But to all who believed him and accepted him, he gave the right to become children of God. They are reborn! This is not a physical birth resulting from human passion or plan—this rebirth comes from God.

JOHN 1:12-13

What is the will of God? The will of God is revealed in the context of our personal relationship with him. To know the will of God, we have to be part of his family. We can know the will of God the Father only if we have been "reborn" by the Holy Spirit into the Father's family. We do this by believing in Jesus and accepting him as Savior. "But to all who believed him and accepted him, he gave the right to become children of God. They are reborn! . . . This rebirth comes from God" (John 1:12-13). How can we be sure that we are part of God's family? God promised it: "You are all children of God through faith in Christ Jesus" (Galatians 3:26).

When we have become members of God's family, we will want to learn what brings our Father pleasure, and we will begin to understand what the head of our family wants for us. As children grow older and get to know their human father, they soon come to understand what pleases or displeases him, brings him honor or shame, delights or disappoints him. They also grow in their perception of his hopes and dreams for them.

Have you joined the family? The Father is waiting to welcome you. Are you already in the family? Then talk to God. He's not hiding his will from you—he wants you to know it, but he also wants you to know him. He will guide you one step at a time.

TO READ: *John 1:19-28*

THE KING IS COMING

John replied in the words of Isaiah: "I am a voice shouting in the wilderness,
'Prepare a straight pathway for the Lord's coming!'"
JOHN 1:23

J ohn the Baptist said he was the servant sent before the King to prepare
the pathway. What did he mean? When Eastern kings and emperors
visited their realms, a servant was always sent ahead to prepare the pathway.
Torrential downpours often caused roads to cave in and mountains to slide
down onto the highways, blocking traffic. The servant's job was to make
sure the highways were repaired, with all the holes filled in, so the way was
fit for the king!

This custom was familiar to the people of John's day. So when John
cried out, "Prepare a straight pathway for the Lord's coming," the meaning
was unmistakable. The people knew their national road in Israel needed
repair—the Jews served Rome. The people had family problems—personal
paths to clear up too. Their lives were a mess of rubble that needed
attention. The Jews knew that Isaiah the prophet had said that when the
Messiah came, he would restore all things (Isaiah 11:12). John told them
the King was coming, and it was time to pick up a shovel and get to work.

Repentance is taking up a shovel and showing God you mean
business. It's being sorry enough to make restitution where possible.
Then the King will come!

TO READ: *John 1:35–51*

THE SILENT YEARS

Philip went off to look for Nathanael and told him, "We have found the very person Moses and the prophets wrote about! His name is Jesus, the son of Joseph from Nazareth." "Nazareth!" exclaimed Nathanael. "Can anything good come from there?" "Just come and see for yourself," Philip said.

JOHN 1:45-46

J esus got his training for the ministry at home in Nazareth. We know very little about those thirty "silent years." We do know Joseph died (though we are not sure when), making Jesus head of his earthly family, the breadwinner. He lived as a part of a small country community and plied a trade. These years belong to Mary and to Jesus' brothers and sisters. Apart from these things, we know nothing.

The Gospel writers respect the silent years and do not intrude. Jesus used that time to prepare himself for his spiritual calling.

Do you live in a Nazareth? Perhaps you feel that there is nothing special about your hometown. Maybe your family is an ordinary one, which does pretty routine things. You have a so-so job and your life goes on its way, uninterrupted with much trauma. Did you know that these "silent years" are important?

The mundane atmosphere of your Nazareth does not mean you need to be a mundane Christian. "Nazareth living" can be a test of your commitment to Christ. If God called you to leave home and begin to serve him today, would you be ready? Seminaries do not servants make! Nazareths do! If these are your silent years, make sure they are busy ones. If you cannot serve God in Nazareth, he will never send you to serve him anywhere else.

TO READ: *John 3:1-21*

I NEED TO BE
BORN AGAIN

"So don't be surprised at my statement that you must be born again."

JOHN 3:7

H ave we received spiritual life? Let us consider whether God's "wind" has changed us or if our life looks just the same today as it always has.

Jesus explained to Nicodemus that he needed to be born from above. "I assure you, unless you are born again, you can never see the Kingdom of God" (John 3:3). Nicodemus had been born physically when God "breathed into [him] the breath of life" (Genesis 2:7), giving life to his body and soul. But there was something more. Now this teacher of Israel needed to be born spiritually. The life of the Spirit needed to bring life to Nicodemus's spirit, which in a way was an even greater miracle than that of his physical birth.

Jesus told Nicodemus, "Don't be surprised at my statement that you must be born again" (John 3:7). First Jesus said "you"; then he added "must." The word *you* in Greek is plural—all who want to enter God's kingdom must first be born again. Jesus showed that this was an eternal matter, that life in the kingdom of God could not even begin without the activity of the Holy Spirit. Jesus explained that Nicodemus must be related to him by being "born again." That can be brought about only by the work of the Holy Spirit. If this was true for Nicodemus, a great teacher of Israel, it is certainly true for all of us. We must be born again.

TO READ: *John 3:22-36*

THE BEST MAN

*John's disciples came to him and said, "Teacher, the man you met on the
other side of the Jordan River, the one you said was the Messiah,
is also baptizing people. And everybody is going over there
instead of coming here to us."*

JOHN 3:26

Talk about pressure! Jesus' disciples were baptizing just around the
bend of the river from the place John was baptizing. Can you
imagine Jesus setting up a church on your block? What would that do to
your congregation?

John's answer is an example to all Christians who struggle with
jealousy when their ministry is threatened by someone else: "I am filled
with joy at his success" (John 3:29).

How can you say "I am filled with joy" when you are losing people
to another church? Maybe you are leading a Bible study. Some "new kid
on the block" begins a meeting the same night as yours. One by one, your
people disappear. How do you handle that? Or you are teaching an
elective seminar at a convention. Six women come into your room, while
the speaker across the hall has to ask you for some of your empty chairs!

John said, in essence, "Jesus is my friend. He is the bridegroom, and
the best man never competes!" We need to remember that we are only
and ever the "best man." The One who must get all the glory is Jesus. If he
chooses to diminish my responsibility and give it to another, that is his
prerogative. After all, it is his wedding!

John lived by a very simple principle: "He must become greater and
greater, and I must become less and less" (John 3:30). When we live by
the same principle, we, too, will be able to say, "I am filled with joy."

TO READ: *John 4:1–8*

VALUABLE VIRTUES

He had to go through Samaria on the way.

JOHN 4:4

We were getting ready to do a "values survey" in our community. Being charged with the responsibility of women's ministries at our church, I needed to know what women thought in order to better serve and minister to them. We decided to collect data from five thousand ladies concerning their sexual, social, and spiritual values. Coming across the biblical record of Jesus' conversation with the woman of Samaria in John 4, I realized he was using the "survey method" as well! This gave me great encouragement, and I avidly researched his methods and noted the good results!

First of all, I noticed that he talked with the woman *when* he was wearied with his journey (John 4:6). Though faint with hunger and waiting for his disciples to bring meat, he knew that his "meat" was to do the will of the One that sent him. Jesus watched for every opportunity to interview people on the most personal levels concerning their values, without thought of the cost to himself.

Then I noted *where* he questioned the woman. He chose a center of ordinary daily activity—the village well. He did not go to the synagogue when seeking to answer the cry of lost sheep. He knew he would find such hungry souls outside church boundaries. We have to ask the right people the right questions in the right places if we are to have the glorious chance to give them the right answers.

TO READ: *John 4:9-15*

TIPS ON TALKING

The woman was surprised, for Jews refuse to have anything to do with Samaritans. She said to Jesus, "You are a Jew, and I am a Samaritan woman. Why are you asking me for a drink?"

JOHN 4:9

How can we start a conversation about God? Start talking about things the other person understands. Jesus started with a bucket! Next, make sure you show interest in people as people. Jesus cared about the Samaritan woman's personal problems, and she knew it. Don't be sidetracked. The woman wanted to start arguing about which church to go to, but Jesus reminded her that it was the Person she worshiped that was important, not the place of worship.

Don't be shocked. Know your world and what's going on out there; there is a difference between isolation and separation. Jesus was never isolated from sinners, but he was separate from sin. Next, realize that sin is a symptom of the real problem—a soul-thirst only God can quench. Tell people that Jesus is the answer to their thirsty quest. Don't be afraid to talk about salvation, souls, and sin; Jesus did.

Talk naturally. You should be able to talk about your faith as freely as you do about your family. Jesus made spiritual talk easy and comfortable for others, because it was easy and comfortable for him. Be sure not to put on a special voice when you talk about God—use your usual one!

And, finally, don't run after your prospective converts; Jesus didn't. When they've had enough, let them go—but pray for them. And then watch them come back with their friends. What joy! Talking of truth satisfies as nothing else can. You may even conquer your appetite the way Jesus did, just with the fullness of it all!

TO READ: *John 4:16-26*

A HEART FOR WOMEN

*"For you have had five husbands, and you aren't even married
to the man you're living with now."*

JOHN 4:18

J esus had a heart for women. The disciples were astonished to find him speaking with a woman, especially a woman of the despised Samaritans—a woman who had had five husbands and who was living with a sixth man at the time she talked with Jesus! Yet Jesus saw her need. She thirsted for relationships to fill her empty life. "Wouldn't you like to have that thirst quenched?" Jesus inquired.

We would do well to ask all thirsty women the same question. With broken marriages behind them, many women are searching for their identity, their happiness in a meaningful union. But you can't quench spiritual thirst with a marriage—however meaningful it may be! "God is Spirit," Jesus reminded the woman of Samaria (John 4:24). His Spirit is like living water and quenches our thirst. "Please, sir," said the woman, "give me some of that water" (John 4:15).

Today we can ask him to do that for us, too. We can simply say, "Jesus, I need you; Jesus, I want you; give me this water." We will need to leave our sinful lives behind us as the Samaritan woman left her bucket, but then, like the woman at the well, we'll never thirst again.

> *Jesus, I thirst—*
> *Quench me;*
> *Jesus, I hunger—*
> *Feed me;*
> *Jesus, I'll tell—*
> *Send me.*

TO READ: *John 4:27-30*

WHAT WILL THEY SAY?

Just then his disciples arrived. They were astonished to find him talking to a woman, but none of them asked him why he was doing it or what they had been discussing.

JOHN 4:27

Thinking about the story of Jesus and the woman at the well made me realize how many of us live crippled Christian lives because of "what *they* might say." "They" can be Great-aunt Alice, my husband or child, my sophisticated friend, or even the gossip at the women's club. Jesus didn't bother himself with what "they" might say about his conversation with a despised woman because he cared deeply about what God had already said! That's why he made himself of no reputation and humbled himself, and that's why we must do the same. Jesus told us that as the Father had sent him, so he would send us (John 20:21).

Years ago I got to know a rough street boy. After he became a Christian, he asked me to go with him to talk to his friends. "Where are they?" I inquired.

"In the pub," he answered.

"Oh, I couldn't go in there," I quickly responded. "Whatever would people say?" I was pretty sure that if I were to go into a place like that, the church organist would happen by as I entered with my new friend.

"He made himself of no reputation," God reminded me. "Now go and do likewise." So I went—because I tried to care more about what *he* had already said than what *they* might get around to saying. "Lord, humble me and may you find me fighting to be faithful, rather than seeking popularity. May I care about *your* reputation and learn to let you care about mine."

TO READ: *John 4:31-38*

REAPING THE
GRAIN OF GRACE

"Do you think the work of harvesting will not begin until the summer ends four months from now? Look around you! Vast fields are ripening all around us and are ready now for the harvest."

JOHN 4:35

L ook around you," said Jesus to his disciples. "Vast fields . . . are ready now for the harvest," he exhorted them. Squinting against the midday sun, the disciples followed Jesus' gaze. Coming up the hill toward the village well were the men of Samaria, led by the woman to whom Jesus had been talking. Of course it was the men that the woman went to first. Men were her weakness, but men she knew, men she loved, and men she would tell about "a man who told me everything I ever did" (John 4:29). Coming to Jesus, the men entreated him to stay with them, and he graciously accepted their invitation.

I am sure the disciples weren't sure about it all, but Jesus, who "had to go through Samaria" (John 4:4), knew he "had to" stay two days with the woman and her friends (John 4:40). And the inevitable miracle happened— many believed that Jesus "is indeed the Savior of the world" (John 4:42).

This, then, was the harvest Jesus spoke about to his disciples. To see similar possibilities, we will need to "look around." The disciples, assigned the mundane task of procuring bread from the village mill, had forgotten the Bread of Life who walked by their side. We must raise up our eyes to him daily and then follow his gaze to the harvest fields that are white already!

> *Hard I look—*
> *I see Thee,*
> *I follow Thine eye—*
> *I see them—*
> *Running—Ready—Ripe*
> *Send me forth, a harvester.*

COME AND DRINK

On the last day, the climax of the festival, Jesus stood and shouted
to the crowds, "If you are thirsty, come to me! If you believe in me,
come and drink! For the Scriptures declare that rivers of
living water will flow out from within."

JOHN 7:37-38

What a real experience of deep soul happiness we find when we receive from Christ the free gift of the Holy Spirit. We discover, through the Holy Spirit, an inexhaustible fountain of life in Christ. We can come with our bucket of faith and put it into the fountain with faith and prayer, drawing out spiritual blessings. Then, like the woman Jesus met at Jacob's well, we can run back to our thirsty, needy world to share the Good News with our friends (John 4:28).

As the prophet Isaiah promised, "With joy [we] will drink deeply from the fountain of salvation!" (Isaiah 12:3). Joy is very important. Without joy, our fountain of life becomes bitter. Not too many people will readily drink from a poisoned fountain. And not too many folks will be eager to accept a drink of anything from a person with a sour face!

But perhaps you're not feeling bitter; instead, you feel that your fountain of life is running dry. Perhaps you feel like someone has dumped "dirt" (such as worry, fear, or doubt) in your well and dried you up, blocking the flow of God's Spirit. You need to ask God to reopen the well, so you can once again draw up the blessings of the Holy Spirit and give refreshment to those around you.

Jesus spoke of a beautiful experience that can be ours. All who are thirsty should listen, believe, and drink. Put in your bucket, and when you draw it out, share the refreshment of God's Holy Spirit with others.

TO READ: *John 8:1-11*

A NEW START

"No, Lord," she said. And Jesus said, "Neither do I. Go and sin no more."

JOHN 8:11

H ave you ever felt like you have been "caught in the very act" by the religious community or some other group? If so, you will be able to empathize with this unnamed woman.

One day Jesus faced a group of religious leaders who dragged out in front of him a woman they had caught actually committing adultery. The law said she and the man involved should be stoned to death. However, the religious leaders brought only the woman to Jesus. You can almost hear them sneering, "If this man Jesus claims to be the Son of God, let's see what he does with this situation!"

The point of this story is not the woman's sin but the calling of sinners. Jesus, the Savior, offers forgiveness and a new start to any who will repent. There was no doubt that the woman had sinned. Jesus did not dispute the fact that she had committed adultery. Nor did he dispute that this was against God's law—one of the Ten Commandments in fact (Exodus 20:14). But Jesus chose to forgive her. In the process he taught the religious leaders a lesson about their own sinfulness! They slunk away, unable to cast stones because Jesus had forced them to look inside their own hearts! Jesus didn't condemn the woman either. But then he added, "Go and sin no more" (John 8:11).

"Go and sin no more" is where new life begins.

GRAVECLOTHES

And Lazarus came out, bound in graveclothes, his face wrapped in a
headcloth. Jesus told them, "Unwrap him and let him go!"

JOHN 11:44

I magine waking up from the dead, only to find that you can't move—
you're awake but bound tightly by strips of cloth. Think what this
experience must have been like for Lazarus. He heard Jesus' words calling to
him, "Lazarus, come out!" (John 11:43) and had no choice but to obey. He
struggled to his feet and shuffled to the entrance to his tomb and out into
the sunlight. Standing in the midst of stunned and wondering neighbors, he
found himself unable to see or move his hands. Straining to hear sounds he
couldn't fathom, he realized the incredible fact of his resurrection. He was
back on earth, imprisoned in his graveclothes. Eager hands unwrapped the
stifling cloth from his face, his body, his arms, his legs. Lazarus was set free
to start life anew. Many of the witnesses believed in Jesus at that point
(John 11:45), and God was glorified.

When Jesus rose again, he left his graveclothes behind too (John
20:3-7). Graveclothes don't belong on the living. Graveclothes belong
on those in the grave.

Are you wearing graveclothes? What did you bring into your Christian
life that should have been left behind? What binds your mouth, your
hands, your feet, and keeps you from glorifying God? Listen to Life
himself. He is saying that you need to have your graveclothes unwrapped
and thrown away. This will be a testimony of what Christ has done for
you in giving you new life. Throw away your graveclothes; they are poor
dress for a living person!

TO READ: *John 13:1-20*

ADONAI

"You call me 'Teacher' and 'Lord,' and you are right, because it is true."
JOHN 13:13

I saw the Lord. He was sitting on a lofty throne, and the train of his robe filled the Temple," said Isaiah (Isaiah 6:1).

Adonai speaks of master-ownership. "You call me Adonai and so I am," said Jesus Christ to his disciples. God revealed his ownership of us through Israel and expects our obedience and respect.

There are good masters and bad masters. God is a good master—one who makes sure his servants are properly cared for and reimbursed for their services. Paul delighted to call himself a slave and to serve the Lord Christ, never doubting that God was his master, and marveling at the rewards of his servitude.

Do you ever worry that Christianity will reduce you to servitude? I have news for you—it will! But it will turn out to be glad and willing service—a voluntary offering. You will soon count it a privileged calling.

Our master is master of the universe, of the people in it, and of their destiny. He is master of our earthly masters. He is master of our situations, master of our trials and our joys. He is the master master!

I hear people talking about making Jesus Christ Lord or master of their lives. They cannot do that. They cannot make him what he is already. He is Adonai, and you and I had better get around to acknowledging him as such.

SEPTEMBER

TO READ: *John 13:1-20*

KNOW POWER

"You know these things—now do them! That is the path of blessing."
JOHN 13:17

People who leave their graveclothes behind them act, speak, and walk quite differently.

A young teacher accepted Christ. Dead to God, he was called by Christ out of the tomb of his troubles and loosed from his graveclothes. "Whenever teachers are on playground duty in my school," he told me, "the rest of us rip them to shreds behind their backs. Since I've found Jesus Christ, I can't find it in my heart to do that anymore!"

Another woman, who worked in a factory, held her own with the coarsest of men, her language turning the air around her a royal blue. The day after she walked forward at a Billy Graham crusade, a man sidled up and made a snide remark. She stood there, listening in silence. "What's up with you?" the man asked in amazement. "Last night I lost half my vocabulary," she said simply. Her graveclothes lay at the foot of the cross where they belonged.

But how do you find the power to live without the old, familiar graveclothes that have been so much a part of your old life? Sometimes, as in Lazarus's case, you need a helping hand. At other times, God frees your hands to remove them yourself. He tells you to put off the rags of the old life. We are to remove lying, stealing, laziness, bad language, bitterness, and clamor (Ephesians 4:26-31).

"Know power" works. "You know these things—now do them!" said Jesus.

TO READ: *John 14:1-14*

THE TRUTH
ABOUT THE TRUTH

Jesus told him, "I am the way, the truth, and the life.
No one can come to the Father except through me."

JOHN 14:6

W hat did Jesus mean when he said that? Did he claim to have a corner on all truth? Was he suggesting that other religions are false?

The Bible tells us that God does not *have* truth, he *is* truth; he is equal to his attributes. This means we can have tremendous assurance that what he has told us stands. "God is not a man, that he should lie" (Numbers 23:19). Truth includes the idea of faithfulness. We can depend upon God's being the truth, telling the truth, and explaining the truth to us.

Jesus Christ, God incarnate, is the true Truth about the truth! First of all, he is the Truth about God. "No one has ever seen God. But his only Son, who is himself God, is near to the Father's heart; he has told us about him" (John 1:18). Second, he is the Truth about humanity. He told us that people are basically evil (Mark 7:21-22), and that we love darkness rather than light (John 3:19). Third, he is the Truth about salvation. There is a way sinful people can live with a holy God. It's very simple, really. The holy God must forgive their sins.

Since Jesus claimed to be the true and holy God, we can believe him when he tells us that "everyone who believes in him will not perish but have eternal life" (John 3:16). You can't trust the word of many people anymore. But I have news for you—you *can* trust Jesus!

TO READ: *John 14:1–14*

FOLLOWING JESUS' EXAMPLE

*"The truth is, anyone who believes in me will do the same works I have done,
and even greater works, because I am going to be with the Father."*

JOHN 14:12

W hat does it mean to follow Jesus' example? Certainly we cannot do what he did. Let's take a look at three aspects of Jesus' ministry that teach us about how we, frail humans, can follow his example.

First, Jesus was a master teacher, and to follow his example we must obey his teachings. But Jesus' teaching cannot be followed without Jesus' power. We cannot live the Christian life without the Christ who lived it. People cannot be neutral about Jesus. We cannot follow his teachings without accepting the truth of everything he said and without accepting Christ himself by the Holy Spirit.

Second, Jesus lived to please his Father, not himself or other people. There will be times when we are reviled and must bless, or are forsaken and must walk alone. In such situations, we will need to keep our focus on pleasing our heavenly Father, not ourselves or others.

Finally, Jesus depended on his Father for power. If Jesus depended on God to raise the dead, we too can depend on God for any power we need. Jesus said, "Anyone who believes in me will do the same works I have done, and even greater works" (John 14:12).

It takes a lifetime to learn to be like Jesus, but it's worth every minute of it! His love is ours for the knowing. His strength is ours for the taking. His power is ours for the asking. As Jesus lived by the power of the Father, so can we (John 6:57).

TO READ: *John 14:15-21*

CHEEKY CHARLIE

"He is the Holy Spirit, who leads into all truth. The world at large cannot receive him, because it isn't looking for him and doesn't recognize him. But you do, because he lives with you now and later will be in you."

JOHN 14:17

D id you know the Holy Spirit can live in you? When Jesus told the disciples this, they couldn't grasp what Jesus meant; and sometimes it's hard for us to understand, too.

I remember listening to a street preacher trying to explain how Jesus could come and live inside the heart through the Holy Spirit. A man in the crowd, called Cheeky Charlie, a professional heckler of open-air speakers, shouted out, "Nonsense! How can Jesus come and live in your heart? Why, I've just passed a butcher's shop and seen a heart hanging in the window—it's nothing but a blood pump!" The preacher, well used to Cheeky Charlie's interruptions, asked him if he ever went "courting," and if he ever looked deep into his sweetheart's eyes and said, "Darling, I love you with all my blood pump." Charlie got the point.

The word *heart* is used as a figurative expression for the seat of the mind, will, and emotions—the deepest part of our being. God, through the Holy Spirit, wants to invade that region and live there! This is what makes a person a true Christian.

Jesus described the experience of the infilling of the Holy Spirit both as a well and as rivers of water. Doesn't that sound like a refreshing experience? Do you want to know how the Holy Spirit comes to live in you? You simply have to ask him. Invite him to come into your life. He will. Jesus promised he would.

TO READ: *John 14:22-31*

THE HELPER

"But when the Father sends the Counselor as my representative—
and by the Counselor I mean the Holy Spirit—he will teach you everything
and will remind you of everything I myself have told you."

JOHN 14:26

I s your memory a thing you forget with? Are you good at remembering
birthdays, wedding anniversaries, the names of your in-laws' family? How
about Scripture? Are you good at memorizing verses from the Bible? We are
told to hide God's Word in our hearts, and it will "check" us when we think
of sinning (Psalm 119:11). Jesus promised his disciples that he would send
the Holy Spirit into their hearts to help them remember his words. That
promise was for all disciples in all ages—people like you and me!

But even the Holy Spirit can't help us remember what we've never
taken the trouble to learn! Some people seem to think the Holy Spirit is a
magic wand standing in the corner of our minds. When we are too lazy to
learn something, we somehow expect him to cheat for us by whispering
the right answer in our ear. But he won't do that. He never said he would.
Our Lord said the Holy Spirit would be sent to teach us all things and
would then help us to remember what had been taught.

Now I don't know about you, but my memory needs help. It stands
to reason that I might need heavenly help when it comes to heavenly
things. But I must learn the spiritual concepts, do the studying, and work
at the memorizing. Only then will my heavenly Helper aid in the recall of
all that hidden treasure of wisdom in the vault of my heart.

A COMMON FOCUS

"I no longer call you servants, because a master doesn't confide in his servants. Now you are my friends, since I have told you everything the Father told me."

JOHN 15:15

How precious are Christian friendships! While we may have many kinds of friends in many different stages and walks of life, friendships with other Christian women can prove to be the most precious because we can share a spiritual bond. We are in tune with each other when we talk about Jesus.

When Jesus talked to his disciples near the end of his life, he explained that they were more than simply followers or servants; they were friends: "I no longer call you servants, because a master doesn't confide in his servants. Now you are my friends, since I have told you everything the Father told me" (John 15:15). That shared knowledge of the Father gave Jesus and the disciples a special depth of friendship.

An essential component of Christian friendship is sharing what we're learning from our heavenly Father about life's experiences. There is nothing that brings you closer to your Christian friends than sharing how God is a comfort in a bereavement you didn't expect, a divorce you didn't want, or a sickness you weren't anticipating. Life's lessons learned at the foot of the cross make for deep friendships! Exchanging mutual knowledge of Jesus not only gives you a common focus, it gives you shared secrets to treasure. If your friendships are lacking depth and appear shallow and trivial, try sharing a lesson you are learning about your heavenly Father. If you initiate it, you and your friend will probably soon be chatting away. The time you spend together with your friend will never be time enough!

TO READ: *John 16:1-15*

CONVERSION

*"And when he comes, he will convince the world of its sin,
and of God's righteousness, and of the coming judgment."*

JOHN 16:8

How can we possibly live the Christian life without Christ? We can't! It is the Holy Spirit who makes the life of Christ ours!

The Holy Spirit convicts us of sin. When someone first told me I was a sinner, I was most indignant. But after I thought about it, I began to feel uneasy, then guilty. This change of attitude was the Holy Spirit's work in my life.

The Holy Spirit convinces us that Jesus is the only answer to our sins (John 14:16-17). The same person who had the courage to talk to me about my sin problem also explained that Jesus had come to earth to take my punishment for me. She told me I needed to turn away from living for myself and to walk in God's way. It wasn't just her persuasive arguments that converted me to Christ—there was a power in her words. The Holy Spirit was using my friend to convince me of the truth of these things.

The Holy Spirit commands and empowers us to witness (Acts 1:8), commissions us to care (Acts 2:44-45), and consecrates us to serve (Acts 6:1-5). One of the miracles of conversion is a new focus and redirection of our activities. There is a pervading sense that time must now be used to help others know the Lord. We become other-oriented, instead of self-centered and self-absorbed. A great sense of God's purpose for our life will begin when we receive Christ by his Spirit. He will never leave us.

TO READ: *John 17:1-26*

KNOWING GOD

"And this is the way to have eternal life—to know you, the only true God,
and Jesus Christ, the one you sent to earth."

JOHN 17:3

K nowing God is imperative for salvation—you can't go to heaven
unless you know God through Christ. In his prayer for his disciples,
including those who follow him today, Jesus said, "This is the way to have
eternal life—to know you, the only true God, and Jesus Christ, the one
you sent to earth" (John 17:3). People need to know that God can be
known.

Knowing God does not involve knowing everything about him (we'd
have to be God to know all that). But God has given us knowledge that is
totally adequate for personal salvation. God has given us this knowledge
of himself in five main ways:

1. **Nature**—nature reveals the Creator (Psalm 19:1-4; Romans 1:20).
2. **Conscience**—God has put into people's hearts a natural understanding
   of right and wrong (Hebrews 10:16).
3. **The Ten Commandments**—God's requirements for people (Exodus
   20:1-17).
4. **Old and New Testaments**—all that we need to know to be saved and
   to live for him (Psalm 119:55, 68, 73; 2 Timothy 3:16).
5. **Christ**—if we would know God, we must know Christ. (John 1:14;
   10:30; 14:6-9).

God has given all the information people need in order to turn to
him and be saved. Knowing Jesus is the way to have true peace and eternal
life with God. Come to Jesus and find God. Then begin the adventure of
knowing God more and more every day, and begin the anticipation of
knowing and enjoying him forever.

TO READ: *John 19:28-37*

MISSION ACCOMPLISHED

When Jesus had tasted it, he said, "It is finished!"
Then he bowed his head and gave up his spirit.

JOHN 19:30

I t is finished!" Jesus was shouting in triumph, witnessing to heaven and earth and sea that the work of redemption was accomplished. These were not the whimpering words of a defeated man, but the victory salute of a conqueror. Will we be able to say, "It is finished," when our time comes? Not about the work of redemption, for only One could accomplish that—but about the work of telling the world about him. Will we cry, "*I am* finished" or "*It* is finished" when God calls us home?

Recently I heard of a young Christian man who died in an accident. He had lived his short life for his Lord, making every happy moment count. His life had not been "cut off" as some suggested, but completed. If we have sought to finish the work he has given us to do (notice it does not say that we are to finish the work he has given someone *else* to do!), then like our Savior we will be able to commit our spirit into the Father's keeping—in peace (Matthew 27:50). Jesus, because he was Jesus, could say, "Spirit, go home." We are not God and do not have the capacity to make our spirits obey us. But when God says to us, "Spirit, come home," we shall go. May our missions be accomplished and a glad cry of "It is finished" be on our lips!

FAITH IS THE BEST HANDKERCHIEF

Mary was standing outside the tomb crying,
and as she wept, she stooped and looked in.

JOHN 20:11

The angels in white, "sitting at the head and foot of the place where the body of Jesus had been lying," asked Mary, "Why are you crying?" Mary answered, "Because they have taken away my Lord . . . and I don't know where they have put him" (John 20:13). Tears, even necessary ones, can distort our vision. The distraught woman "glanced over her shoulder and saw someone standing behind her. It was Jesus, but she didn't recognize him." Just see what tears can do! She, supposing him to be the gardener, said to him, "If you have taken him away, tell me where you have put him, and I will go and get him" (John 20:15).

How can you mistake the risen Son of God for a gardener? Quite easily—if tears do not turn into triumphant faith. Belief in the Resurrection is the best handkerchief I know! Mary was mourning her Christ, her Savior, the One who had cast out the demons that had tormented her. Beside herself with grief, she shed her necessary tears. But there came a moment when a question needed to be asked: *"Why* are you crying? Who are you looking for?"

Faith realizes that Christ is alive! Then *who* can cry? Are you in shock? In mourning? Can you not see the Christ presenting himself to you as the answer, even to death? Can you hear his voice calling your name? Mary's tears prevented her from seeing her Savior. Let faith dry your eyes, look up, look around—then look ahead!

TO READ: *John 20:19-23*

THE FIRST AND FINEST MISSIONARY

He spoke to them again and said, "Peace be with you. As the Father has sent me, so I send you."

JOHN 20:21

God had one son, and he sent him to be a missionary. "For God so loved the world that he gave his only Son" (John 3:16). Jesus' mission was to go on a cross-cultural journey to tell the people he found about God. He left his home and family, traveled a long way, and identified with the people. He learned their language, ate their food, wore their clothes, and endured their sicknesses. He lived among the poorest folk in the obscurest village, and understood the deepest needs of the community.

But he also kept abreast of the national and international news and was articulate in expressing his biblically based views on the issues in focus. After thirty years of preparation, he began his preaching, teaching, and healing ministry. He went about doing good. He drew large crowds of people to hear his sermons, yet he always had time to listen and love the individual.

In the world's eyes, he failed in his missionary endeavors and was crucified for his trouble. But in God's sight, his mission was gloriously accomplished, and he returned home to a marvelous welcome and a grand reward. He paid the ultimate price a missionary is ever asked to pay—laying down his life for his God on the foreign mission field. But like other humble servants that followed after him, he lives forever in heaven, surrounded by his converts. Jesus was the first and finest missionary!

TO READ: *John 20:24-31*

DOUBTING THOMAS

They told him, "We have seen the Lord!" But he replied, "I won't believe it
unless I see the nail wounds in his hands, put my fingers into them, and
place my hand into the wound in his side."

JOHN 20:25

When most of the disciples first saw Jesus alive after his crucifixion, Thomas had not been with them. When the other disciples told him about the fact of the Resurrection, Thomas replied, "I won't believe it unless I see" (John 20:25). Some of us are skeptical like Thomas was. We find it very easy to doubt what we cannot see or touch. The word *doubt* implies uncertainty, not knowing which way to take. Doubt itself is a choice, a matter of the will.

Perhaps we too are suspicious by nature, wanting hard evidence before we'll go out on a limb about anything. We choose to believe what we believe; we choose to doubt what we want to doubt. The enemies of Jesus chose to deny his resurrection; they chose to believe that choosing to believe in the resurrection of Jesus Christ leads to joy, peace, and the experience of his risen life in us. The living Christ is the biggest reason we tell others about our faith. Paul, writing to the Corinthians, said, "If Christ has not been raised, then your faith is useless" (1 Corinthians 15:17). No other religion in the world boasts that its founder was actually God who became a man, was killed, yet rose again from the dead. Such claims should certainly be investigated! Even if you are skeptical by nature, like Thomas was, it is safe to investigate your doubts by taking them directly to Christ. Let him help you choose to believe!

TO READ: *John 20:24-31*

LOGOS

But these are written so that you may believe that Jesus is the Messiah,
the Son of God, and that by believing in him you will have life.

JOHN 20:31

God's *logos* is God's Word. In Revelation 19:13, it is used as the title of the Son of God. The Logos was one who did not merely keep company with the Godhead, but was deity himself (see 1 John 1:1)—one in whom all the treasures of divine wisdom were embodied. This logos became flesh and lived among us (see John 1:14). "We saw him with our own eyes and touched him with our own hands . . . the Word of life," John said (1 John 1:1). His name is Jesus! He is the Word of Life and the light of all people.

The light of the Logos overcame the darkness of a lost world. In fact, Jesus Christ was God's ultimate Word of light for our lost, dark days. Hebrews 1:1-2 tells us: "Long ago God spoke many times and in many ways to our ancestors through the prophets. But now in these final days, he has spoken to us through his Son." God has nothing more to say to us than he has already said, for he has said, "Jesus"!

So if "Jesus" was the most important thing that God has ever said, why don't we listen? Why don't we try to understand what God seeks to communicate to us? If Jesus, God's best thought, is not worth one of ours, there's something wrong! God's Logos came into the *cosmos* that the world should pay attention to him. The apostle John wrote about these things so that we could "have life" (John 20:31).

TO READ: *John 21:1-15*

A SPIRIT OF COMPETITION

After breakfast Jesus said to Simon Peter, "Simon son of John, do you love
me more than these?" "Yes, Lord," Peter replied, "you know I love you."
"Then feed my lambs," Jesus told him.

JOHN 21:15

Peter left his beloved blue, blue Sea of Galilee, his nets, his fish, and
all that was dear to follow Jesus. But Peter left something more
important than all of these things—his spirit of competition!

When he and Andrew had been business partners with the sons of
Zebedee, there had always been a sense of competitiveness. James and
John and old Zebedee had managed to do better than Peter and Andrew,
but Peter knew fishing. What's more, he had the physique. Look who
pulled the net ashore with 153 fishes in it (John 21:11)!

But Jesus asked Peter for that competitive nature on the seashore.
Breakfast had been eaten and Jesus asked, "Do you love me more than
these [the other disciples]?" Peter had been sure he loved the Lord more
than all the other disciples put together. Why, he had even told the Lord
so in front of them! But after three denials, he had to humbly admit he
had not beaten the others to it, in the matter of loving!

If we are to shepherd the Lord's sheep together, there is no room for
a spirit of competitiveness—the sort of spirit that says I am more loving or
more capable than others. We need to cooperate in brotherly love if the
sheep are to be fed. Do you need to give your competitive nature to Jesus?

TO READ: *John 21:15-23*

BREAKFAST WITH JESUS

*Once more he asked him, "Simon son of John, do you love me?" Peter was
grieved that Jesus asked the question a third time. He said, "Lord, you know
everything. You know I love you." Jesus said, "Then feed my sheep."*

JOHN 21:17

H ave you ever noticed how our senses aid memory? For example, the
scent of a rose brings a huge wave of nostalgia to my British heart.

After his resurrection, Jesus appeared to his disciples on a beach,
having made a charcoal fire and cooked their breakfast (John 21:9). Of all
of them, Peter must have caught his breath as he smelled the acrid smoke.
It surely surrounded him with memories of an awful night not too long
before when he had stood shivering as he warmed himself by another
charcoal fire (John 18:18).

Now, on a beach, the resurrected Jesus was cooking breakfast for
Peter and the others over a charcoal fire. After that meal, the Lord asked
Peter three times, "Do you love me?" Can you imagine how that question,
triggered by his recent failure, must have pierced Peter's soul? Yet Jesus let
Peter know that, in spite of his failure, Peter could be forgiven. What's
more, the resurrected Lord told him that he had special work for Peter
to do.

Are you willing to let go of your past sins? Loving and serving God is
a learned art—with many failures along the way. Peter could have told the
Lord to go away because he was not worthy to serve him. He could have
killed himself in despair, like Judas Iscariot did (Matthew 27:5). Instead,
Peter allowed Jesus Christ to forgive him, cleanse him from his sins, and
fill him with the Holy Spirit so that he could serve his Lord powerfully.
We can do the same.

TO READ: *John 21:15-23*

SOMETHING FOR NOTHING

Once more he asked him, "Simon son of John, do you love me?" Peter was grieved that Jesus asked the question a third time. He said, "Lord, you know everything. You know I love you." Jesus said, "Then feed my sheep."

JOHN 21:17

D iscipleship is not giving something for nothing; discipleship is giving nothing for something! Peter had nothing to give Jesus except his failure. Jesus took it, forgave it, and said, "Feed my sheep." When you have just made a total idiot of yourself in front of your friends, your enemies, and, indeed, the whole world, how incredible to hear Jesus commission you to serve him again!

Peter had served Jesus for three years. In his opinion, he had been giving him something for nothing. Hadn't he given Jesus the benefit of his strong body and personality, his time, his energy, his enthusiasm? *And all for nothing,* Peter must have thought proudly to himself. He had not charged Jesus for his services, or demanded special rooms or treatment when they traveled together.

But after the Cross, Peter was a broken man. He had denied his Lord and had followed him afar off. He came to realize discipleship is not giving something for nothing; discipleship is giving nothing for something!

Jesus loves us when we fail. We come to the end of our fleshly effort to be something or to do something and lay our nothings in his hand, and he gives them back to us, dressed in something new. He gives us hope for the future, a job to do for him, a sense of being needed after all, his power to overcome, and a great sense of worth. Now that's something!

Thank you, Jesus!

TO READ: *John 21:15-23*

THE COST OF GIVING OUR CHOICES TO JESUS

"The truth is, when you were young, you were able to do as you liked and go wherever you wanted to. But when you are old, you will stretch out your hands, and others will direct you and take you where you don't want to go."

JOHN 21:18

D iscipleship not only involves a call, a commitment, and a commission; it involves a cost—the loss of our independence. Our responsibilities take hold of our rights and lead them to places we would not choose to go.

Jesus spoke of this to Peter. Peter was crucified upside down. That surely was not the way Peter would have chosen to die! But he had no choice. When we are truly his disciples, Jesus makes our choices for us.

The thing that matters most to us is freedom—to dress ourselves as we wish, to come and go when we please, and to use our hands to shape our own destiny. Yet in one sentence, Jesus told Peter that discipleship would cost him all these freedoms. Another will dress him; cruel men will force him to walk to a dreadful, inverted cross, where his hands will be stretched out and his freedom to hold his own destiny, crucified.

Not all of us will be called to glorify God by such a death. But we are certainly called to glorify God by our lives. Commitment costs. Yet we need to remember the cost will be rewarded with a crown. When Jesus had finished talking with Peter about this matter, he said to him, "Follow me" (John 21:19). Peter gave his choices into the hands of Jesus and obeyed. Will we?

TO READ: *Acts 1:1–11*

YOU WILL
RECEIVE POWER

*"But when the Holy Spirit has come upon you, you will receive power
and will tell people about me everywhere—in Jerusalem, throughout Judea,
in Samaria, and to the ends of the earth."*

ACTS 1:8

I t's easy for us to talk about our vacation, grandchildren, or new job. It's harder for us to talk about the Lord.

Jesus said salvation must be preached "to the ends of the earth." No place is to be missed, no one left out. When Jesus gave his disciples their marching orders, he told them to begin at Jerusalem, the place of their worst experiences and greatest failures. They were then to go on to Judea, the place where their neighbors and Jewish relatives lived and knew the worst about them. After that, they were to go on to Samaria, the place of their worst prejudices. From there they were to go to the ends of the earth.

Actually, it is often easier to go to the farthest parts before attending to the nearest. We feel we are too well known in our "Jerusalem," so we fear that people won't believe us. But we need to start there. And whether we are in Jerusalem (our own town), Judea (our own state), Samaria (the home of our enemies), or the ends of the earth (where languages and cultures are completely different), Jesus has promised to be with us "always, even to the end of the age" (Matthew 28:20). He would not give us a command without the power to do it. We need to go and be witnesses of the gospel. We will receive power to communicate his word effectively.

TO READ: *Acts 2:1-21*

WITH GREAT EFFECT

"'In those days I will pour out my Spirit upon all my servants,
men and women alike, and they will prophesy.'"

ACTS 2:18

A fter he ascended into heaven (Acts 1:9), Jesus told his disciples to stay in the city of Jerusalem until he sent them what his Father had promised—the Holy Spirit—who would dress them with the dynamic they would need to preach repentance and forgiveness of sins to all nations.

And then the day came! Suddenly the Holy Spirit fell on those waiting people, accompanied by special supernatural phenomena. All of them were filled with the Holy Spirit and began to speak in other languages as the Spirit enabled them! These languages enabled foreigners in Jerusalem to hear in their native tongues "the wonderful things God has done!" (Acts 2:11). This, explained Peter, is what Joel had prophesied.

The Holy Spirit is a gracious gift, and he is also a "generating gift." He generates the power to be witnesses. It's all quite impossible without the Holy Spirit, who gives us the power to testify about him with great effect to the ends of the earth.

We can start by telling people that Jesus died and rose again. We can make sure they understand that he wants to forgive their sin and give them the Holy Spirit.

Some will mock, and some will be indifferent or, worse, belligerent. But some will respond. That, however, isn't our business; that part belongs to God. Our business is to tell them; it's God's business to turn them around. We must only do our part; we can be quite sure God will do his. He promises to give our message great effect.

WISE MEN STILL SEEK JESUS

The members of the council were amazed when they saw the boldness of Peter and John, for they could see that they were ordinary men who had had no special training. They also recognized them as men who had been with Jesus.

ACTS 4:13

How could these men, who've had no special training, know so much? the members of the council wondered. Here was this rough fisherman, Simon Peter, giving an excellent little sermon to the elders of Israel. He was difficult to discredit because the cripple whom Peter and John had healed was standing right there with them—rather telling evidence to the power of the risen Christ (Acts 4:14)!

At this point, the Bible tells us, the members of the council "recognized them as men who had been with Jesus"!

Christ is wisdom, and knowing him makes us wise. Those in this world who think themselves wise are fools in God's sight because they count the knowledge of him irrelevant. It's better to be childlike in your understanding of Christ, than an old person in your mere human knowledge.

When you've been with Jesus for a little while, you begin to discern what is really important. And it's what we learn of him that will make the world marvel. Do you have lots of degrees or a bright mind that you have tuned to the world's pitch? What gifts are these? You may be "forever following new teachings, but . . . never understand the truth" (2 Timothy 3:7), and what a waste of God-given intelligence! Wise people seek Jesus first, then use their gifts to glorify him.

TO READ: *Acts 5:1-11*

LYING TO GOD

Then Peter said, "Ananias, why has Satan filled your heart?
You lied to the Holy Spirit, and you kept some of the money for yourself."

ACTS 5:3

I n the versions of the Bible that I first read, the Holy Spirit was often referred to as the "Holy Ghost." As I read the Bible, I discovered the Holy Spirit was a Person—in fact, the third Person of the Trinity—and not a shrouded being.

I also found I could treat him as a Person. I could resist him (Genesis 6:3), insult him (Hebrews 10:26-31), stifle him (1 Thessalonians 5:19), and grieve him (Ephesians 4:25-31). The most sober realization and conviction of all dawned upon me as I read Acts 5:1-11—I could lie to him!

The story tells of Ananias and Sapphira, who sold a piece of property and laid the proceeds at the feet of the apostles. Their sin lay not in the fact that they only brought half of the price, but that they *said* they brought all of it!

How often have I lied to the Holy Spirit? I thought. "You have all my time," I had told him when I first became a believer, yet that was just not true. "You have all my money," I had intoned in a pious platitude at a prayer meeting. "Not so," the Spirit whispered in my ear! "You have all my heart," I had promised many, many times.

How glad I am that God does not deal with us as he dealt with Ananias and Sapphira. If he did, I would not be writing this book! The Holy Spirit is a Person, and I need to apologize to him and ask his forgiveness.

THE "JUST US"

Saul was one of the official witnesses at the killing of Stephen. A great wave
of persecution began that day, sweeping over the church in Jerusalem, and
all the believers except the apostles fled into Judea and Samaria.

ACTS 8:1

W hen the first persecution arose around Stephen, the Christians were scattered abroad. Acts 8:4 tells us they "went everywhere preaching the Good News about Jesus." In other words, they gossiped the gospel. A good definition of "preaching" is the communication of truth through personality.

Ordinary people fleeing for their lives told other ordinary people along the way the reason they were on the run. This was the way the Good News was carried to the uttermost parts of their world. There were leaders among them, even though the apostles stayed in Jerusalem. But the majority of the people were just like you and me—ordinary folk.

It is the same today. God wants ordinary people to tell other ordinary people about his Good News of salvation. The leaders can't do it all. The leaders can help us to know what to communicate, and the evangelists can show us how to lead people to Christ. But if our world is to be reached, it will take every single one of us passing the news on to another.

I was invited to some meetings in Atlanta. I asked the lady who had called to inquire about my coming what church or organization she represented.

"Well," she replied a little shyly and hesitantly, "it's just us." I found out the "just us" were a bunch of God's ordinary people gossiping the gospel. It was a sheer delight to serve them!

TO READ: *Acts 16:11–15*

DOWN BY THE RIVERSIDE

On the Sabbath we went a little way outside the city to a riverbank, where we supposed that some people met for prayer, and we sat down to speak with some women who had come together.

ACTS 16:13

Lydia, a Jewish proselyte, a seller of expensive purple cloth, was accustomed to going to the place by the river where the Jews met for prayer and joining the worshipers. We learn that "she was a worshiper of God" (Acts 16:14).

We also can learn a valuable lesson about the sort of prayers God heeds and answers. Lydia was heard by God. Prayer precedes conversion; God hears the prayers of a grandmother concerned for her grandchild, a husband concerned for an unbelieving wife, or simply the prayer concerned for himself—as in Lydia's or Cornelius's case. It's important to encourage people who are seeking a relationship with God to pray, because prayer also prepares the heart to receive the living Word of God. Paul, having had a vision of a *man* from Macedonia asking him to "come over here and help us" (Acts 16:9), found instead a *woman* who was waiting to listen at the place where prayer was made. He lost no time sitting down and explaining the gospel to Lydia. I love Paul's flexibility!

Prayer truly prepares the heart. The Lord opened Lydia's understanding, and she "accepted what Paul was saying." After she and her household were converted, she begged Paul and his friends to stay with her. The beautiful story of Lydia reaffirms our belief in the power of prayer. We are reminded that prayer precedes conversion, prepares the heart, and stimulates us to ministry.

TO READ: *Acts 16:11–15*

A LYDIA PLACE

She was baptized along with other members of her household, and she asked
us to be her guests. "If you agree that I am faithful to the Lord," she said,
"come and stay at my home." And she urged us until we did.

ACTS 16:15

B e my guests," said Lydia to Paul and Silas. Lydia "urged" them—in other words, she wouldn't take *no* for an answer. So Paul and Silas accepted her offer of gracious hospitality.

Hospitality has been defined as "the love of strangers," and all through Christian history, the homes of believers have been the places where both strangers and friends have gathered for worship, friendship, healing, and help. Paul told the Roman Christians to practice hospitality (Romans 12:13); and Paul honored Gaius, a Roman whose hospitality he and the church enjoyed (Romans 16:23). On the island of Malta after a shipwreck, Publius, "the chief official of the island," welcomed Paul, Luke, and their companions to his home and fed them for three days (Acts 28:7). Paul healed Publius's father while he was there, and a stream of blessing began on the island (Acts 28:8-10).

If nonbelievers, like Publius, and brand-new believers, like Lydia, welcomed strangers hospitably, then how much more should we, who have known the Lord for much longer, show hospitality? The problem often lies in western busyness and fractured, scattered families. The words, "Come and stay with me," are seldom heard.

Over the years our home has been "a Lydia place." The world has been invited into the heart of our family, and we have found, as Lydia undoubtedly did, that when we live in a home without walls, everyone benefits.

TO READ: *Acts 20:13-38*

WHEN IT'S TIME
TO SAY GOOD-BYE

*"And now I entrust you to God and the word of his grace—his message that
is able to build you up and give you an inheritance with all those
he has set apart for himself."*

ACTS 20:32

S tanding in a busy airport, I watched people meeting and greeting,
sighing and crying! Saying good-bye is no fun at all.

Paul was saying good-bye to his friends, the leaders of the church in
Ephesus. He was on his way to Jerusalem, not knowing what was ahead,
but conscious of the fact that he would never see these Ephesian believers
again (Acts 20:25). How would they fare? Would they make it without
him? This must have made it very difficult for Paul to trust them into
God's care and get on that boat! However, he was able to say, "And now
I entrust you to God and the word of his grace."

How do you trust God when it's time to say good-bye? How do you
sail away to a college campus after leaving home as a vulnerable child?
How do you move on to another ministry and pass the baton to other
leaders who you feel are not quite ready? The secret is to realize that you
are trusting God and his grace, not any earthly man or woman, to keep
and watch over these precious people! They are safe in his care. When you
know that it is time to say good-bye, put your work, your child, your
spiritual followers, your parents into God's safekeeping. Pray that his
grace will be their keeper and sustainer while you are away. Then trust
God to do the rest.

TO READ: *Acts 23:1–11*

TAKING THE
EASY WAY OUT

That night the Lord appeared to Paul and said, "Be encouraged, Paul.
Just as you have told the people about me here in Jerusalem, you must
preach the Good News in Rome."

ACTS 23:11

P aul tried hard to be a good servant and witness, but it got him into
an awful lot of trouble in a lot of places. Acts 21 records Paul's return
to Jerusalem after his third missionary journey. When Paul went to the
temple, some Jews from Asia incited a riot (Acts 21:27-36). But Paul
actually used the opportunity as a captive to speak to a captive audience.
Paul refused to be intimidated by the terrible treatment he received. God
gave him the power to avoid taking the easy way out.

We may not have had a dramatic conversion like Paul's, but all
believers have seen Jesus as their Savior with eyes of faith and have been
appointed as servants and witnesses to that fact. We may never be hounded
and persecuted as Paul was, but we may well be tempted to take the easy
way out when the heat is on. The devil will try to discourage us when people
laugh at our beliefs or tear our reputations apart, but we can overcome our
fears by being obedient to the heavenly vision God has given us.

Are you being tempted to give up or give in? Let the risen Christ
encourage you as he encouraged Paul: "Be encouraged, Paul. Just as you
have told the people about me here in Jerusalem, you must preach the
Good News in Rome" (Acts 23:11). We too must be obedient to our
vision from heaven until all our work is done! We can be sure God will
stand with us until the end.

TO READ: *Acts 26:4-32*

SITTING ON THE FENCE

*Agrippa interrupted him. "Do you think you can make
me a Christian so quickly?"*

ACTS 26:28

I t's not enough to be almost persuaded; it's not enough to decide that
you will become a Christian . . . later. You can be almost persuaded, but
lost! You can take your time and sit on the fence—but that will assure you a
place with the devil and all his angels!

Sitting on the fence is easy. You can sit on the fence every Sunday at
church. Thousands of respectable people do it every week. It's not very
comfortable, but it certainly can be done.

Perhaps you don't want to bother God by asking him to pick up his
pen and write down your name in his book. Or maybe you want to wait a
while and live a little first. "Lord, make me holy—but not just yet," you
pray! After all, you've heard that God can be such a spoilsport!

Maybe you are waiting for your best friend to make a decision—
you've never been the first to make a move.

If you want to go to hell, simply do nothing. So what do you need
to do to make absolutely sure you *don't* go to hell and *do* go to heaven? If
you want to get off the fence, then all you have to do is jump. It will be a
leap that lands you safely in the arms of Jesus! It will be the best thing you
ever did.

OVERLOAD

The next day, as gale-force winds continued to batter the ship,
the crew began throwing the cargo overboard.

ACTS 27:18

During a storm at sea, the sailors had to lighten the overburdened ship (Acts 27:14-20). Many times we need to lighten our own ships so we don't go under!

When I was a small child my father took my sister and me down to the Liverpool dockyards to see the merchant ships that were bringing us food in the middle of the blitz during World War II. I noticed a painted waterline around the center of each vessel.

"What's that for?" I asked my father.

"That's to show the people loading up the ship how much it's made to carry. If they put too much on so the line disappears, the boat will sink. If they put too little inside, it won't be filled full enough to do what it was made to do. Each boat is made by its builder to carry just the right amount."

I have often applied that picture to my own life. God has made me quite a large cargo ship. I can carry a lot—but there is still a "waterline" I need to watch. If I'm not taking anything on for God, I will feel strangely light and unfulfilled. If, however, I say yes to everything, I'll soon be at the bottom of the sea!

Realize that God is your boatbuilder. He knows who you are, how big your hold is, and what he wants you carrying. The way to fulfillment lies in keeping close enough to hear his still small voice and in being obedient. Happy sailing!

TO READ: *Romans 12:1–11*

DELIGHTING TO DO THE WILL OF GOD

Don't copy the behavior and customs of this world, but let God transform you into a new person by changing the way you think. Then you will know what God wants you to do, and you will know how good and pleasing and perfect his will really is.

ROMANS 12:2

I have so many choices," a young student confided to her teacher. "If only God would write me a letter and tell me what to do."

"He has written you a letter," her teacher replied, handing her a Bible.

"But, where is my answer?" the student asked, bewildered, as she thumbed through the pages.

"It's in there somewhere," her mentor answered. "It may not be one specific verse in one chapter, but rather a principle found in many places throughout the whole book. You could well discover it in a study of the life of a patriarch, the wise sayings of Solomon, or the instructions of Paul. You may find that Jesus directly addresses your dilemma, or you may not. But one thing I can tell you: If you really want to know God's will because you want to delight him, and if you're willing to consistently read your Bible, you will find your answer. God has promised that those who seek will find."

The crux of the matter is that little word *if*. If you are willing to consistently study God's Word, only then will you find God's "good and pleasing and perfect" will (Romans 12:2). We have to consistently read, study, and digest God's Word.

God doesn't hide his will. He speaks specifically to many situations in his Word. He gives general principles for people to apply to many other types of situations. He gives his Spirit for wisdom. He wants to show you his "good, pleasing, and perfect" will. Then he wants you to delight in doing it.

TO READ: *Romans 12:12-21*

MY PART

Do your part to live in peace with everyone, as much as possible.
ROMANS 12:18

I'm glad the Bible says to live in peace with everyone "as much as possible." Sometimes it is not! But I can't use that as an excuse. Have I really done my part to make it possible? The Scripture does say, "Do your part" or as another translation puts it, "As much as lieth in you." God depends on me to do my part! Did I confront the person? Did I write a letter, call her on the phone, ask a wise friend to intervene? Once I have done the things that only I can do and honestly can think of nothing else that can be tried, then I can rest, and pray, and wait for God to intervene.

The hardest part is the part that depends on the other person! Sometimes an offended or hostile adversary will reject my overtures and throw my best efforts back in my face. But I must remember that I am responsible only for my attitude—not for his or hers. I must seek to live peaceably with "everyone." If only Paul had said "most everyone," or "some people," or "your friends and other people you like," or "the people who like you"— but he didn't. Peace will require all my effort at all times to put it all right with *everyone*. But don't forget, Paul does say "as much as possible." If it is, then God will bring reconciliation. If it is not, he knows—so I can stop blaming myself and rest in the knowledge that I have done my part!

OCTOBER

TO READ: *Romans 16:1–9*

STANDING BY
THE FAMILY

Our sister Phoebe, a deacon in the church in Cenchrea,
will be coming to see you soon. Receive her in the Lord, as one
who is worthy of high honor. Help her in every way you can,
for she has helped many in their needs, including me.

ROMANS 16:1-2

A single parent once looked around her Sunday school class and said with gratitude, "I have been so alone, but you are my family now." She had found the joy of being adopted into God's family and of having sweet fellowship with her believing family in a local congregation.

Christians have two families—their natural family and the spiritual family of God. Paul called Phoebe "our sister." This term implies a special relationship in a spiritual family. God embraces all who have been born of the Spirit and draws them into his family.

Phoebe was not only a sister, but a servant, too. The word for "servant" is *diakonos,* from which we have the word *deacon.* In Romans 16:2, Paul calls her "a helper of many" (NKJV). In that verse the word *helper* means "one who stands by another." So Phoebe was a woman of some consequence, a patroness of the saints, and she was apparently entrusted to be a courier of Paul's letter to the saints in Rome. At some time in Paul's ministry, God used Phoebe, whose name means "bright," to light his weary way, lift his load, and stand by him.

All of us can be such lights, and we can lighten the loads of other saints. Perhaps not all of us will be called to such positions of prominence as Phoebe, but all of us can care for the poor, the oppressed, and the orphaned. All of us can find great joy in standing by the family of God.

TO READ: *1 Corinthians 3:10-17*

OUR SPIRITUAL WORSHIP

*But there is going to come a time of testing at the judgment day to see
what kind of work each builder has done. Everyone's work will be
put through the fire to see whether or not it keeps its value.
If the work survives the fire, that builder will receive a reward.*

1 CORINTHIANS 3:13-14

I am often asked, "Will Christians be judged if they have accepted
Christ?" The answer is yes. We must all stand before the judgment seat
of Christ to "receive whatever we deserve for the good or evil we have
done in our bodies" (2 Corinthians 5:10). It doesn't say, "All of us will
appear before God's judgment seat—except me!" Believers will not be
condemned for sin because their sin has been blotted out, canceled,
nailed to Christ's cross (Colossians 2:14). But believers will be judged for
the good and the bad they have done. The quality of what they have done
with their lives will be tested.

Paul called believers "builders." All people are building something
with their lives. Some are building their dream castles, others their empires
of influence. Some are building temples to their own fame. What are you
busy building? Are you building anything in the kingdom of God? Are you
building friendships with a view to leading someone to Christ, or building
a ministry to children, women, or to the needy? Will your life's accomplishments survive the fire of God's testing? In other words, will God find your
"building" to be made of gold, silver, and jewels—having eternal value?

The rewards are described in the Bible as crowns—such as the crown
of righteousness (2 Timothy 4:8) or the crown of life (Revelation 2:10).
The Lord Jesus will crown the builders who have built well. When we
build up God's kingdom, we offer Christ true spiritual worship, and we
will receive a reward.

NOT MY STUFF

My conscience is clear, but that isn't what matters.
It is the Lord himself who will examine me and decide.

1 CORINTHIANS 4:4

There was a time in my life when I held myself responsible for every bad thing that happened. I used to take personal responsibility for trouble in the women's work at church (I should have known what to do), the breakdown of other's marriages (I should have given them better marriage advice), and even our golden retriever's bad behavior in the neighborhood. Yes, I even took blame for the dog!

When we allow ourselves to play the blame-yourself game, the ensuing guilt dries up the soul, withers the spirit, and makes for depression. Don't do it. As Paul put it, to let it be a very small thing to be judged by others. In fact, he says he didn't even trust his own judgment about himself. He kept a clear conscience and would let the Lord show him the truth.

That's not to say that we shouldn't own what is ours. As a young mother trying to be patient with my children, it was easy to blame the little imps for my impatience and irritation. However, I learned that the children did not create my mood, they simply revealed it. I couldn't blame my children for my bad-tempered attitude—that was "my stuff" and I needed to deal with it. As Paul stated, God alone must judge each one of us. He will set the record straight. Some of us, however, need to stop taking responsibility for things that are not our stuff!

TO READ: *1 Corinthians 10:1–11*

WHEN BAD EXAMPLES ARE GOOD

These events happened as a warning to us,
so that we would not crave evil things as they did.

1 CORINTHIANS 10:6

Where can we look for examples of godly people, for heroes and heroines? The Bible! The writers of the New Testament often used examples from the Old Testament to stimulate us in holy living. But they also pointed out some of the bad examples as well.

We can learn from both the good and the bad. When Paul reminds his readers of what occurred "to our ancestors in the wilderness long ago" (1 Corinthians 10:1), he points out that the believers can learn from those mistakes. The records of bad examples are supposed to stop us from choosing a wrong lifestyle.

It's not difficult to find bad examples if we just look around. Sometimes those in leadership, who are very visible, are bad examples. Leaders of government, public officials, educators, and especially church leaders ought to be conscious of the fact that their public and private morality should line up. Our leaders should be examples of what is good. But when they aren't, we can learn how *not* to live. Bad examples do not give us license to sin, but they should warn us about the consequences of ungodly actions.

Bad examples should stimulate us to wholesome living in the light of Christ's return. Bad examples can sometimes be examples that work for our good—showing us what we don't want to be and what we don't want to experience. We can begin by deciding to be a godly example to those around us.

TO READ: *1 Corinthians 10:12-33*

ESCAPING
TEMPTATION'S POWER

*But remember that the temptations that come into your life are no different
from what others experience. And God is faithful. He will keep the
temptation from becoming so strong that you can't stand up against it. When
you are tempted, he will show you a way out so that you will not give in to it.*

1 CORINTHIANS 10:13

I've always disliked tests. But now that I am a teacher myself, I know
there is no other way to help students evaluate, learn, and grow than
by putting what they've learned to the test.

The tests that come into our lives are meant to deepen our walk with
God. "When your faith is tested, your endurance has a chance to grow . . .
you will be strong in character and ready for anything. . . . God blesses the
people who patiently endure testing" (James 1:3-4, 12).

But tests are different from temptation. God may test, but he never
tempts. That's Satan's realm. Temptation is universal and happens to the
best of us! Temptation is not a sin—after all, Jesus was tempted (Matthew
4:1-11). It's how we handle the temptation that becomes the issue. God
promises that even when Satan does his dirty work in sending an enticing
temptation our way, God will not allow it to be too strong for us, and he
will provide a way of escape.

Facing temptation humbles us because sometimes we give in and
find ourselves in a sticky situation with God and others, needing to
repent! We have to know our own sinful nature well enough to know
where temptations will strike. Then we must be ready with Scripture so
that we can send Satan packing. After all, that's what Jesus did!

TO READ: *1 Corinthians 15:51-58*

WHEN

When this happens—when our perishable earthly bodies have been
transformed into heavenly bodies that will never die—
then at last the Scriptures will come true.

1 CORINTHIANS 15:54

Have you ever sat by the side of someone you love who is being slowly swallowed up by death? If you have, you will know how hard it is to believe this verse. How you long for someone to come along and stop it all! If only a great big giant could walk into the room and swallow up death, who is busy swallowing up your dear one! It is all like a dreadful nightmare, except it is many times worse than a bad dream because it's real. On the one hand, you can't seem to wake up and have the shadows disappear, and on the other, you can't go to sleep without having a cloud of despondency follow and surround you so tightly that you can't get your breath.

It was at such a bitter, despairing time as this that I found 1 Corinthians 15:54: "When this happens—when our perishable earthly bodies have been transformed into heavenly bodies that will never die—then at last the Scriptures will come true: 'Death is swallowed up in victory.' " Oh, blessed "when." Oh, gentle promise of God. And who shall there be who is strong enough to digest death? Why, the Lord God—it is he! The Lord God will wipe away the tears from all faces and ransom our people from final destruction.

"O death, bring forth your terrors! O grave, bring forth your plagues! For I will not relent!" he promised (Hosea 13:14). Take courage, dear friend, there is a time—a moment—a "when."

TO READ: *1 Corinthians 15:51–58*

THE VICTORY IS OURS, THANK GOD

How we thank God, who gives us victory over sin and death through Jesus Christ our Lord!

1 CORINTHIANS 15:57

Death, and with it the termination of human possibilities, comes to all of us, small and great, rich and poor, young and old. What place does the word *victory* have in the same sentence as the word *death?*

When Christ rose from the dead, he demonstrated immortality of the soul. He killed death through the Resurrection and blew hell wide open (Hosea 13:14).

This truth, mixed with faith and the comfort of the Spirit, is intended to give us relief as we face the passing of someone close to us. Clark Pinnock says, "God is God not only of the sweet by and by, but of the bitter here and now!" As we believe the promise of victory over death, God will turn "the beating time" into "the blessed time."

If the last enemy is death, and Christ has defeated him, we can know that death is already retreating, wounded and bleeding to his own end. But a mortally wounded animal is the most dangerous animal of all. He will do as much damage as he can to anyone that dares to venture near. Watch him warily and with respect, remembering that in a little while he will be gone forever—and in that rejoice. As we stand helplessly by, watching dark death snatch our dear treasures away from us, let us remember that death cannot but loose our beloved ones into God's loving arms.

TO READ: *1 Corinthians 15:51–58*

NEVER, EVER USELESS

So, my dear brothers and sisters, be strong and steady,
always enthusiastic about the Lord's work, for you know
that nothing you do for the Lord is ever useless.

1 CORINTHIANS 15:58

M any people have a dread of living in vain. I read about a man who left a request in his will that his ashes be used in egg timers so that his life would not be a total write-off! The Bible tells me that my labor in the Lord is never useless. That's why I need to be steadfast and immovable in my determination to seek out the work that is his will for my life; and once I find it, I must do it with all my strength, all my days, keeping all eternity in mind.

Working for Jesus Christ and his kingdom has eternal repercussions. Are you ever so despondent that you feel you may as well end up in an egg timer? Come to God through Christ—ask him to help you spend your time wisely, and you will not feel that your life is empty and frustrating. However, if you begin to serve him, you may run into another problem. You will probably discover there is never enough time to accomplish everything that needs accomplishing!

"What do people get for all their hard work?" Solomon asks (Ecclesiastes 1:3). Solomon was the wisest of men, yet he still had his egg-timer moments! Paul, knowing believers get discouraged, told us that the secret of a meaningful life is to be enthusiastic in the work of the Lord.

TO READ: *2 Corinthians 1:1–11*

COMFORTED
TO COMFORT

He comforts us in all our troubles so that we can comfort others.
When others are troubled, we will be able to give them
the same comfort God has given us.

2 CORINTHIANS 1:4

How can I comfort others if I haven't known what it is to be comforted myself? To effectively administer encouragement, it helps to have experienced the comfort of God myself. In my own life I have experienced God's comfort at many times in many ways. I have received his mercy, healing, and help. God did not comfort me only to make me feel better, but so that I can comfort others in their pain and difficulty.

Every believer can have a ministry of encouragement because every believer has experienced pain or difficulties of one kind or another and has been comforted by God. It's hard to think beyond our own needs when trouble hits home, but the comfort we receive from God will be just the comfort others are waiting for!

Paul wrote about his own hardships, pressures, and despair, but he saw a twofold purpose behind them. One purpose was that Paul and his companions learned to depend, not on themselves, but on God. The second purpose behind Paul's sufferings seems to be that the Corinthian believers needed to learn how to pray for those experiencing hardship. A ministry of comfort is born from trouble, but those in trouble must be bathed in prayer. There is a comfort, born in others' prayers, that always lifts the spirit, strengthens the will, and sets the heart on fire for God. None of this could happen without troubles.

Are you aware of those around you who need comfort? God has comforted you so that you can comfort them.

TO READ: *2 Corinthians 10:1–18*

A SPIRITUAL SELF-IMAGE

For some say, "Don't worry about Paul. His letters are demanding and
forceful, but in person he is weak, and his speeches are really bad!"

2 CORINTHIANS 10:10

P aul had heard what some in the church at Corinth were saying about
him. It's hard when you are criticized unkindly—it can make you feel
awful about yourself. Paul's healthy self-image shows us how to let God
hold us up when others put us down.

Paul realized he was being evaluated by people who were just
comparing themselves with others. Each of us has a proper sphere of
service, determined by the limits God sets (2 Corinthians 10:13). Each is
placed in the kingdom and gifted for kingdom work by God. Paul didn't
worry about being compared to others—he just wanted to make sure he
fit God's plan. Paul measured himself by God's commendation. He may
not have been a trained speaker, but he knew what he was talking about.
Paul's overriding compulsion was to teach the truth in every way possible.
Whether he did it better or worse than someone else did not deter his
plans, and it should not deter us either.

We need to get a handle on the things we do best and learn to live
with the things we do less well in areas where we are less gifted. But we
shouldn't let other people's evaluation of our personality, gifts, or service
be overplayed in our lives. Our gifts, calling, and personal boundaries are
set by God alone. Believers should be happy with God's boundaries and
glad to operate within them. A healthy spiritual self-image gives us
freedom to work for Christ, whatever we hear them saying about us!

A THORNY PROBLEM

To keep me from getting puffed up, I was given a thorn in my flesh, a messenger from Satan to torment me and keep me from getting proud.

2 CORINTHIANS 12:7

My friend and I had been talking about the way adversity forces us to trust God. "I've lived twenty years with a thorn in the flesh," my friend remarked. "How do I learn dependence now that the thorn is out?" We agreed that pride and fleshly energy take over so easily when the need to depend is removed. If we feel strong and confident *apart* from God—watch out!

Yet all of life will not necessarily be one long chapter of accidents. What about the times "the thorn" is removed or we find ourselves between thorns? To depend even when the sun shines is a real test of maturity. It helps to pray a lot. Prayer gives us a sense of our inadequacy at all times and this helps us lean on the Lord.

To be reminded of his Person reminds me of my person, and that will surely help me to depend! Isaiah, seeing God high and lifted up, saw himself low and cast down (Isaiah 6). A season of prayer will help us to stop saying "Wow is me" and make sure we say "Woe is me"! Physical thorns can be in our fleshly nature until the day we die and should keep us in constant dependence on the Spirit of God to make good his strength in our weakness. This way we will *glory in his power* and not in our own strength.

TO READ: *Galatians 5:16-26*

THE DIVINE PROMPTER

*But when the Holy Spirit controls our lives, he will produce this kind of fruit
in us: love, joy, peace, patience, kindness, goodness, faithfulness, gentleness,
and self-control. Here there is no conflict with the law.*

GALATIANS 5:22-23

What is the evidence of the Holy Spirit's working in us? Present-
tense Christianity doesn't live itself out in memories of past
churchgoing but vibrates with vitality in the here-and-now. Our "sinful
nature loves to do evil" (Galatians 5:17), and it can easily be fed with
wrong food, such as what we see on TV, what we read, and what we
think about.

Even after we become believers, we still have that sin nature, and it
declares war on the Holy Spirit. The reason for this conflict of interests
between the old and new natures inside a Christian is that the old nature
wants to go on being sinful and selfish, while the new nature of Christ,
imparted by the Holy Spirit, wants to be just like Christ! "The Spirit gives
us desires that are opposite from what the sinful nature desires" (Galatians
5:17). Christ urges us not to give in to the selfish, insistent voice that tells us
to shut our ears to the Spirit's prompting and do our own thing. He urges us
to heed his whisper and obey his word. The prompter at a play stands in the
wings, eyes fastened to the script. If an actor stumbles, the prompter is quick
to prompt so that the actor can do and say the right thing at the right time.
We need to listen to *our* prompter, Christ himself.

We are to keep in step with the Spirit. Only with his help can we live
the holy lives that God wants us to live.

IN STEP

If we are living now by the Holy Spirit, let us follow
the Holy Spirit's leading in every part of our lives.
GALATIANS 5:25

When we first come to faith in Christ we feel we can conquer the world—with God's help, of course! We wonder if the Spirit will be able to keep up with us. After a little going, a little knowing, and a little growing, we begin to realize this "walk" of faith requires training, stamina, and expertise. We cannot help asking ourselves the question, "How long will I be able to stay caught up with the Spirit?" Further down the hard course of life, tripped up by sin, or distracted, like Martha, by much serving, or just plain jaded with the constant fight of faith, we find ourselves fervently echoing Paul's exhortation to simply "follow" the Holy Spirit.

God delights to hear and answer that request. He wants us to *follow*. He doesn't wish to see us galloping ahead or dragging behind, but following, going where he goes, marching as one person toward the finish line.

The Holy Spirit is described in Scripture as the Helper. He will not walk *for* us—he will walk *with* us and *lead* us; and make no mistake about it—he won't stop going even if we do. There is grace to help in time of need: strength for the day, confidence for tomorrow, direction in the dark, company in the light—even power to plod—and it's all within our reach. It is his to supply, and it is ours to use.

TO READ: *Galatians 6:1–10*

LONELY LOADS

Share each other's troubles and problems,
and in this way obey the law of Christ.
GALATIANS 6:2

There is a time for everything, a season for this and a season for that. There is a time to bear a care in solitude, and a time to share a prayer with a friend. We need the wisdom to know when to shoulder responsibility, when to delegate, and when to cast it all upon Jesus—our incomparable Burden-bearer.

Sometimes I have to have a cry, then wash my face and get on with it! I know I must bear the thing alone. Another day, when I was burdened beyond belief after watching a loved one suffer, a friend came to me and touched my hurt with tenderness, mending the raw edges of my helplessness. Such love brought a blessed buoyancy that helped more than I could tell. Someone cared enough to help make my burden bearable. Yes, there is a season for sorrow, a time to bear another's burdens.

But there comes a time when only God's shoulders are broad enough to carry the weight of my worry. Then crushing burdens become carried burdens. Yoked to him, I can plow my lonely furrow, walk a straight path, cope with the intolerable, and figure out the impossible. Then, having been carried, I am sent on my way strengthened to help carry another. I need to pray: *Show me when to share, Lord; commission me to carry, Lord. And teach me not to burden one of your special children, if I must bear my burden alone!*

TO READ: *Ephesians 1:1-14*

DINNER PLATES

*This letter is from Paul, chosen by God to be an apostle of Christ Jesus.
It is written to God's holy people in Ephesus,
who are faithful followers of Christ Jesus.*

EPHESIANS 1:1

P aul wrote many letters to the groups of believers scattered around
Asia Minor, and in many versions of the Bible, he addressed these
"holy people" as "saints." A "saint" in the New Testament sense was a
saved sinner. It is through faith in the Lord Jesus Christ that a sinner
becomes a saint.

But what does the word *saint* mean? The Greek words *hagios* for
"saint" and *hagiazo* for "sanctify" are related. The vessels in the temple
were sanctified—set apart for God and for his service—and so are ordinary
people who come in faith to Jesus Christ. All New Testament believers are
holy people—saints—regardless of their progress or growth.

Paul addresses his letters to ordinary believers who were called by
God to be saints, just as surely as Paul was called by God to be an apostle
(Romans 1:1).

Some people protest the word *holy* or *saint,* saying they don't want to
be called by such a high and holy title. It means they have to live up to it!
Too many Christians want to be saved by the Lord, yet live like the devil.
When once we realize that being a true Christian means being "Christianly"
true in character, and when we decide to live in obedience to our calling,
then God will set us aside for his very special service, just as he did the
vessels in his temple.

Whether we like it or not, we are holy people, saints. We bear the
responsibility of his name and should live accordingly!

TO READ: *Ephesians 1:1–14*

MUCH MORE

How we praise God, the Father of our Lord Jesus Christ,
who has blessed us with every spiritual blessing in the
heavenly realms because we belong to Christ.
EPHESIANS 1:3

P aul says God has blessed us in the realm of spiritual experience with a special benediction. The Lord thinks so highly of the people he created that he commanded certain things be done for them—thus blessing them.

The Old Testament tells us about Noah and his family who were sheltered in a huge boat from God's judgment. Then after forty days and nights, the waters receded and their boat rested on Mount Ararat. What a lovely picture of the things God wants to do for us! We deserve the judgment of God for our wrongdoing; but Christ is our life-saving boat, and sheltered in him we escape the retribution due to us.

But Christianity is not escapism. Christianity is opening the door to a whole new world—a spiritual Mount Ararat. As Romans 5:10 puts it, "For since we were restored to friendship with God by the death of his Son while we were still his enemies, we will certainly be delivered from eternal punishment by his life." Major Ian Thomas explained it this way in a sermon: "Christ's death makes us fit for heaven—Christ's life makes us fit for earth!"

Becoming a Christian means understanding God's judgment and sheltering in Christ; being a Christian means exploring Mount Ararat—the heavenly slopes of spiritual experience. It's hard to take in anything more once we have grasped the meaning of the Cross, but the "much more" of the gospel leads us into spiritual blessings and heavenly experiences that will bring a song of praise and love from our hearts.

ELECTION

Long ago, even before he made the world, God loved us and chose us in Christ to be holy and without fault in his eyes. His unchanging plan has always been to adopt us into his own family by bringing us to himself through Jesus Christ. And this gave him great pleasure.

EPHESIANS 1:4-5

One of the key mountaintop blessings we read about in the book of Ephesians is election. The word means "selection," "nomination," or "appointing." The loving God Almighty, who knows all things, chose us to be his children.

To those of us who struggle with a negative self-image, the doctrine of election gives a great sense of worth. Watch a shy teenage girl chosen by a handsome boy to attend the senior prom. She knows that he picked her out beforehand. See what that does for her confidence! See a "plain Jane" blossom into vibrant womanhood when she gets engaged. Her fiancé had all the world to choose from, and he chose her.

Growing up with a beautiful and popular sister led to a lot of disappointments for me. The boys would always look at her before they looked at me. In school she was a student leader as well as the captain of the tennis team. She was always getting chosen for something. Then Jesus chose me to be his disciple and friend. My whole world changed, and I was content.

When you experience and embrace the love of God in your own heart and mind, you will realize that he wanted you to be his very own—as if there were no one else but you in the whole wide world. You are a valuable, eternal person, chosen by God for a personal relationship. It just doesn't get any better than that!

TO READ: *Ephesians 1:1–14*

REDEMPTION

*He is so rich in kindness that he purchased our freedom through
the blood of his Son, and our sins are forgiven.*

EPHESIANS 1:7

Another blessing recorded in Ephesians is the purchase of our freedom—
redemption. The word *redemption* means "to buy back with a ransom."
The slave market is in Paul's mind as he tries to find images to convey the
state of our spirits as slaves to sin and the love of our Redeemer, paying
with his own precious blood the ultimate price for our freedom. Some
think that because Christ died, all receive redemption automatically. Not
so! We have to say thank you and take advantage of that freedom by
walking away from our old master and serving the One who has bought us
with such a price—whose service is perfect freedom!

An African chief raided a village and took captive a young boy. The
child became his favorite servant. Years later the boy's aged parents,
having spent years sacrificing, took their very lives in their hands and
journeyed afar to lay the redemption money at the chief's feet and claim
their now-grown son. Free to go, the son declined, choosing to stay and
serve his master. His sorrowing parents returned to die alone in their old
age. A few years later the chief died, and according to custom, the favorite
servant was buried alive with him to keep him company in the afterlife.
The young man had refused to be redeemed.

What a tragedy occurs for those who refuse to be redeemed by the
one who loves them! Have you refused to be redeemed? That is a very
dangerous thing to do!

TO READ: *Ephesians 1:1–14*

A CELESTIAL AGATHA CHRISTIE

God's secret plan has now been revealed to us; it is a plan centered on Christ, designed long ago according to his good pleasure.

EPHESIANS 1:9

I s God's will a mystery to you? This verse tells us that God has made known to us his "secret plan." Such are our spiritual blessings in heavenly places!

Do you think of God as a sort of celestial Agatha Christie who delights in fooling you? Do you believe that when you finally get to heaven the last chapter will tell all? Well, this is not what is meant by the word *secret.* God is speaking here of previously hidden truths that are now divinely revealed. He wants us to know them. Paul may have had the secret, mysterious religions of his day in mind when he used this word. These religions were secret societies whose mysteries were revealed only to initiated members. If we have been initiated into the kingdom of God, by receiving God's Spirit, the secrets of that kingdom are ours. The same thought is found in 1 Corinthians 2:9-10: "No eye has seen, no ear has heard, and no mind has imagined what God has prepared for those who love him." But God has revealed them to us through his Spirit. For the Spirit searches all things—yes, the deep, secret things of God.

Spiritual truths are not found in human wisdom but rather are revealed by God. The promise of Scripture is that we have received "his Spirit (not the world's spirit) so we can know the wonderful things God has freely given us" (1 Corinthians 2:12). Furthermore, it is God's *good pleasure* that we should know them! There's no mystery here!

TO READ: *Ephesians 1:15-23*

PEOPLE WHO DON'T NEED PRAYING FOR

Ever since I first heard of your strong faith in the Lord Jesus and your love
for Christians everywhere, I have never stopped thanking God for you.
I pray for you constantly.

EPHESIANS 1:15-16

What motivates you to pray? Bad news? That seems to be a pretty common motivation. There's nothing like a good crisis to drive us to our knees! When trouble confronts us, we tend to pick up God like a crutch, only to discard him when trouble is past! But good news, not bad news, is Paul's motivation. He teaches us a much-needed lesson, showing us how to pray for people who don't need praying for! Paul describes these Christians at Ephesus as having lots of faith in God and lots of love for each other. These Christians were living a life full of joy and making their mark in society. "Why waste valuable prayer time on them?" some may ask.

There are so many needy Christians, sick people, and marriages in trouble. First of all, Paul tells us to undergird and protect the strong ones in prayer. That's important. The devil keeps his sharpest arrows for his most effective enemies. The apostle prays that these Christians might know the Lord Jesus even better than they do already. He prays that they will have hearts flooded with light, so that they can see something of the future God has called them to share. He prays that they will experience strength of will through God's power.

This is a fine passage of Scripture to use in praying for those who don't need praying for. Use it—believers will thank us for making mention of them in our prayers.

TO READ: *Ephesians 1:15-23*

ADEQUATE

I pray that you will begin to understand the incredible greatness of his power
for us who believe him. This is the same mighty power that raised Christ
from the dead and seated him in the place of honor at
God's right hand in the heavenly realms.

EPHESIANS 1:19-20

P aul talks of the working of God's "mighty power" on our behalf. "I pray that you will begin to understand the incredible greatness of his power for us who believe him," that same mighty power that raised Christ from the dead and seated him in the place of honor at God's right hand in heaven. If you've ever seen a dead body, then you will be able to under-stand a little of the power it must take to restore it to life! It will take more power than sending an astronaut to the moon and bringing him back again! After all, *people* have the power to do all that! But people do not have the power to raise the dead. God did that when he raised Christ, and now he tells us that the same power works in each believer! That means his mighty power in me is adequate for any situation.

A man from Australia bought a Rolls Royce in England and took it home with him. However, he neglected to find out the horsepower. He wrote to the manufacturer, but received only the terse British reply, "Adequate!" The British firm believed that that was all the owner of the car needed to know.

We don't need to know how God's power works, we only need to know that his power in us is available and wholly "adequate." Use it to its full advantage for God's kingdom!

TO READ: *Ephesians 1:15–23*

OVER MY HEAD
BUT UNDER HIS FEET

And God has put all things under the authority of Christ,
and he gave him this authority for the benefit of the church.

EPHESIANS 1:22

A dear friend was journeying with me to a conference and began to share the story of her thirty-year marriage. "If you had told me two years ago that my husband would walk out and leave his three lovely children and his wife after thirty years, I would have said you were crazy," she said soberly. "But here I am. I still think of my oldest boy on the day my husband left, saying, 'But Dad, you've always said Mom is one in a million.' 'Well, now I've found one in a billion,' he coolly replied, and walked out of our lives. For a few months I was swamped," she continued. "But then I found Christ, and the Scriptures told me that anything 'over my head' was under his feet! I learned that his mighty strength would work for me. I read that Jesus Christ my King was triumphant, and that in him, I could be triumphant, too!"

I told my friend—my brave and beautiful friend—that kings of ancient times put their feet on the neck of their enemies in a symbolic gesture, and that God our King had put his foot on the neck of his enemies, too.

What situation are you facing that is over your head? Remember, whatever is over your head is under his feet—and therefore, under yours, too. Ephesians 2:6 says that God has "raised us from the dead along with Christ, and we are seated with him in the heavenly realms—all because we are one with Christ Jesus."

A WOMAN OF ACTION

For we are God's masterpiece. He has created us anew in Christ Jesus,
so that we can do the good things he planned for us long ago.

EPHESIANS 2:10

O ther translations of this verse say that we are to "do good works, which God prepared in advance for us to do," and "Long ago he planned that we should spend these lives helping others."

These "good things" are not actions that get us into heaven, but are rather the tasks awaiting us once we enter there! And that doesn't mean we have to die first. We enter heaven the day heaven enters us! "Heaven came down and glory filled my soul," says the song. When Jesus Christ comes into my life, I enter heaven on earth—I *am* seated with him in heavenly places. Once that union with Christ is established, what a relief to discover that God has something for me to do!

I'm a woman of action, and the idea of sitting around on a misty pink cloud playing a harp is not my idea of heaven!

What a joy it was for me to discover that God has prepared some people that needed helping, and that he had prepared me to help them! That brought a real sense of worth and purpose to my life.

Some people don't know how to find others who need help. One practical lesson I have learned is this: If possible, never say no to opportunities. If you become known as a willing servant, you will soon be given someone to serve. That's one way to find the "good things" that God has prepared in advance for you to do!

TO READ: *Ephesians 2:11–22*

BECOMING

*In those days you were living apart from Christ. You were excluded from
God's people, Israel, and you did not know the promises God had made
to them. You lived in this world without God and without hope.*

EPHESIANS 2:12

P aul talks to the Ephesians about citizenship. He reminds them that at
one time they were strangers from the things of God, "living apart
from Christ . . . excluded." He may have been using a reference to the
greatly coveted and privileged Roman citizenship (Acts 22:28).

The Greeks called those who lived outside their cities "pagans." The
Jews also spoke disparagingly of the *ethne* or Gentiles, meaning those
outside the knowledge of the God of Israel. Instead of thinking of them as
those with whom they should have shared their knowledge of Jehovah, the
Jews created a sense of alienation. But now these Ephesian Gentiles, these
outsiders, had stepped inside the promises of God and had become true
citizens of the heavenly kingdom. "But now you belong to Christ Jesus,"
Paul says. "Though you once were far away from God, now you have been
brought near to him because of the blood of Christ. For Christ himself has
made peace between us Jews and you Gentiles by making us all one people.
He has broken down the wall of hostility that used to separate us"
(Ephesians 2:13-14).

Stuart lived for seven years in America as a registered alien. The day
he became a United States citizen, I watched the brotherly hugs and
handclasps and knew that the unseen wall had been broken down!
Becoming a citizen of a great nation is a good thing, but becoming a
citizen of heaven is even better!

BELONGING

Together as one body, Christ reconciled both groups to God by means of his death, and our hostility toward each other was put to death.

EPHESIANS 2:16

I f the wall of hostility has indeed been broken down by the death of Christ (Ephesians 2:13-14), why then do so many people inside the kingdom still meet a stone wall where true fellowship is concerned? Why does the wall still divide black and white, rich and poor, those with social status and those without? I believe it is because Christians have not been taught that the basis of their unity is "belonging."

Unity begins when we get our theology straight. If the wall has been broken down and yet the wall is still there, it is because someone has been building it up again! What is a wall? It's a barrier—something that includes others and excludes you. We sense it, though it be unseen, between people inside the church. We see different factions with religious and personal differences. Yet our unity is in belonging. For through him we *all* have access by one Spirit to the Father. He sees all of us kneeling down at our bedsides at the end of the day!

I must not be a builder of walls. I must lay down my trowel and use my hands rather to reach out to my brother and sister in love. I need to keep acting as if the barrier isn't there; I need to walk through it and speak into years of silence. I must write another letter and extend another dinner invitation. I must do what I can to make sure others know I believe in belonging!

TO READ: *Ephesians 3:1-13*

WHOSE PRISONER?

*I, Paul, am a prisoner of Christ Jesus because of
my preaching to you Gentiles.*

EPHESIANS 3:1

W as Paul the prisoner of Nero? Not in Paul's thinking. Paul believed
that "everything that has happened to me here has helped to
spread the Good News" (Philippians 1:12). He firmly believed nothing
could happen to him without divine permission. Paul knew God had a
plan for his life, and that it was no accident that he was in jail. He was
able to say, and did quite regularly, "I don't know what the future holds,
but I know the One who holds the future." No, Paul did not believe he
was a prisoner of the Gentiles, but rather a prisoner of Jesus Christ for the
sake of the Gentiles. Paul was more attuned to his calling than to his
circumstances, and cared more about the people whom he served than
about the personal consequences of his service.

When I was a young mother with three children under school age, I
came to a similar conclusion about my situation! I lived in a small house,
kept prisoner by my responsibilities to my family. But because of those
confining duties, I began to know the older ladies who lived around me.
I was able to say, "I am not a prisoner of my circumstances, but rather a
prisoner of Jesus Christ for these dear ladies!"

What circumstances imprison you? Are you a prisoner of Christ for
the sake of someone else? Once you recognize this, your attitude will
change and so will your actions. Just whose prisoner are you?

TO READ: *Ephesians 3:14-21*

BODY LANGUAGE

*When I think of the wisdom and scope of God's plan, I fall to my knees and
pray to the Father, the Creator of everything in heaven and on earth.*

EPHESIANS 3:14-15

P aul was kneeling before the Father. No matter that a Roman guard
was in the room, perhaps even chained to him; no matter whether
the guard was scoffer or brother. Paul was on his knees.

You know, seeing someone pray has great impact! I will never forget
one instance when I was a student and had been sent with a message to the
president of the student body. Knocking briefly, I rudely burst into the girl's
room and found her at prayer. The sight of this beautiful girl, unashamedly
bowing her knees to the Lord Jesus Christ, had a profound effect on me. I
was somehow angry with her because she made me feel awkward, and yet
her very body language preached an eloquent sermon of commitment that
I badly needed to hear! I would not have listened to her words, but I could
not ignore her message.

We do not always have a quiet room to run to. Sometimes the most
important praying must be done in the midst of turmoil, people, and
problems! I don't think any one of us will be forced to have our quiet
time as Paul did, accompanied by the clanking of chains! It's so easy for
us—but we don't do it! People like Paul, prisoners for Christ, pray for *us!*
It's time that free people prayed too!

TO READ: *Ephesians 3:14-21*

GROUNDED IN LOVE

*And I pray that Christ will be more and more at home in your hearts as you trust
in him. May your roots go down deep into the soil of God's marvelous love.*

EPHESIANS 3:17

P aul prayed that the Ephesian Christians would be strengthened
internally. He prayed for power in their inner spirit. He asked God
that Christ would so settle down in their hearts and lives that their hearts
and lives would be settled down. He begged God that the young believers
would put their roots downward and bear fruit upwards. He wanted the
church to be grounded in love, for to be established in love *is* the
Christian life.

This love requires renewal in the inner spirit. If the inner spirit is
starved, the outer person will show it. If we ourselves are malnourished,
we will be lethargic, self-absorbed, and disinterested in anyone else's
misfortunes. But as we make Christ at home in our hearts, he will
constantly shed abroad his love, supplying us with the ability to love
the "whole family" in heaven and on earth (Ephesians 3:15).

If only Paul hadn't said that! If he had said that we were *part* of a
family, or that there were a couple of family members he would like us to
try to get along with . . . but he didn't. He reminds us that we are part of
the "whole family," a family that needs loving and that is going to take a
whole lot more love than just mine. It's going to take Christ in the inner
spirit—in all of us!

TO READ: *Ephesians 3:14-21*

BENT KNEES, WET EYES, AND A BROKEN HEART

May you experience the love of Christ, though it is so great you will never fully understand it. Then you will be filled with the fullness of life and power that comes from God.

EPHESIANS 3:19

W hat equipment do I need if I am going to serve the Lord, sir?" a young missionary recruit asked a veteran Christian. The old saint quickly replied, "Bent knees, wet eyes, and a broken heart!"

The bent knees were mentioned first. The hardest thing for a missionary to do is to remember to bend them, because there are so many holy and good substitutes! There is the sweet fellowship with other great missionaries. There is the edification of fellow national believers. There is the corporate time of prayer that the staff enjoys each day. There are family devotions around the breakfast table with the children. But the bent knees that lead to the wet eyes that result from a broken heart come from the isolation of the soul.

The most important transactions take place alone—absolutely alone! That is the time when you are able to comprehend, to really grasp what is the breadth and length and depth and height of the love of Christ.

One day Jesus looked out on a needy multitude and was moved with compassion (Matthew 14:14). The word *moved* could well be translated "convulsed." That deep, deep love came from Christ's time spent alone with his Father—with bent knees, wet eyes, and a broken heart!

Missionaries, of course, are not the only ones who need to practice bent knees! If a missionary is "an ordinary person called to do extraordinary things with very little help," then that includes all of us!

TO READ: *Ephesians 4:1-10*

OUR VOCATIONS

*Therefore I, a prisoner for serving the Lord, beg you to lead a life worthy
of your calling, for you have been called by God.*

EPHESIANS 4:1

When it was time for me to leave high school and go to college, the
"vocational" teacher interviewed me to see if I had any idea of
what I wanted to do with my life. "What vocation do you have in mind?"
she asked me sternly. I went to a school that expected its graduates to
pursue a vocation—no, not vacation—vocation! The idea of simply
leaving to "get a job" was unthinkable.

Since the vocational opportunities for girls in my day were somewhat
limited to the teaching and nursing fields, I hastily said "teaching," though
to be honest, the thought had never occurred to me till then! I had been
taught that those privileged with higher knowledge are called to higher
vocations! Certain behavior was expected of us—a worthy walk anticipated.
I was left with no doubt that I had an obligation to live in a manner that
would not besmirch the name of my school.

It is even more important for Christians who have "learned" Christ
to live in a manner that does not besmirch the name of their Savior. This
manner of living is described as a "walk." It's not a leap of faith, not one
giant stride, but to quote my husband, "One simple, practical step after
another. Certainly, as in ordinary walks, some steps will be greater than
others, a few will be harder than others, and some will lead to higher
ground than others, but the spiritual life is a walk."

Are we living a life worthy of our calling in Christ?

MAKING ALLOWANCES

Be humble and gentle. Be patient with each other,
making allowance for each other's faults because of your love.

EPHESIANS 4:2

Are you good at making allowances for people? Or do you have ridiculously high expectations?

Our lives should say, "I make allowances for people," for this is the language of love. Forbearance is a divine quality. Romans 2:4 talks of the kindness, tolerance, and patience of God. His followers should do no less. We ought to willingly make allowances for one another *because* we love one another. This means I should hold back my quick judgment and should not evaluate or dissect people's motives.

What a challenge to walk through life like this! Are we making allowances for our teenagers, for example? I remember Pete, our youngest, growing daily right out of his socks—at fourteen years of age he was six-feet four-inches tall. Quite an achievement over such a small amount of time! But I didn't make allowances for his grand accomplishments! His schoolwork zeroed; around the house he was lazy and undisciplined; he couldn't be bothered even to pretend he wanted to go to church anymore! "No wonder!" laughed the wise counselor I resorted to in deep distress. "He's put everything he's got into blood and bones and height!" I got the point and made allowances.

Bishop H. C. G. Moule has said that forbearance is "allowing for each other's frailties and mistakes; aye, when they turn and wound you 'in love,' finding it easy to see with their eyes and if need be to take sides with them against yourselves!" That's making allowances!

NOVEMBER

TO READ: *Ephesians 4:1–10*

BEFORE IT FALLS APART

Always keep yourselves united in the Holy Spirit,
and bind yourselves together with peace.

EPHESIANS 4:3

D o you make every effort to maintain the unity that already exists between Christians? We are exhorted to make that our goal.

My sister, who has been a valuable model to me in maintaining excellent personal relationships, said one day, "I refuse to have a row with that girl—life's too short to fall out with anyone." We can refuse to have a row if we want to. That is making an effort to keep what we already have— unity. The problem is that if we have unity among ourselves, we sometimes ignore or neglect it. We start to work on it only when a relationship falls apart! But we must get to work *before* it falls apart. We must endeavor to maintain it. We do that by building an already good relationship into something even better. That takes time and effort.

We have good relationships with our church staff, but they can always be better. We schedule regular times to eat, to have fun, and to pray together. It's such a comfort and delight to meet with people on the same spiritual level as ourselves and enjoy a time of maintaining our unity!

I have a friend who often spends time with me—playing tennis, talking, shopping, or just relaxing—and she never fails to say before she leaves, "Let's pray together." It's just a brief glance heavenwards, but what a bond of peace it adds to our relationship!

What practical things are you doing to maintain the unity of the Spirit?

TO READ: *Ephesians 4:1-10*

MAJORING ON MAJORS

There is only one Lord, one faith, one baptism.
EPHESIANS 4:5

The basis for the unity that we have with other believers is set out for us in Ephesians 4:4-6. The little word *one* appears often. There is *one* body, and Christ is the head. A body is an earthly vehicle whereby a spiritual being gets around in a physical environment. We are to be vehicles for his actions. We are *one* in the Spirit, for we have access by one Spirit to the Father. All who have the Spirit have one common hope—that one day we shall be like him.

We have *one* Lord, too. When David gathered his band of distressed and discontented men around him in the cave of Adullam, he became captain over them. Those men saw each other, not so much as potential threats, competitors, or enemies, but as comrades in arms united by their leader (1 Samuel 22:2).

We have *one* faith, sharing the same vital truths concerning the Lord, his work, and purpose. We share *one* baptism, for we are all baptized into the body of Christ (Galatians 3:27). All believers see baptism as a rite of identification with the Lord Jesus. It should be a unifying factor, for in every baptism there is a statement of relationship to the risen Lord.

Lastly, we have *one* God and Father of all. If we can keep in mind the many things we agree upon, we will maintain the unity of the Spirit through the bond of peace.

TO READ: *Ephesians 4:1-10*

THE LOVELIEST
SYMPHONY OF ALL

*However, he has given each one of us a special gift according to the
generosity of Christ. That is why the Scriptures say, "When he ascended to
the heights, he led a crowd of captives and gave gifts to his people."*

EPHESIANS 4:7-8

D id you know you have a spiritual gift that was given to you for the
church's benefit? My husband was asked to visit a family who was
thinking of joining our church. "Pastor Briscoe," began the father, "what
does your church have to offer my family?"

"What does your family have to offer my church?" replied my
husband. He explained that the policy of our fellowship is to help people
discover their spiritual abilities and exercise them for the good of the whole.

Paul explains that persons are gifts (Ephesians 4:11). There have
been apostles who had a distinctive position, prophets with inspired
utterance, evangelists with the ability to spread the Good News, and
pastors and teachers to shepherd the flock under Christ. All these people
are there to teach the believers to do the work of ministry (Ephesians
4:12). The greatest mistake people can make is to think of church as a
spectator sport.

Paul also writes that gifts are given to *all* Christians. Each one of us has
a special gift (Ephesians 4:7). Each gift is different, and there is a diversity as
subtle and beautiful as the spots on a leopard, snowflakes on the grass, or
grains of sand on the seashore. Each personality with its matching gifts is
unique, but, like a note in a chord of music, or an instrument in an orchestra,
it is intended to blend with others so that the message of salvation becomes
the loveliest symphony of all.

TO READ: *Ephesians 4:17-32*

EASY PREY

*With the Lord's authority let me say this: Live no longer
as the ungodly do, for they are hopelessly confused.*

EPHESIANS 4:17

♡

A warning is necessary if you are a new Christian living among old pagans. Your lifestyle has to be different! How do the pagan nations live? People wander in a world of illusion and futility (Ephesians 4:18). Love has become lust, and their darkened understanding says that what is temporal is eternal, and what is eternal is irrelevant. Spiritual experience is not for people living in the real world, they say!

This worldly thinking is the result of calloused hearts (Ephesians 4:18). People sin and get away with it, then stick out their chins and say, "See, the sky didn't fall on my head!" They are greedy, wanting more of everything even though they have most everything. They indulge in outrageous conduct, living without care for high personal standards or social sanctions, and they have a passion for sexual indulgence at the expense of others. This is how the nations without Christ walk about this earth. They become so indifferent, even to the sanctity of human life, that they reduce everything to the mighty dollar.

The story is told of a man's watching another man drown in Hong Kong harbor. The drowning man begged the observer to jump in and save him, but the man refused until a passerby offered him some money! Not every unbeliever behaves in such a callous way, but every unbeliever, with no mighty checking power within, has the potential for all of the above. Alone against the foe, the Christless one is easy prey.

TO READ: *Ephesians 5:1-14*

IMITATORS

Follow God's example in everything you do,
because you are his dear children.

EPHESIANS 5:1

O ur son Pete wanted a bird! His sister had left for college, and he was feeling lonely. Without giving the matter much thought, I bought him a cockatiel. When Pete emerged from the bathroom after the first and last training session with his new-found friend, "Cornbread" (we found out later he should have been called "Cornelia") was relegated to a life within the walls of the cage in Pete's room. "Talk to him, Pete," I urged my son over the next few weeks; but the novelty of the pet wore off and my urging was to no avail. We donated Cornbread to a friend (now an enemy!) and told her, "Don't worry when you hear deep breathing in the middle of the night!" The poor bird had heard nothing more than Pete's deep, slumbering sighs, and so had imitated them! Have you ever heard a cockatiel deep-breathe? It's eerie.

But all of us learn by imitation, by following others' examples. Paul said, "Follow my example, just as I follow Christ's" (1 Corinthians 11:1). We are to watch carefully, listen acutely, and pick up every inflection of our master's voice!

Would we want people following our example? The very fact that we are being watched should force us to deal with our erratic behavior and not cause others to stumble. Jesus had some hard words about people who cause others to fall. He said it would be better if stones were tied around their necks and they were cast to the bottom of the sea (Luke 17:2)!

TO READ: *Ephesians 5:15-20*

BUYING TIME

Make the most of every opportunity for doing good in these evil days.
EPHESIANS 5:16

We must buy up the opportunities we have before the night comes. This is the day of opportunity. Our church took a survey of two thousand women in our community to find out what they were thinking, and how our women's ministry could best meet their needs. Out of all of those interviewed, only a handful of women were hostile or refused to talk with us. We need to buy up the opportunities with the many who are interested and searching.

Colossians 4:5 tells us to "live wisely among those who are not Christians, and make the most of every opportunity." Paul goes on to explain that in this wise walk, our speech must be salty (there will be a tang to it) so that we may know how to answer every person. Making the most of every opportunity means cultivating the "know-how" of argument and debate. Making the most of every opportunity means that by our very lifestyle, we will engender some questions from others.

Once in a train full of rowdy, drunken football fans, a young Christian was sitting quietly, reading. An old gentleman, observing first the drunks and then the young man, said to him, "You seem to have found the secret to life—do you want to share it?" Our young friend lost no time "making the most of the opportunity"!

We must ask God for a great sense of urgency so that we can make the most of every opportunity to serve and share him.

TO READ: *Ephesians 5:15-20*

LIKE A CUP
UNDER A FAUCET

Don't be drunk with wine, because that will ruin your life.
Instead, let the Holy Spirit fill and control you.

EPHESIANS 5:18

H ave you ever been drunk?" a man asked me. I confessed I had not.
"I have," he said. "Everything was affected. My eyesight, my
balance, and my judgment!"

Interestingly, Paul uses drunkenness to teach us about the fullness of
the Spirit. Don't be controlled by drink, but be controlled by the Spirit, he
says. Let the Holy Spirit affect the way you look at things and the way you
walk. Being filled with the Spirit will be a happy experience. God will not
make us miserable if we let him rule us. Our hearts will be singing all day
long, and in fact, we will be able to thank God always for all things! (See
Ephesians 5:19-20.)

Paul doesn't say to have *some* of the Spirit for *some* things. Christianity
is a religion of "alls." It's an "all or nothing" faith in an all-sufficient God.
The Holy Spirit is to "fill and control" us. Once the Holy Spirit fills us and
gains control, he can enable us to do what he tells us to do!

Like a cup under a faucet, our lives must be held under God's Spirit.
If we grieve or pull back or lie to him, confession will be necessary or we
shall lose the fullness. Notice I didn't say lose the *Spirit*—but the fullness.
Once the Holy Spirit comes into our hearts as resident and not as renter,
he comes to stay! It is up to us to make him as comfortable as possible in
our lives.

TO READ: *Philippians 1:1–19*

THE THINGS
THAT HAPPEN TO ME

And I want you to know, dear brothers and sisters, that everything
that has happened to me here has helped to spread the Good News.

PHILIPPIANS 1:12

W hen you're pressed for time or in a bind, it's hard to think of those around you.

I was trying to finish up a big writing project and meet my deadlines. I boarded the plane and settled down to study. The man next to me began to read my notes over my shoulder! *O Lord*, I prayed, *I don't have time to talk. I need to get ready for the challenge of the day.*

He is the challenge of the day, the Lord seemed to say.

The man began to question me, and I somewhat reluctantly put my books away to give him my full attention. Later, as we began to land, a light aircraft spun across our path, and our pilot dived sharply, narrowly avoiding a collision. Everyone screamed—including me!

"I bet you just said a prayer or two," my companion gasped, ashen-faced.

"You bet I did," I replied, "but I'm ready to go! That doesn't mean it won't be scary getting there, but God has my life in his hands!"

"I'm not ready to go," the man said quietly. "I'm scared to death!"

"Maybe you've been scared to *life*," I suggested.

I cannot afford to shut myself off behind my Bible from the people who live in the world. People come first, before papers that have to be written or study that needs to be done. It's a lesson I have to learn over and over again.

TO BE OR NOT TO BE

For to me, living is for Christ, and dying is even better.
PHILIPPIANS 1:21

Hamlet, the prince of Denmark, paced around the battlements lamenting, "To be or not to be; that is the question." Hamlet believed that if he went on living, it would be grim, but if he died, it would be worse!

Paul the apostle walked around his cell, faced with an identical dilemma: "To be or not to be." His attitude, however, was different from Hamlet's. "I long to go and be with Christ" (Philippians 1:23), he said, using a military term meaning "to strike the tent." The tent of his body was being dismantled. He had certainly lost a peg or two in his travels! As he contemplated moving camp and setting up his "new tent" in heaven's land, he could be pardoned for ruminating that this would be "far better."

However, he was acutely aware that he had a duty of obligation toward all his spiritual children, not the least of whom were his beloved Philippians. "But it is far better for you that I live," he agreed, as if caught in an eternal debate. "If I die," said Paul, "it will be marvelous; if I go on living, it will be great!" You can't do much to a person who lives by *that* philosophy.

Are you like Hamlet or Paul? Can you say, "For to me, living is for Christ," or would you have to say, "For me, to live is misery, anger, hopelessness, depression"? The Christian has Paul's philosophy of joy—it is the legacy of God's children.

TO READ: *Philippians 2:1–4*

A VOLUNTARY HUMILITY

Don't be selfish; don't live to make a good impression on others.
Be humble, thinking of others as better than yourself.
PHILIPPIANS 2:3

Being one in spirit and person means minimal strife in the church, even when we are very different. "Do nothing out of selfish ambition or vain conceit" (2:3, NIV), exhorts Paul.

When any hint of self-seeking or unworthy ambition motivates our actions, look out! If vainglory, which is simply a cheap desire to boast, is the best that we can manage, we shouldn't join a church. We'd split it!

In pressing toward our goals, to what extent do we use people as rungs on our climb? What happens to the people in our lives, to our Christian service, to our effectiveness as a believer?

Do we really consider others "better" than ourselves? Do we look to the interests of others before our own (Philippians 2:4)?

Why do our churches attract so much criticism? Is it not because we spend all our time fighting each other rather than fighting the devil? Why is there so much strife in the church choir? "When the devil fell out of heaven, he fell into the choir," responds a cynic! Must we be prima donnas?

We can achieve almost anything we want if we are willing to forfeit the credit! For some of us, that will require a radical change of attitude. Voluntary humility is the hardest thing on earth to achieve. For the Christian, it *must be* if we are to be like him.

TO READ: *Philippians 2:5-18*

A BIBLICAL HUMILITY

Your attitude should be the same that Christ Jesus had.

PHILIPPIANS 2:5

Humility is a view of ourselves learned at the feet of our Savior. Humility is born from a sense of dependence, not a false depreciation of ourselves. Biblical humility gives knowledge of *derived* worth. "I am worth something *because* of him," we can say. I am worth dying for; I was worth creating, saving, sanctifying, glorifying. But none of this is apart from him. When we say we are worth *anything* apart from him, we are in trouble!

Humility was frowned upon in the ancient world. If a person was humble, he was considered a cringing object and was despised. Jesus Christ taught us the virtue of humility, and Jesus Christ was the supreme example. Jesus was meek and humble in spirit, and Paul says, "Your attitude should be the same that Christ Jesus had" (Philippians 2:5).

It is good to check up on ourselves once in a while. We need to ask ourselves, "What can I do today that will elevate the interests of the people around me above my own?" We can get so preoccupied with the cultivation of our own spiritual life, that we can miss the noble traits of others.

We must search for and recognize the good qualities in fellow believers and emulate them in our own lives. If we would be like Jesus, we must humble ourselves.

TO READ: *Philippians 3:1-11*

YES, HE DID—
NO, HE DIDN'T

As a result, I can really know Christ and experience the mighty power that
raised him from the dead. I can learn what it means to suffer with him,
sharing in his death.

PHILIPPIANS 3:10

Didn't Paul already know Christ? Well, as Campbell Morgan puts it, "Yes, he did—no, he didn't!" Didn't Columbus discover America? Yes, he did—no, he didn't! We are still discovering America! That's how it is when we meet Christ. We are introduced to him, and then the lifelong relationship begins. Just as the full discovery of America was left to people who would press on to explore the land, so the full realization of God will take investigation on our part.

But just how do we get to know him? We first discover him in the Old Testament. Jesus said, "The Scriptures point to me" (John 5:39). Then we develop close fellowship with Jesus through the Gospels. We see the pen portrait of him in Matthew, Mark, Luke, and John and look hard till the Lord Jesus lives in those portraits and can step out of the book into our consciences.

Campbell Morgan wanted to get to know his Lord and Savior Jesus Christ better, and so he spent three years following him through the Gospels. "After that time," he said, "I got such a vision of the splendor of my master that I've never been the same since."

When we've read of him in the Old Testament, followed him through the Gospels, and seen him as he is in the book of Revelation, then we will know the Lord! How long has it been since you were introduced to Jesus Christ? Do you really know him? Would you have to answer: "Yes, I do—no, I don't"?

MODEL MODELS

Dear friends, pattern your lives after mine,
and learn from those who follow our example.
PHILIPPIANS 3:17

Ⓖ

After I gave the commencement address for a modeling school, I watched the girls walk across the platform to receive their graduation certificates. They were perfectly poised and coifed with just the right amount of cleverly applied makeup in just the right places! They were, I mused, model models. Lastly, their popular teacher stood up to receive a standing ovation from the girls. It was then that I understood why the girls looked as they did. They were obviously her followers. She was perfectly poised and coifed with just the right amount of cleverly applied makeup in just the right places!

That is really what following, or being a disciple, is all about. Paul told the young Christians in the church at Philippi to watch how he lived the Christian life and do the same. He knew how important it was for those eager young believers to have a model.

This does not mean we should proudly set ourselves apart, put ourselves on pedestals, or pretend we are something special. Always remember that even the great apostle Paul did not count himself to have arrived at perfection (Philippians 3:13). We are to be models of growth, not models of perfection. That is the key!

Paul draws attention to other unknown, godly people and says, "learn from those who follow our example." Could Paul point us out as a model for younger Christians? Could you and I ask others to join in following our example?

TO READ: *Philippians 4:1-5*

JOY—WHENEVER, WHEREVER!

Always be full of joy in the Lord. I say it again—rejoice!
PHILIPPIANS 4:4

W e are to be "full of joy in the Lord" (Philippians 4:4). If we know how to do that, we won't be depressed by our circumstances.

We are not told to rejoice about the tragedies of life, but we are encouraged to rejoice *in the Lord* when hard times come. He promises to comfort us when we are mistreated and to help us to bravely endure when we suffer. We will be able to survive our circumstances with his help because he has already survived his circumstances as the God-man, Jesus of Nazareth. In Christ we have available to us all the support of heaven.

We are to rejoice in our relationship with him *always*. That doesn't mean just when the sun is shining; it means when it rains, hails, snows, and even if a tornado hits our life! *Always* means "always."

Joy is the badge of the believer. Paul, writing from his prison cell, emphasized the inability of circumstances to stifle his enjoyment of the Lord. "Be full of joy," he exhorted the beloved Philippian believers, "I say it again—rejoice!" (Philippians 4:4). When we can't praise him for what he has allowed, we can thank him for who he is in the midst of what he has allowed! This does not mean that we do not mourn with those who mourn, but it does mean that we point discouraged people to Jesus—the source of joy.

TO READ: *Philippians 4:6–9*

A GRADUATED WORRIER

Don't worry about anything; instead, pray about everything.
Tell God what you need, and thank him for all he has done.

PHILIPPIANS 4:6

Now there's a mouthful! "Don't worry about anything," Paul says blithely, as if it's as easy as falling off a log.

When I was a little girl, I worried my shoes would shrink. After all, I had heard my teacher say my sandals were getting too small. When I was a teenager, I worried that I wouldn't get a date. When I got engaged, I worried I might be in a car wreck the eve of my wedding. When I had my first baby, I worried he would fall into the washing machine and drown! When my children became teenagers, I worried they wouldn't get a date (or get a bad one), or they might be in a car wreck on the eve of their wedding, or their children might fall into the washing machine and drown!

There's no end to the possibilities for worry. You'll never run out of things to worry about! Being a graduated worrier, I have had to learn some hard lessons about what worry does to me—and my family! Worry does not empty tomorrow of its problems; it simply empties today of its strength.

But more important, worry betrays a lack of trust in God's care. That's what really helped me to realize that lack of trust in God, the seedbed of worry, is *sin!* Now I can do something about that. I can repent of it and be determined to sin no more! My God delights to lend his strength to such resolve. "Trust me," he says. "Don't worry about anything."

TO READ: *Philippians 4:8-23*

GOD'S GATEKEEPERS

And now, dear brothers and sisters, let me say one more thing as I close
this letter. Fix your thoughts on what is true and honorable and right.
Think about things that are pure and lovely and admirable.
Think about things that are excellent and worthy of praise.

PHILIPPIANS 4:8

Paul names eight "gatekeepers" that should stand in the gateway of our thinking.

First, as our mind is fed information, we should ask ourselves, "Is it true?" God's own truth can be our measure.

Then we should inquire, "Is it honorable?" Does the thing I hear have a noble ring to it? Is the action I am being asked to take respectable?

Next we need to determine, "Is it right?" Is it just and fair? We can search the Gospels and see if Jesus addressed the issue. What did he say was right?

When we consider what we watch on television or at the movies or what we read, we should inquire, "Is this pure and lovely?" Will this data I am feeding into my mind result in godly love and beautiful actions?

What's more, we need to ask, "Is it admirable?" Is what I am thinking about praiseworthy and well reputed? Does it sound attractive or appealing?

Finally, we must consider, are we thinking what is "excellent and worthy of praise"? I'm sure many of us would have difficulty labeling most of our thought life as *excellent*. We should hold our thoughts above the world's thoughts. Reach for a star; don't settle for mediocrity.

If we would all determine to allow only that which calls down the approval of God into our thought patterns, then we would be well on the way to experiencing continual peace of mind. So if you value the approval of God, Paul concludes, "fix your thoughts on" these things.

TO READ: *Colossians 2:1-23*

FILLING UP
THE EMPTINESS

For in Christ the fullness of God lives in a human body,
COLOSSIANS 2:9

Human beings living without Christ long for a completeness that somehow they know there should be yet they sense isn't there. They are conscious of something missing in their lives.

This sense of lack, of incompleteness, is a result of how we were created. We were created for fellowship with God. But as a result of the Fall, God is distant without Christ, and the unregenerate person is very often aware of it.

Once a person is saved from sin and filled with the Spirit, however, the "lack" is filled up with God. In every dimension of our life, we begin to experience healing and wholeness. How does this happen? When the Spirit fills our life with God's presence, we feel his healthiness in every part of our life—spiritually, morally, and mentally. Saved people recognize that they are new creations, indwelt by God himself.

You can be full of yourself, full of good intentions, full of pleasures, full of ambition and drive and yet at the end of the day find yourself as empty as a drum. To be a partaker of the very nature of God, however, means sharing in the divine fullness—and there is no fullness like God's fullness! Do you have a busy life but still feel empty? Through Christ you have been reconciled to God; through Christ you can have peace with God. You were made by God, for God. The remedy that gives health and wholeness is in God's fullness!

TO READ: *Colossians 3:1-25*

"WHAT TO DO?"

*Work hard and cheerfully at whatever you do, as though you were working
for the Lord rather than for people. Remember that the Lord will give you an
inheritance as your reward, and the master you are serving is Christ.*

COLOSSIANS 3:23-24

The people in Liberia have many problems. But when they come to an
impasse, they simply smile a marvelous Liberian smile, shrug their
shoulders, and say, "What to do?"

Coming from a culture that tends to believe that people can do
anything they want to do if they try hard enough, we may think that this
sounds like a weak excuse. However, simple acceptance of the situation
may be the first step to the realism required to live amidst trying circumstances without falling apart.

Christians should be willing to wait upon the Lord until we are told
what to do—and herein lies our rest. In acceptance we find peace. Once
instructed, however, we must "work hard and cheerfully." Enthusiastic
"doing" delights the heart of God! Our daily "doing" must not be for our
earthly honor or success either. We must not "do" for people so that people
will "do" for us! Instead, we must "do" for people as though we are "doing"
for God.

My mother-in-law was a great example of this text. Whenever she
cleaned a pair of shoes, they shined as if Christ were going to wear them;
whenever she cooked a meal, she cooked it as if Christ were joining us for
dinner. And she was satisfied to receive her "reward" from him!

> *Dear Lord—when I know not "what to do,"*
>   *still me.*
> *When you've shown me "what to do,"*
>   *fill me,*
> *That I may "do" your will with all my might!*

TO READ: *1 Thessalonians 2:17–3:13*

MY HEAVENLY OSCAR

After all, what gives us hope and joy, and what is our proud reward and crown? It is you! Yes, you will bring us much joy as we stand together before our Lord Jesus when he comes back again. For you are our pride and joy.

1 THESSALONIANS 2:19-20

Did you know that there will be an awards day in heaven? When it comes, God will give crowns to his faithful servants who have preached the gospel or have led people to Christ.

The Thessalonian converts were Paul's crown, and they gave him much joy: When Paul spoke of the Thessalonian believers as a crown of joy, he was thinking of his reward as an evangelist. Some have a special gift for evangelism, but we are all to be witnesses and win people to Christ. Those who do this will experience "much joy" when our Lord Jesus returns.

What other awards will be given in heaven? A crown of righteousness will be given to all who have been eagerly looking forward to Christ's second coming (2 Timothy 4:8). You could call this a "crown of readiness." Those who have cared well for God's flock, the church, will receive the shepherd's crown (1 Peter 5:1-4). God will give a crown of life to those who "patiently endure testing" (James 1:12).

During the Oscar presentations, I have been struck by the way every recipient takes the platform to thank the people who have made it possible for him or her to win. When the "heavenly Oscars" are presented, all of us will want to take our opportunity to thank the one who made it possible, the Lord. And unlike the earthly Oscars, the heavenly Oscars have no limit—there are plenty of rewards for everyone! Everyone, that is, who is faithful to the Lord.

TO READ: *1 Thessalonians 4:1–18*

BEING WHOLLY WHOLE

God wants you to be holy, so you should keep clear of all sexual sin.
1 THESSALONIANS 4:3

W hat is God's will for my life? What does God want me to do? These are very important questions. But one thing God wants of us has nothing to do with *doing,* but rather with *being.* Before we ask God what he wants us to do, we need to understand and accept what he has already said we must be.

God wants his people to be holy, and this requires us to give up our sin. In a process called "sanctification," God works to transform our behavior to his holy standards. This happens in the lives of all who have accepted Christ as Savior, in whom the Holy Spirit is working to make them more like Christ. Because we will not be perfectly holy until heaven, our sanctification requires constant repentance from sin. Repentance involves turning away from our sins, from all that hinders us from being set apart for God's special use, from all that keeps us from being holy.

If you are struggling to find out what God wants you to do with your life, you need to ask yourself these questions: *Will what I am contemplating doing mean I will be more like Christ by doing it? Will I be more holy, more whole than before?* The answers to these questions should help you to decide!

God calls us to be holy. When we are set apart for him, we will be able to serve him—in our family, in the church, and in the world. This is the will of God!

TO READ: *1 Thessalonians 5:1-28*

SAYING THANK YOU

No matter what happens, always be thankful,
for this is God's will for you who belong to Christ Jesus.
1 THESSALONIANS 5:18

W hen the scriptures say, "This is God's will for you," we need have
no doubts that what is being said *is indeed* God's will for us!

Are you in the habit of saying thank you no matter what?
Another version of the Bible says: "Give thanks in all circumstances"
(1 Thessalonians 5:18, NIV). Notice the verse doesn't tell us that it's
God's will for us to give thanks *for* all circumstances, but *in* all
circumstances. Paul was writing to the Thessalonians, who were
suffering difficult things in difficult times. Yet he told them to give
thanks!

In the middle of a nightmare, we can give thanks that "weeping may
go on all night, but joy comes with the morning" (Psalm 30:5). In the pain
of bereavement, we can thank God for the comfort of his "rod" and "staff"
in our "dark valley of death" (Psalm 23:4). When others reject us for our
beliefs, we can thank God that he accepts us fully and unreservedly, and we
can be thankful for friends who believe as we do. In all things there will be
something for which we can praise and thank God. When we can't praise
him for what, in his sovereign will, he has allowed, we can praise him for
who he is in the middle of it.

Dare we thank God for such things? Yes! *No matter what happens,* give
thanks!

TO READ: *2 Thessalonians 3:6-15*

WORKING WHILE WE'RE WAITING

And I say to the rest of you, dear brothers and sisters,
never get tired of doing good.
2 THESSALONIANS 3:13

S ome of the believers in Thessalonica were so convinced that the Lord's second coming was imminent that they decided it was useless to work for their living! Paul was horrified by this, so he told the idlers, in no uncertain terms, to earn their own living, following the example he gave them while he was with them.

As we await his return, Jesus prays for us that our faith and our strength will not fail (Luke 22:32; John 17:15-17). He doesn't want us wilting while we're waiting! Think about it—Jesus worked hard. He spent years working for his living. And when he did kingdom work full-time, he was never too harried to heal, never too faint to fight for a soul, never too tired to talk with those who sought him, never too weary to listen in love. And yet, because he experienced our human nature, he knows how tiredness can weaken our body, and he understands what it is like to be on the edge of tears. Now, as we continue his work on earth by doing good and building the kingdom, Jesus rejoices in heaven over the sheep on earth coming into the fold.

A journey with Jesus is not an easy thing. You won't get to your destination without sand in your sandals and dirt in your hair, but you will have the incalculable joy of his company. His abundant sympathy and his "Well done" at the end of the day will be worth it all.

TO READ: *2 Timothy 3:1-17*

THE LIBRARIAN

You have been taught the holy Scriptures from childhood,
and they have given you the wisdom to receive the salvation
that comes by trusting in Christ Jesus.

2 TIMOTHY 3:15

The Bible is like a library. It has a historical section, a poetry shelf, and a collection of wisdom literature. There are practical helps for daily living. If you are musically inclined, there is a section just for you. If you like human interest stories, there are lots of biographies and autobiographies. There are even books that look into the future!

When you visit a library, you need to know how it is arranged so you can quickly select the material of your choice. Take some time to sit down with God's Word and familiarize yourself with its layout. Then try to read something from each section in the course of the year, so you will have a balanced view of the whole.

The Holy Spirit is like the librarian. His job is to answer your questions, see to your complaints, and encourage you to become an accomplished reader. In the end though, *you* have to sit down and read the book. The librarian cannot do that for you; neither can the other people who use the library!

Many of us treat our Bibles as we treat our public libraries. Some of us never even bother to get a card. Others of us start a book, never finish it, and find ourselves fined for keeping it too long. That's a shame! It will always cost you if you make a habit of doing that! It will cost you the encouragement, wisdom, and instruction that are available to you. Become a book lover. Read in God's library today.

TO READ: 2 Timothy 3:1-17

THE STAMP
OF AUTHENTICITY

All Scripture is inspired by God and is useful to teach us what is true
and to make us realize what is wrong in our lives.
It straightens us out and teaches us to do what is right.

2 TIMOTHY 3:16

Some people doubt the authenticity and reliability of the Bible. For example, they think that because the four Gospels contain variations, the Gospels contradict themselves. So how reliable are the Gospels?

If you saw a fashion show with three of your friends, and then you all came home and talked about it, would you all recount the same thing in exactly the same way? Of course not! Each of you would describe the same "happening" from your different perspectives and in your own words. This is precisely how the four Gospel writers came to record the same events a little differently.

Their reasons for writing played an important part, too. Matthew wrote especially for the Jews. Mark on the other hand, wrote primarily for the Christians in Rome. Luke wrote for the Gentiles. John wrote to a more general, nonbelieving audience. The Holy Spirit used the Gospel writers' personalities and diverse writing styles in the Gospel accounts as we have them. No wonder there are differences—but the important thing to remember is that the message is the same! The writers may have conveyed the Good News with contrasting style and color and with different audiences in mind, but the divinity and humanity of Christ, the redemption of humanity, and the resurrection of the dead were similarly revealed through their pens. The variations of their Gospels only stamp them with authenticity!

You can believe what God's Word says about itself. It is totally reliable. Put your trust in its promises, and obey its precepts. You will not be disappointed.

TO READ: *Hebrews 2:1–18*

DRIFTING AWAY

So we must listen very carefully to the truth we have heard,
or we may drift away from it.

HEBREWS 2:1

W hat is this truth that we must listen to so carefully?
Christ is Lord. After fulfilling his mission on earth to pay for our sins, Jesus Christ, our risen Savior, "sat down in the place of honor at the right hand of the majestic God of heaven" (Hebrews 1:3).

Christ is supreme. Christ is, in fact, greater than the angels, greater than the greatest of people, and greater than the devil and all his emissaries. Jesus is Lord, and his word is true, so we must fall on our face and worship him.

The first-century Christians, to whom the letter of Hebrews was written, knew these facts yet were in danger of drifting away from the truths that they had received.

Is it really any different today? *To drift away* is literally "to flow by; to slip away." If only we would so earnestly endeavor to stay securely moored to the truths we have learned about Christ. The warning of Scripture is clear: "We must listen very carefully to the truth we have heard, or we may drift away from it" (Hebrews 2:1). The readers of this letter were established believers, and yet the pressures of their circumstances were such that they were willfully neglecting the basic tenets of their faith, and they began to drift away. We must be warned by their example—we need to be disciplined and pay more careful attention!

TO READ: *Hebrews 3:1-19*

TODAY

*That is why the Holy Spirit says, "Today you must listen to his voice.
Don't harden your hearts against him as Israel did when they rebelled,
when they tested God's patience in the wilderness."*

HEBREWS 3:7-8

Quoting Psalm 95, the writer of Hebrews pleaded twice with the Jews, "Today you must listen to his voice" (Hebrews 3:7, 15). God's word never changes. Like the Old Testament psalmist and the New Testament letter writer, we have only today. Yesterday is gone, and tomorrow is never certain. Today is what counts. Will you listen to his voice *today*?

"But how do I hear his voice?" you ask. We hear it first by listening to what he has already said in his word. Daily we must expose ourselves to God's voice through Bible reading, worship, and prayer.

Suppose, for example, that at work today your boss makes a pass at you. He's a married man. You may feel flattered or even tempted, but as a Christian you know that the Bible is very clear on matters of fidelity in marriage. You could pass the buck by saying to yourself, "Jesus will say no for me. I can do nothing; he will do it all!" But as you wait for Jesus to say no, nothing happens. Then you discover that *you* have to say no—and you have to say it *today*, at that very moment! Once you have said no, however, the power to keep on saying no will be supplied.

Jesus expects us to be obedient, to make right moral choices, to strive to stay in his place of blessing by living holy lives. What is Jesus saying to you today? Are you listening? How must you respond today?

TO READ: *Hebrews 6:1-20*

AS LONG AS LIFE LASTS

Our great desire is that you will keep right on loving others as long as life lasts, in order to make certain that what you hope for will come true.

HEBREWS 6:11

How do we "keep right on loving others as long as life lasts" (Hebrews 6:11)? It seems an impossible task, especially when we feel wrapped up in our own concerns and problems. We do it by faith and patience, realizing that this is the best way we can show God how much we love him. It's fine to tell God you love him but far better to show him. And one way we show him is by loving other Christians.

Whenever we call a friend in trouble and take time to listen to her struggles, whenever we take small children off a single mother's hands to give her a break, whenever we pay the electric bill for a student struggling financially to stay in Bible school, we show God how much we love him. Whenever we visit a grandmother in a nursing home who loves Jesus but has no relatives to care for her, whenever we spend our vacation building a house for the homeless, whenever we give to missions till it really costs us something, we show God how much we love him!

What do you do for other Christians? It's not enough to pray for them or just say we love them. God sees our heart and watches our life. He knows what we are doing, and when he sees us love and care for his people, he will not forget to reward us! As long as life lasts, keep on loving!

341

TO READ: *Hebrews 10:11-22*

THE VEIL

*And so, dear friends, we can boldly enter heaven's Most Holy Place because
of the blood of Jesus. This is the new, life-giving way that Christ has opened
up for us through the sacred curtain, by means of his death for us.*

HEBREWS 10:19-20

I n times past, the priest was the mediator between God and Israel.
Since the Resurrection of Christ, *he* alone is the "one Mediator who
can reconcile God and people" (1 Timothy 2:5). He is our High Priest.
Israel's high priest would enter the Most Holy Place where God dwelt
and offer the blood of a lamb as a sacrifice for the people, that they
might be made one with God.

When Jesus' flesh was rent on Calvary, the veil or curtain that hung
across the entrance into the Most Holy Place was also torn in two, making
entrance into God's presence possible. We can call God "Father" and come
freely before him to "find grace to help us when we need it" (Hebrews
4:16).

When our children were growing up, their father traveled a great
deal. When he returned, he needed to catch up with mountains of work
that were always waiting for him. Since his study was at home, I tried to
keep the door shut and the children outside! But he would always open
the door and tell me to leave it that way. "I want the kids to know I am
always accessible to them," he would say. The children would run in and
out whenever they had a need or a want, a kiss or a hug for Daddy.

That is how our Father in heaven would have it, too; Jesus made that
possible!

OUR THINGS OR HIS THINGS?

And let us not neglect our meeting together, as some people do,
but encourage and warn each other, especially now that the
day of his coming back again is drawing near.

HEBREWS 10:25

A s a boy of twelve, Jesus had said to his parents, who had been
looking for him, "You should have known that I would be in my
Father's house" (Luke 2:49). Jesus' focus in life—even as a young man—
was his Father's business. This is what he was about.

What are we about—our things or his things? Jesus' "things" included
being in the temple listening and asking questions (Luke 2:46). Years later
he taught in the synagogues (Luke 4:14-15). When he went to his hometown, Nazareth, "He went as usual to the synagogue on the Sabbath"
(Luke 4:16).

If we, like our Lord and the apostle Paul, want to be doing God's
business, we, too, must meet with a body of believers. We will never
find a perfect church, and if we do, we should be careful not to join it,
lest we spoil it! We should make our presence felt in our church! If the
church is a group of God's people, God promises that he will be there.
He said, "For where two or three gather together because they are mine,
I am there among them" (Matthew 18:20).

Fellowship is a very important part of our spiritual life, for it keeps
our faith burning. If a coal falls out of a fire, it will soon go out. Believers
need to be an active part of a local church. As we focus individually and
collectively on God's things, God is pleased.

TO READ: *Hebrews 11:1–12*

PRAYING ACCORDING TO THE INSTRUCTIONS

So, you see, it is impossible to please God without faith.
Anyone who wants to come to him must believe that there is a God
and that he rewards those who sincerely seek him.

HEBREWS 11:6

One of the things that discourages some from praying is the fear that they won't do it right. For example, it says in Hebrews 11:6 that whoever comes to God must believe. But what if I feel I don't believe enough? How do I measure my faith, or how does God measure it? Do I have to do it right in order to get my prayers answered?

If you buy a cake mix and then ignore the instructions on the box, you can't blame the manufacturer if the cake flops! It's a little the same with prayer. We need to read the instructions:

- We must come in faith, believing that there is a God who will hear us and reward us (Hebrews 11:6).
- We must willingly let God examine our heart (Psalm 139:23-24), confess our sins (1 John 1:9), and then repent (Acts 3:19).
- We can pray even if we feel that our faith is small (Matthew 17:20).
- We must consider if there are any of our relationships that need mending. Then we need to go and try to make them right (Matthew 5:23-24).
- We must come to prayer by asking in Jesus' name and for his sake.
- We can ask ourselves, "Will the answer to this prayer glorify Jesus and extend the work of the kingdom?" (John 14:13).

As you practice the discipline of prayer and try to keep these basic things in mind, you'll find yourself on the way to doing it right. What's more, the more you practice, the nearer to a "perfect cake" you'll get!

DECEMBER

TO READ: *Hebrews 12:1-13*

COACH OF THE YEAR

*Therefore, since we are surrounded by such a huge crowd of witnesses
to the life of faith, let us strip off every weight that slows us down,
especially the sin that so easily hinders our progress. And let us run
with endurance the race that God has set before us.*

HEBREWS 12:1

C hrist is our example as we run life's race. As a good coach, he himself competed in the same "sport"—he lived this life on earth. He even died "a shameful death" (Hebrews 12:2). Why? "Because of the joy he knew would be his afterward." So we, too, look forward to the prize—the joy—that will be ours. Christ stands at the winning post and receives us to glory. The prize is to fall into his arms and hear him say, "Well done! You finished the race. You persevered. You did not drift away from the moorings of the truth of your faith. You hung in there." We may *drop over* the finish line in total exhaustion—just as long as we don't *drop out* of the race. Christ endured, so we must not "become weary and give up" (Hebrews 12:3).

The Bible talks of "the race that God has set before us" (Hebrews 12:1). What does that mean? When our two oldest children were running cross-country in high school, the coach would always make sure they arrived at the course early so they would have enough time to walk the course before actually having to run the race. He wanted them to know the difficult humps and bumps of the course.

Tough assignments require tough training, but we can make it. All we have to do is look at Jesus. "We do this by keeping our eyes on Jesus, on whom our faith depends from start to finish" (Hebrews 12:2). The Coach is cheering you on! Look to him.

TO READ: *Hebrews 13:1-25*

WHEN PARADISE ISN'T ENOUGH

Stay away from the love of money; be satisfied with what you have.
For God has said, "I will never fail you. I will never forsake you."

HEBREWS 13:5

It's so easy to be discontent. The more we have, the more we seem to want.

Eve faced such discontent even in Paradise. She allowed herself to become dissatisfied with what God had given her. She wanted more. She believed the snake when he told her that she could (and should!) have more. Then Paradise wasn't enough for Eve (Genesis 3:1-19). Can you imagine how that could be? Yet the snake still tries to tell us that there must be something else that enough money could buy us that would really satisfy our discontentment.

Are you like Eve, thinking you should have more? Have you become dissatisfied—not enough money, not a big enough home? Perhaps you feel that you're not smart enough, thin enough, or beautiful enough. Perhaps you're rebelling against the role to which God has currently called you— and you want (or feel you deserve) more. Are you looking afar for "paradise"?

You need not look any further than your heart. Paradise is found in obedience to God, service for God, and a deep knowledge of God. As long as we believe that paradise can be purchased and furnished with our own hands and means, we will be doomed to discontentment. Once we put spiritual life before material living, paradise will be our home. God has promised never to leave us and never to fail us. To accept ourselves as God created us, to do what he wants us to do today, and to revel in his love for us—*that* is paradise.

TO READ: *James 1:19-27*

THE SOUND OF SILENCE

My dear brothers and sisters, be quick to listen,
slow to speak, and slow to get angry.

JAMES 1:19

Listening works wonders! Loving silence has no sound, but tells the one sitting next to you that you care. It can say to the hurting heart, "I want to free you to think about yourself, your failures, and your goals. Because I love you and am interested in you I am willing to sit in silence with you."

Can you sit with a friend without talking? Can you sit with your husband in silence? Or do you, as I tend to, complete all his sentences for him? That particular habit irritates him to distraction, but I find myself doing it anyway. It's such fun to guess the ending of his story and race him there! I have to confess, though, that both God and Stuart have been working on me lately to exert more self-control. I am learning to use a short reply, because it invites more response! I have thanked God that he has graced me with a companion, and I have reminded myself that he is indeed a companion and not a competitor in a word game!

I have learned to listen and discover with joy the unusual and unique facets of the one I love. I pray hard to fight down my impulsive, emotional response and let him talk.

For this I need to rely on Jesus. I have discovered that God is delighted to tame my tongue and tune my ear; and whenever he has been allowed to do so, he has filled my heart with the knowledge that listening with love brings love in return!

TO READ: *1 Peter 1:1–25*

ENJOYING JOY

You love him even though you have never seen him.
Though you do not see him, you trust him; and even now
you are happy with a glorious, inexpressible joy.

1 PETER 1:8

As my husband and I minister, hardly a day goes by without our hearing someone say, "Why me, why now, why this? Why was my daughter maimed in an accident? Why was my sister left with four small children to raise? Why was my husband laid off—again?"

Peter was writing to believers who were "living as foreigners" in other lands (1 Peter 1:1). He told these believers not to be surprised by the troubles and trials that they were experiencing for following Christ. These people had never even seen Jesus. Yet they saw him with eyes of faith. For some people, seeing is believing. Thomas, Jesus' disciple, was like that. Jesus told him, "You believe because you have seen me. Blessed are those who haven't seen me and believe anyway" (John 20:29). In other words, believing is seeing! So Peter wrote, "You love him even though you have never seen him. Though you do not see him, you trust him; and even now you are happy with a glorious, inexpressible joy" (1 Peter 1:8).

Are you finding it difficult to be full of joy when life is full of hurt? Does God seem far away? Peter reminds us to trust God, even though we cannot see him or even see him working. Rejoicing with inexpressible joy can be our experience, too. Joy even in trouble is part and parcel of the wonderful salvation Christ wants us to enjoy. "[Our] reward for trusting him [is] the salvation of [our] souls" (1 Peter 1:9). Now that's joy we can enjoy!

TO READ: *1 Peter 3:13-22*

WAITING FOR PEOPLE TO SAY THEY'RE SORRY

*Those who disobeyed God long ago when God waited patiently while
Noah was building his boat. Only eight people were saved from
drowning in that terrible flood.*

1 PETER 3:20

O ne of the things that leads to frustration is waiting, especially
waiting for people to say they're sorry. For this, not even the
patience of Job will help us. We need the patience of God.

God knows how to wait patiently. How long did God wait for a
world at odds with him to say it was sorry? As long as it took Noah to
build the ark! God waited, but still a sinful world refused to repent.

When God was on earth in Christ, reconciling the world to himself
(2 Corinthians 5:19), he waited thirty-three years—all his life—for some
people to say they were sorry. These were people he loved—people who
were close to him—people in his very own family! His brothers never did
get around to it while he was alive (John 7:5). It took the Resurrection and
Ascension to convince Jesus' brothers that Jesus was the Christ (Acts 1:14).

We might have to wait our whole life to hear those longed-for
words *I'm sorry.* And some of us may never hear those words at all. But
we have Jesus! He knows how to wait it out patiently. Remember that
patience is a fruit of the Spirit (Galatians 5:22). When we need patience
to wait through heartaches, misunderstandings, and hostility, we have
Jesus. When we need patience to wait for an apology that may never
come, we have Jesus. Patience is love willing to wait out frustration.
Yes, for this we have Jesus.

IF SOMEONE
HAD TOLD ME . . .

As a fellow elder, this is my appeal to you: Care for the flock of God entrusted to you. Watch over it willingly, not grudgingly—not for what you will get out of it, but because you are eager to serve God.

1 PETER 5:1-2

D isillusionment with fellow believers in a church or a mission can take many a young recruit out of ministry. Nobody told me about disillusionment when I started ministering to others.

If someone had told me how easy it would be to get too busy to be blessed, I wouldn't have believed it. Yet even now, forty years after entering the ministry, I struggle *daily* with my devotional disciplines.

If someone had told me that even as we serve God faithfully, God allows painful things to happen to our children, I wouldn't have believed it. Somehow I expected special treatment.

If someone had told me that I would find myself, like Elijah, flat on my face under a broom tree wanting to die (1 Kings 19:4), I wouldn't have believed it. Surely God would help me stay full of energy and not let me totally burn out.

If someone had told me that I didn't have one gift that was expected of me in my role as pastor's wife, I wouldn't have believed it. I did what I could and got others to help do what I couldn't, and we got all the jobs done.

Finally, if someone had told me about all the joy, fulfillment, pure pleasure, laughter, tears, friendships, and love there are in serving Jesus in the place where he has put us—I wouldn't have believed it. But I do now— and for this I humbly praise and adore God! "And I, too, will share his glory and his honor when he returns" (1 Peter 5:1).

TO READ: *2 Peter 1:1–21*

KNOWING JESUS
BETTER AND BETTER

*May God bless you with his special favor and wonderful peace as you come to
know Jesus, our God and Lord, better and better. As we know Jesus better,
his divine power gives us everything we need for living a godly life.
He has called us to receive his own glory and goodness!*

2 PETER 1:2-3

C oming to Jesus is the first step of salvation. The next step, which
stretches into a long relational walk throughout our life, is "to know
Jesus, our God and Lord, better and better" (2 Peter 1:2).

How is this accomplished? "As we know Jesus better, his divine power
gives us everything we need for living a godly life" (2 Peter 1:3). Certainly
this is accomplished in our personal devotional life but also in a local
church in fellowship with other believers. The problem is, what we may
hear in church may work against our knowing Jesus better.

As we read the Bible and get to know Jesus better, we will be better
able to discern what is true or false—whether it comes from outside the
church or within. When we are looking for a church fellowship to join—
and we should—we should ask if it teaches that Jesus died and rose again
and that he is the only way to heaven. We should inquire if it teaches that
the Bible is the inspired word of God. We must study the Scriptures, and
compare what is being taught with what we have studied (Acts 17:10-12).

Growing in Christ means that we will "become productive and
useful" (2 Peter 1:8)—we will begin to exhibit the character qualities of
Christ's disciple (2 Peter 1:5-7). We can ask God to teach us more about
himself. Then we will be able to discern truth from error and can join a
church that teaches the Bible accurately and well.

CHRIST OUR ADVOCATE

My dear children, I am writing this to you so that you will not sin.
But if you do sin, there is someone to plead for you before the Father.
He is Jesus Christ, the one who pleases God completely.
1 JOHN 2:1

J esus had encouraged his disciples to look forward to the Holy Spirit's coming. Even though Jesus was leaving them, he promised to send them "another Counselor" (John 14:16).

The root meaning of the word *counselor* is "one that is called alongside to help." The element of comfort is an important aspect of the Holy Spirit's work, and Jesus used the picture of comforting the desolate as one comforts an orphan. But the word *counselor* also has the idea of an advocate. An advocate is one who is called to one's side to help against an accuser or judge. He is the client's representative who pleads his case and defends his reputation, guarding and administrating his property.

Jesus Christ is our Advocate with God: "There is someone to plead for you before the Father. He is Jesus Christ, the one who pleases God completely" (1 John 2:1). The Holy Spirit holds the spotlight on Jesus Christ, showing us Jesus' worth and enlightening our heart and mind to understand his work. When I was a young person without any Christian influence, unchurched, and ignorant of the facts of the gospel message, there were times when I was conscious of my need of God. When alerted to Christ as the answer, I was thoroughly ready to receive him. The Holy Spirit put Christ—my advocate and friend—in the spotlight so I could see him clearly.

With Christ as our counselor and Advocate, let us give ourselves unreservedly to him and to his work. That way many will see and follow him.

TO READ: *1 John 5:1-12*

TAKING GOD
AT HIS WORD

And this is what God has testified: He has given us eternal life,
and this life is in his Son. So whoever has God's Son has life;
whoever does not have his Son does not have life.

1 JOHN 5:11-12

I f eternal life is the life of the eternal one, it follows that we have eternal life now if we have him. Have you asked Christ into your heart?

First John 5:13 says, "I write this to you who believe in the Son of God, so that you may know you have eternal life." We can *know that we have,* not *hope that we may receive.* Lots of people think they have to wait till they get to heaven to see if they can stay there. But you can know that you have eternal life now! Thank him for that.

Our daughter used to ask Christ into her life every single night as she said her prayers. I tried to tell her she didn't need to go on asking. He had promised to come in the first time, and she could trust him to do what he said. One day I sent her to answer the doorbell. It was her friend. "Ask her in, Judy," I said, and she did. Ten minutes later I asked my daughter, "Why don't you ask your friend in to play with you?"

"She's in already, silly!" replied my little girl. I reminded her that Jesus was the same. She got the point.

"If you . . . open the door, I will come in," Jesus said in Revelation 3:20. What is more, Christ has told us that he comes in to stay. He shuts the door behind him, and no one can open it. Jesus Christ does not change his mind about eternal things.

SUFFERING REVEALS THE FACE OF GOD

It was the Lord's Day, and I was worshiping in the Spirit. Suddenly, I heard a loud voice behind me, a voice that sounded like a trumpet blast.

REVELATION 1:10

If you were to visit the beautiful island of Patmos, you might be cured of feeling sorry for John who was exiled there "for preaching the word of God and speaking about Jesus" (Revelation 1:9). Yet though his surroundings were beautiful, the island was still his prison.

But no exile or prison could stop John from worshiping. John wrote, "It was the Lord's Day, and I was worshiping in the Spirit" (Revelation 1:10). When John was "in the Spirit" on the Lord's Day, he saw the Lord as he had never seen him before! Suffering for this testimony of Jesus did not cloud the face of God but rather revealed it (Revelation 1:12-16).

Perhaps it's hard for you to be "in the Spirit" on the Lord's Day. Maybe you feel like you are on an island, isolated by circumstances, separated against your will from those you love. If you will stay in touch with the God who has allowed these circumstances, you will see Jesus as you have never seen him before. So don't waste the pain.

Suffering helps you see God as you've never seen him before—just as John did. It also helps you see aspects of Jesus' character in a whole new way—just as John did. Once, on the Mount of Transfiguration, John had seen the glory of God in Christ; here he saw more of that glory. Whenever we are "in the Spirit," God will show himself to us. We can let suffering drive us deeper into God and know that he's waiting.

TO READ: *Revelation 1:1–11*

THE JESUS CONNECTION

It said, "Write down what you see, and send it to the seven churches:
Ephesus, Smyrna, Pergamum, Thyatira, Sardis,
Philadelphia, and Laodicea."

REVELATION 1:11

To whom did John write from his island of exile? He wrote to ordinary people who were connected to him because he was connected to Jesus. The Jesus connection is a marvelous thing!

Someone led Janet Smith to Christ. She got sick and was taken to the hospital in the town where I was a student. When I, too, got sick and was taken to the same hospital, I was wheeled down a long corridor by a starched lady with a grim face and laid neatly in a bed beside Janet Smith. And Janet led me to Christ. Soon after I got better and went back to college, Penny, a freshman, became my "little sister." As her "big sister," my responsibility was to look after her. I did—I led her to Christ! Penny grew in God, and the next year, she led her "little sister" to Christ.

This is what the Jesus connection is—a network of blessing, an intriguing mystery that will all be explained one day. But till then, the joy of being part of it all is enough. Whoever and wherever you are, you can be part of it, too! John didn't let the fact that he was isolated worry him. When he was able to travel and preach, he did; when he couldn't do that anymore, he found a way to continue as God's special agent in the Jesus connection—he picked up his pen and papyrus and went right on with his work!

TO READ: *Revelation 1:12–20*

THE GOLD SASH

And standing in the middle of the lampstands was the Son of Man.
He was wearing a long robe with a gold sash across his chest.
REVELATION 1:13

Have you ever wondered what Jesus looked like—what it would have been like to see him? I have. We are not given a physical description of Christ our Lord in his humanity, save that we know he lived within a human body. We do know, however, what he looked like in his divinity. John, the apostle, saw him with his own eyes and tried his best to capture that vision of the glorified Christ for us.

He was told to write what he saw in a book and send it to the seven churches in Asia (Revelation 1:11). This sight of Jesus would help the disciples in these young churches, who were facing prison, persecution, and death, to be faithful to the end. John also wrote to people who were being told that Jesus was a nobody and assured them that Jesus was a somebody—a poor unknown carpenter on earth, but the King in heaven.

He was "wearing a long robe with a gold sash across his chest" (Revelation 1:13). Only the most important people wore long garments and only kings wore golden sashes. In the Old Testament Scriptures, such a sash (sometimes called a "girdle") worn around the waist denoted power and authority. Such sashes were worn by taskmasters. But when the sash was worn around the chest, it denoted faithfulness and affection.

John was in terrible trouble just because he was a Christian, but when he saw the gold sash, he remembered how much he was loved! Do you need to remember that too?

TO READ: *Revelation 1:12-20*

WHITE, WHITE HAIR

His head and his hair were white like wool, as white as snow.

REVELATION 1:14

T he word *white* is used to emphasize great importance. Christ's hair was "white like wool," said John. When shepherds sheared the sheep in those days, two sorts of wool were gathered. One sort was an ordinary off-white wool used for everyday garments; the other sort was the pure white wool kept to make the most expensive clothes. When Daniel had his vision of the Ancient One, he noted the white, white hair as well: "I watched as thrones were put in place and the Ancient One sat down to judge. His clothing was as white as snow, his hair like whitest wool. He sat on a fiery throne with wheels of blazing fire" (Daniel 7:9).

White hair speaks of eternity, of Christ's agelessness, of the dignity of his endless days. It gives a feeling of security. Just knowing he's been around that long helps when I feel very young, inexperienced, and unsure of myself! White hair says, "I am wise. I understand many things because I have lived forever." Christ's age was no ordinary "off-white" age like yours and mine. His white, white hair tells us he existed before the ages themselves and lives outside of time, wise beyond measure, knowing all things.

He promises us white, white hair too, one day. That's the sort of hair we shall have in eternity. As he said to John, "I am the living one who died. Look, I am alive forever and ever!" (Revelation 1:18). Because he lives, we shall live also. The disciples in the persecuted churches needed to hear that!

EYES OF FIRE

And his eyes were bright like flames of fire.

REVELATION 1:14

C hrist's piercing eyes penetrated one's innermost thoughts and being. Peter knew what it was like to have Jesus look at him with those eyes, "like flames of fire." After Peter had denied him, "the Lord turned and looked at Peter. Then Peter remembered that the Lord had said . . ." (Luke 22:61). When Christ was on earth, he had the ability to look at people and make them remember broken promises and words spoken with conviction but never fulfilled!

Christ in heaven has a perfect view of everything: "Everything is naked and exposed before his eyes. This is the God to whom we must explain all that we have done" (Hebrews 4:13). He sees within as well as without: "People judge by outward appearance, but the LORD looks at a person's thoughts and intentions" (1 Samuel 16:7).

When I was a very small child, I can remember hiding behind a sofa, thinking no one could see me! *Even God is looking for me,* I said to my small self with satisfaction. I grew up to realize God never has to look. He sees me hiding; he comes to me and faces me with what he sees. Trying to hide from God is useless. It is best to acknowledge the things we both see and have him deal with the issues of our lives. There is no other sensible course of action to take, for "his eyes [are] like flames of fire."

TO READ: *Revelation 1:12-20*

FEET LIKE BRONZE

His feet were as bright as bronze refined in a furnace.

REVELATION 1:15

W hen John saw the glorified Christ, he saw that his feet looked like bright bronze. Bronze, an alloy of copper and tin, was used extensively in Old Testament times. This ordinary material was used for the sanctuary (Exodus 25:3), fashioned into clasps to hold the tent of the tabernacle together (Exodus 26:11), and to make pillars and carts and a bronze sea for the house of the Lord. After Shishak, king of Egypt, came up against Jerusalem and took away the gold shields that Solomon had made, King Rehoboam made bronze shields to replace them (2 Chronicles 12:9-10).

Refined, or "white," bronze was not used for these things because it was extremely costly and heavy. It was too heavy to use for sanctuary vessels that would be moved around or for soldiers' shields that had to be lifted up. John saw that the glorified Christ had feet like refined bronze.

Those feet are capable of trampling the serpent's head (Genesis 3:15); those feet are capable of trampling down the forces of evil. The risen Lord reminded the church at Thyatira about his feet like polished bronze (Revelation 2:18). There were Christians there who were flaunting sexual sin that needed stamping out. There is no place for such things in Christ's church. His feet are a salutary reminder of that fact! What needs stamping out of your life?

TO READ: *Revelation 1:12–20*

WORDS LIKE WATERFALLS

His voice thundered like mighty ocean waves.

REVELATION 1:15

The breakers still pound on the shore of the beautiful island of Patmos, scattering surf like crystal stars along the sandy slopes. John, the prisoner, would have been encouraged by the sound of that mighty pounding. It would have reminded him of the rhythm of God's creation, held in order by the One in control. As surely as the waves chase each other ashore, so is God's order established in the world. God's blessings, like the waves, roll inexorably onward.

John was encouraged by his belief that God would chase his plans into being and make sure they reached the point of no return, sweeping their way up the sandy beaches of people's lives. When John "turned to see who was speaking" to him (Revelation 1:12), he struggled for a valid expression of what he had heard. The best way he found to describe the voice of God was to compare it to "mighty ocean waves"—the mightiest surf that ever pounded a seashore, the biggest breaker ever to break loose of its brothers, the wildest wave ever to dash the bed of the ocean.

Next time you stand at a waterfall, think about that. Then, when you get to heaven, you will recognize his voice! Christ's voice was greater than the thunder of the breakers on Patmos and carried with it the force of many waterfalls. It was a voice to be reckoned with. "Anyone who is willing to hear should listen," said John (Revelation 3:22).

TO READ: *Revelation 1:12-20*

THE MYSTERY

He held seven stars in his right hand.

REVELATION 1:16

J esus said the seven stars were angels or messengers to the churches in Asia. God is not a divine detective story writer, who sits in heaven, trying to think of ways to muddle us up! He wants to make things plain. He told John that he holds the messengers in his hand; he has a grip on them. Commentators differ as to whether these messengers were heavenly or earthly, but whichever, they were in his hand! They may represent anyone who brings God's messages to a church. God sent these messengers to do his bidding. Their job was simply to deliver Jesus' message to the seven churches (represented by the seven lampstands).

It is a comforting thought to me that Christ holds the messengers in his nail-pierced hand. The church is his bride, and he cares about her. Those of us who also have the privilege of being cared for so deeply by Christ need to make sure Jesus' letters do not get lost in the delivery. People's reaction to the message is not our responsibility, but the delivery of that message as Jesus gave it *is* our responsibility! Jesus has his hands full with his messengers, but when John fainted at the sight of the glorified Christ, "He laid his right hand on [him] and said, 'Don't be afraid! I am the First and the Last' " (Revelation 1:17). A vision of him in all his glory will help us to deliver our message.

THE SWORD
OF THE SPIRIT

A sharp two-edged sword came from his mouth.

REVELATION 1:16

The word of God is full of living power. It is sharper than the sharpest knife, cutting deep into our innermost thoughts and desires. It exposes us for what we really are" (Hebrews 4:12).

When Jesus spoke, his words pierced John's soul. The Word of God is like that. The Bible describes itself in many ways: honey, sweet to the taste; a hammer that breaks the rock; a light and a lamp to our path; a seed; and a treasure of gold. Ephesians 6:17 tells us that the Word of God is the sword of the Spirit. There's a battle to be fought. Sometimes we fight it with our lives, and other times we fight it with our words. When we speak up for Christ in a secular situation, we will find that the sword cuts to the quick.

Jesus' message to the church at Pergamum was to "repent, or I will come to you suddenly and fight against them with the sword of my mouth" (Revelation 2:16). They needed to clean up their act and live like Christ.

Jesus has to use his sharp words on Christians sometimes. Once, when I was afraid of losing my reputation if I witnessed, the Lord used the sword of his mouth on me, reminding me that he "made himself nothing . . . and obediently humbled himself" (Philippians 2:7-8). That cured me! It was sharp, and it hurt, but it drove me to my knees and back to him for healing.

TO READ: *Revelation 1:12-20*

FACING IT WITH JESUS' FACE IN MIND!

And his face was as bright as the sun in all its brilliance.

REVELATION 1:16

J ohn had a case of *déjà vu*. During Jesus' earthly ministry, John, the apostle, had never seen his master with pure white hair, holding seven stars in his hand, or with a gold sash round his chest, but there is something about his Lord's glorified face that reminded him of a mountaintop experience in his past.

Jesus had asked John, his brother James, and Simon Peter to go with him up a high mountain (Matthew 17:1). They had been wondering what Jesus wanted to say to them when suddenly an amazing thing happened. Jesus was transfigured before them. "As the men watched, Jesus' appearance changed so that his face shone like the sun, and his clothing became dazzling white" (Matthew 17:2). As John "turned to see who was speaking" on Patmos, he remembered the face of Jesus of Nazareth on that mountaintop (Revelation 1:12). This was the same Jesus, now glorified forever! The blinding light of God, shining through Christ's earthly body, had caused Peter and James and John to fall on their faces, and they were terrified (Matthew 17:6).

Now, years later, John again fell at his feet as dead (Revelation 1:17). John would look into the dark faces of cruel men before his suffering was over, remember his mountaintop experiences, shut his eyes, and see the face of God shining like the sun in its strength. He would find the courage to bear the unbearable, do the impossible, and reflect the light of Jesus Christ.

What are you facing? Face it with Jesus' face in mind!

TO READ: *Revelation 2:1-7*

IF GOD SENT YOU A LETTER

"Write this letter to the angel of the church in Ephesus. This is the message
from the one who holds the seven stars in his right hand, the one who walks
among the seven gold lampstands: . . . But I have this complaint against you.
You don't love me or each other as you did at first!"

REVELATION 2:1, 4

The risen Lord Jesus asked his servant, John the apostle, who was exiled on a small Greek island, to write some letters to a group of churches for him. And that's how we *know* what Christ thought about the church! He wrote to the believers at Ephesus and reprimanded them because they had lost their zeal and love for him and for each other.

What do you think of the church? Do you consider it outdated, boring, cold? Have you ever stopped to think what Christ thinks of it? He tells us in the book of Revelation. The church is not a building; it is the people who meet inside it. It is not somewhere you go, but something you are!

Love motivates us to serve others. When you lose your love for Christ, you lose your love for unbelievers, too. You even lose your love for fellow Christians. Love always wants to please. I enjoyed my teenagers being in love. They usually wanted to help with the dishes! Love doesn't only *help* with the dishes, love *does* the dishes! Love goes the extra mile, or two or three or four! Love stops asking, "What can God do for me?" and starts inquiring, "What can I do for God?" Love sings in the rain, and love always replies to God's letters!

If God sent you a letter telling you he was upset with you for losing your love for him and for others, how would you respond? How would you answer his letter?

TO READ: *Revelation 2:8-11*

JESUS PROMISED

*"Anyone who is willing to hear should listen to the Spirit
and understand what the Spirit is saying to the churches.
Whoever is victorious will not be hurt by the second death."*

REVELATION 2:11

A willingness to suffer often proves the genuineness of love. The small group of Christians who loved the Lord and lived in Smyrna were suffering because they belonged to him. The risen Christ reminded them who he is. "I am the First and the Last," he said to them. "I am the living one who died" (Revelation 1:17-18). That's always a good thing to hear when you may be facing martyrdom!

Smyrna was widely known as the "crown" city because of its beautiful situation, nestled between the gully and the mountain peaks crowned with the most luxurious dwellings and government buildings. How appropriate of the Lord Jesus, then, to encourage the few frightened believers to be "faithful even when facing death, and I will give you the crown of life" (Revelation 2:10).

It helps to know that the Savior knows about our troubles, doesn't it? "I know about your suffering and your poverty," he says (Revelation 2:9). We do not know if the Christians in Smyrna belonged to the lower ranks, or if their unselfish concern for the underprivileged had left them poor. Whatever the reason for their trials, Christ wanted them to know he saw their plight and was preparing a better place for them. What is more, he told them not to fear the journey to the better land, even though the way would lead through prison gates.

Because of Smyrna, suffering believers through the years have been helped to face the first death, by believing they will not be hurt by the second! After all, Jesus promised!

WHERE YOU LIVE

"I know that you live in the city where that great throne of Satan is located, and yet you have remained loyal to me. And you refused to deny me even when Antipas, my faithful witness, was martyred among you by Satan's followers."

REVELATION 2:13

The Christians in Pergamum lived right next door to Satan himself! Pergamum was not a Satan-worshiping city full of witch doctors, but rather a Satan-worshiping city full of priest doctors! The city was famous for its medical library and hospital. It boasted fantastic temples and a theater that seated thirty-five hundred people. Psychiatry and hypnosis were practiced there, and on the top of a huge hill stood the famous temple of Zeus! Was this "Satan's seat," we wonder? In 1871, an altar with the words "Zeus the Savior" inscribed on it was found in that area.

We have to wonder what it would have been like to live in a place like that, daring to believe in Jesus the Savior, the Healer and the Lord of all! Antipas, Christ's faithful martyr, found out what it was like, and sealed his witness with his blood. Others would be faithful to their deaths in that place. Still, the risen Christ had some things against his church there. Basically, many were compromising their faith in the face of the opposition. Error had been mixed with truth, and morals had been corrupted. "Repent," commanded Jesus. "I will give [you] manna that has been hidden away in heaven . . . a white stone, and . . . a new name" (Revelation 2:16-17). Jesus promised he would reveal intimate secrets to those who stand firm, however hard it is!

TO READ: *Revelation 2:18-29*

A GREATER PUNISHMENT

"Anyone who is willing to hear should listen to the Spirit and understand what the Spirit is saying to the churches."

REVELATION 2:29

Thyatira was the church that wouldn't listen. In the Bible, the word *hear* means perceiving with the mind and understanding with the heart. Are we willing to hear what we don't want to hear? Do you ever open your Bible and try not to let the words sink in?

Perhaps you have settled for a cease-fire in the war between a difficult relative and yourself, instead of initiating "peace talks." Maybe you are absorbed by ambition, and you don't want to listen to the Lord tell you not to strive in such a way.

We don't know how the church in Thyatira was born, but it could well have been through Lydia's witness; she was a native of that city (Acts 16:14). Perhaps the people would no longer listen to God's voice through that godly woman, or maybe they just enjoyed their sexual sin too much to give it up. Whatever the reason for their dullness of hearing, the Lord rebuked them for being willfully deaf. The "Jezebel party," those in the church who were tolerating fornication, adultery, and perversion, must be dealt with, Jesus insisted. Jesus explained that he "gave her time to repent" (Revelation 2:21).

God has given us time to repent as well. Some of us need to use our inner ears, to listen to the Spirit, and to give up our sin, sexual or otherwise. Until we do, we risk a much more dreadful punishment than even Satan can devise. We risk the judgment of our God (Revelation 2:23)!

A LESSON FROM HISTORY

"Write this letter to the angel of the church in Sardis.
This is the message from the one who has the sevenfold Spirit of God
and the seven stars: I know all the things you do, and that you have
a reputation for being alive—but you are dead."

REVELATION 3:1

S ardis was a "dead" church. Its Christian members had become overconfident. They remind me of a driver whose gas gauge reads empty, but who believes he has enough gas to get him where he's going!

Sardis lay fifteen hundred feet above the floor of the valley. Gold, found in the river that ran between the foothills, and silver, mined in the area, were made into the first coins here. It was a materialistic culture. At one time, the city had been the political center of Asia Minor. Its name had been synonymous with luxury and opulence. In the end, Cyrus came with his Persian army and besieged the city, taking it easily. Cyrus spared Solon's life as a symbol to posterity of the precarious nature of prosperity. Sardis had been overcome by overconfidence. More than three hundred years later, Antiochus the Great again captured Sardis by finding his way, like a thief in the night, up the seemingly impregnable cliffs.

I suppose, as someone has said, "If history teaches us anything, it teaches us that it doesn't teach us anything!" The Christians in Sardis reading John's letter from Jesus Christ understood when the Lord said to them, "You have a reputation for being alive—but you are dead" (Revelation 3:1). They were also hopefully shaken into repentance when the risen Lord warned them, "Go back to what you heard and believed at first; hold to it firmly and turn to me again. Unless you do, I will come upon you suddenly, as unexpected as a thief" (Revelation 3:3).

TO READ: *Revelation 3:7-13*

THE DOOR
OF OPPORTUNITY

"I know all the things you do, and I have opened a door for you
that no one can shut. You have little strength,
yet you obeyed my word and did not deny me."

REVELATION 3:8

T he church at Philadelphia had been given an open door of opportunity. All they had to do was to walk through it and establish the
kingdom of God on the other side. There is absolutely no rebuke in this
particular letter from Jesus to the Christians in Philadelphia—only
encouragement, though they had "little strength" left to do good to all.

The church had many opponents. False teachers, Judaizers, and
Satan himself pitted their wits against the little group of believers. But
the believers kept true to their Lord and took the grand opportunity to
draw on his strength and to step through those open doors.

God has opened doors of opportunity for us, too—opportunities to
witness freely and to attend Bible classes and growth groups—opportunities
to have Christian friends and fellowship.

It's impossible to stop God's holding the door open. The only thing
we can do is to stand still and refuse to enter through the door of service.
You don't need to be a very strong Christian to step over the doorstep and
begin. You only need to have a "little strength" to do that! Incidentally,
when you walk through the door, Jesus will meet you on the other side
with a new power, a new blessing, and a new name (Revelation 3:12)!

TO READ: *Revelation 3:14-22*

THE HANDLE IS ON YOUR SIDE

"But since you are like lukewarm water, I will spit you out of my mouth!"

REVELATION 3:16

The people who went to church in Laodicea were respectable, wealthy, skin-deep Christians. They appeared to have taken a lukewarm bath of religion.

The city of Laodicea got its water from nearby hot springs, which became lukewarm by the time the city dwellers put it to use. The tasteless, tepid water made a disgusting drink—not cold enough to refresh, not hot enough to give warmth. The Lord Jesus knew the believers in Laodicea would understand him when he accused them of being lukewarm. The Greek words for *hot* and *cold* are emphatic, meaning boiling and frigid. God would have us boiling or freezing toward him, but he despises those who are merely tepid.

When we are lukewarm, we think we "don't need a thing" (Revelation 3:17)—but we are in need of everything. We are really spiritually impoverished, yet we count ourselves religion-rich and think ourselves "mature." It is so easy to be lukewarm. All we have to do is nothing. No growing, no going, no knowing, no sowing! That will do it.

But Jesus would not have it so. Listen—God is counseling his own. Lukewarm we might be, but God wants us either hot or cold.

Jesus stands at the door of every lukewarm heart. He wants to come into our life and bring his cup of rejoicing with him. He would meet us inside our shallow spirituality and heat our cooling ardor into bright flames of love. Open the door—the handle is on your side.

TO READ: *Revelation 3:14-22*

EYE EXAM

"I advise you to buy gold from me—gold that has been purified by fire. Then you will be rich. And also buy white garments so you will not be shamed by your nakedness. And buy ointment for your eyes so you will be able to see."

REVELATION 3:18

The Laodiceans were familiar with the famous medical school that had produced a powder for the cure of ophthalmia, an eye disease affecting many people in the East. Again Jesus uses a familiar illustration to open their eyes to spiritual realities. "Buy ointment for your eyes so you will be able to see" (Revelation 3:18), he counsels the unbelieving believers.

Though they think themselves clothed in their religion, Christ tells them they are "wretched and miserable and poor and blind and naked" (Revelation 3:17), pointing out how obnoxious spiritual pride is in God's sight.

But listen—God is counseling his own. Lukewarm they might be, but God's people they most surely are—and he would be a wonder of a Counselor to them, a Mighty God, their Everlasting Father, their Prince of Peace. Jesus offered them his rightness for their wrongness, urging them to dress their spirits in such a garment of grace that they would "not be shamed by [their] nakedness" (Revelation 3:18).

He stands at the door of every lukewarm heart. He wants to come into our uninterested lives and bring his cup of rejoicing with him. He would meet us inside our shallow spirituality and heat our cooling ardor into bright flames of love.

Enter my heart,
My loving Lord,
Take not a part but the whole—
Quicken my spirit,
Warm my cold mind,
And set me on fire in my soul!

TO READ: *Revelation 3:14-22*

GOD IS A PERFECT GENTLEMAN

"Look! Here I stand at the door and knock. If you hear me calling and open the door, I will come in, and we will share a meal as friends."

REVELATION 3:20

B ut how do I take a leap of faith into the arms of Jesus?" you ask. "I want to go to heaven. I want to get down off my fence, but I need help. Show me how."

First of all, you have to understand four basic things. The first is the fact of sin. Believing you are a sinner means acknowledging that you are not perfect. Having said yes to that, the second thing you need to do is believe that your sin has separated you from a holy God. The third question is: Do you believe God loves you so much that he sent Jesus to save you from the consequences of your sin? If you can say yes to that question, then the last thing you need is to ask God to forgive your sin, come into your life, and write your name in his book in heaven. If you do not know how to ask him, make this prayer your own. "Dear Jesus, I believe you are a holy God, and I realize I am sinful. Forgive me. I want to go to heaven. Thank you for dying to make that possible. Come into my life, Lord Jesus, by your Holy Spirit."

Did you say it? Did you mean it? Then it is done! You are saved! He said so, and God is a perfect gentleman, so you can trust his word! Thank him—right now!

TO READ: *Revelation 5:1-14*

WORTH DYING FOR

And they sang in a mighty chorus: "The Lamb is worthy—
the Lamb who was killed. He is worthy to receive power and riches
and wisdom and strength and honor and glory and blessing."

REVELATION 5:12

In this scene in Revelation, all of heaven joins in a chorus of praise to Christ, the Lamb. Imagine a choir of glorious angels numbering "thousands and millions" (Revelation 5:11). Surely this is a song worth hearing!

Who is the Lamb? He is Christ, the one seated on the throne. What is he "worthy" of? Christ alone is "worthy to open the scroll and break its seven seals" (Revelation 5:5). In other words, Christ can initiate the end of history and usher in the kingdom of God. He proved himself worthy because he was a perfect man, he died to conquer sin and death, and he rose again in victory. Only Christ conquered evil, so he alone is worthy to set in motion the beginning of the end of evil's reign!

For whom did Christ die? For whom did he conquer sin and death? For you and for me. To him we were worth dying for. The provision was himself—the Lamb, who died for you. The Lamb is worthy—the Lamb who was killed. He is worthy because of what he did for us—saving us and making us fit for heaven. You have been made worthy because of the Lamb, who is "worthy to receive power and riches and wisdom and strength and honor and glory and blessing" (Revelation 5:12). We should fall down and worship with all of heaven!

MY WEDDING DRESS

"Let us be glad and rejoice and honor him. For the time has come for the wedding feast of the Lamb, and his bride has prepared herself. She is permitted to wear the finest white linen." (Fine linen represents the good deeds done by the people of God.)

REVELATION 19:7-8

Among the graphic imagery in the book of Revelation is a picture of the church as the bride of Christ. This imagery is spread throughout the Bible. In the Old Testament, Israel is often depicted as God's bride (Ezekiel 16:8-14; Hosea 2:1-23). The symbol of marriage is in the Gospels, too (Matthew 22:1-14; Mark 2:19; John 3:29). Paul made use of the picture of the church as Christ's bride in Ephesians 5:25-27. So it is not surprising that Revelation uses the imagery of marriage.

The picture here is of a bride invited to her own wedding. She is given fine linen to wear as her wedding dress. The bride has not purchased this special dress for herself; instead, the heavenly bridegroom, the Lord Jesus Christ, has already paid for it! The price of that white dress was Christ's blood—his death on the cross. By his death alone believers can have their sins forgiven. Christ then fills their lives by his Spirit.

The bridegroom purchased the wedding dress and invited his bride to the wedding feast. Each one of us has to respond to the Lord Jesus Christ's invitation to our heavenly wedding. When Christ clothes us in the linen of his own righteousness, we are ready for the great day! And oh, what a day that will be! Have you responded to his gracious invitation? Don't forget to RSVP. This is a party you don't want to miss!

TO READ: *Revelation 21:1-27*

HEAVEN

*Then I saw a new heaven and a new earth, for the old heaven and
the old earth had disappeared. And the sea was also gone.*

REVELATION 21:1

Do you believe in heaven? What do you think it is like? Do you
imagine yourself sitting on a pink, damp cloud, playing a harp?
What sort of a place is it?

Heaven is a *pretty* place. Revelation 22:2 tells us fruit never fades
there. I'm always sad when I see the plants fade in my garden. I will never
see them fade in heaven.

Heaven is a *permanent* place. The builder and maker is God, and Christ
is the chief cornerstone (Ephesians 2:20). Heaven is forever because God is
forever. It is a permanent place, filled with permanent people.

No one will ever die in this *painless* place—no one is ever sick
(Revelation 21:4)! Can you imagine a place where there is no more
suffering? Our sorry world needs to hear about a place like that!

Lastly, it is a *perfect* place. The perfect Person, the Lord Jesus Christ,
lives there, and no sin will be allowed to enter heaven (Revelation 21:8).
If sin entered heaven, it wouldn't be heaven anymore!

"We haven't any idea where you are going, so how can we know the
way?" Thomas asked (John 14:5).

Jesus answered him: "I am the way, the truth, and the life. No one
can come to the Father except through me" (John 14:6). Do you want to
go to heaven? Ask Jesus about it. Ask him to forgive your sin. If you do,
heaven will come down and fill your soul!

reference index

topical index

GOD'S FAITHFULNESS
Jan 1, 6, 29, Apr 7, 12, 18, Oct 5

GOD'S GLORY
Mar 9, 21, 22, May 10, June 6, 10, July 22, Oct 11, 23, Dec 10, 17, 29

GOD'S HOLINESS
Feb 23, Mar 28, Apr 6, May 9

GOD'S POWER
Jan 2, 4, 8, 30, Feb 14, 18, 19, Mar 1, 12, 22, Apr 12, May 12, June 11, 25, July 3, 12, 25, Aug 4, 14, Sep 1, 3, 18, 19, Oct 20, 21, 29, Nov 12, Dec 7, 16

GOD'S PROMISES
Jan 2, 6, 8, Mar 26, Apr 1, 11, 15, 16, May 23, 24, 25, 28, 29, June 1, 5, 7, 17, 26, July 2, 9, 13, 14, 23, 25, Aug 16, 18, Sep 4, 5, 18, 19, 29, Oct 5, 6, 7, 19, 24, Nov 14, 24, 29, Dec 2, 8, 9, 21, 22

GOD'S PROVISION
Jan 10, May 18, 27, Sep 8

GOD'S WILL
Jan 5, Mar 26, Apr 15, May 5, June 18, 23, July 12, Aug 18, Sep 29, Oct 19, 26, Nov 20, 21

GOD'S WORD
(see Bible)

GOOD DEEDS
Oct 23, Nov 18, 27, Dec 30
(see also Servant/Service/Serving)

GOSSIP
Aug 26

GRACE
Feb 3, 15, 24, Mar 2, 11, Apr 26, May 3, 7, 10, 13, Aug 11, 13, 27, Sep 25, Oct 13, Nov 28, Dec 27

GRIEF
(see Sorrow)

GUILT
Mar 25, 31, Apr 3, 17, May 11, Sep 7, Oct 3

HATE/HATRED
May 1

HEALTH/HEALING
Jan 16, Mar 24, 30, Apr 16, 21, 24, May 31, June 11, 26, July 4, 17, Oct 9, Nov 17, Dec 18, 22

HEAVEN
Jan 1, 16, Mar 20, 21, Apr 19, May 3, 9, 10, July 14, 21, 22, Aug 12, 16, Sep 8, Oct 16, 23, 24, Nov 19, 20, Dec 9, 12, 22, 28, 29, 31

HOLY/HOLINESS
May 9, June 10, 17, Nov 20

HOLY SPIRIT
Jan 4, 13, 15, Feb 4, 14, 15, 18, 22, Mar 27, Apr 1, 6, 7, 13, 15, May 8, 14, 17, 24, 25, June 6, 7, 10, 15, July 14, 25, Aug 17, 18, 21, 28, Sep 3, 4, 5, 7, 18, 19, 21, 29, Oct 1, 7, 11, 12, 13, 19, 25, Nov 1, 2, 7, 17, 20, 23, 24, Dec 5, 8, 10, 18, 21, 23, 28

HOPE
Feb 21, Apr 6, May 12, 23, June 3, July 13, Sep 16, Oct 24, Nov 2, 19, 27

HOSPITALITY
Sep 24

HUMILITY
Jan 23, June 9, 10, 22, July 1, 2, Aug 9, 10, 22, 26, Oct 5, 31, Nov 10, 11

"IMPOSSIBLE" SITUATIONS
Jan 8, Feb 17, 24, July 3, 15, 25, Oct 14, Nov 27, 30, Dec 19

INTEGRITY
Feb 3, 26, Mar 2, 6

INTERCESSION
Jan 23, Feb 23, Mar 9, July 23

JESUS CHRIST, RELATIONSHIP WITH
Mar 18, 27, Apr 17, 18, 19, 23, May 10, 15, 22, 27, 29, June 1, 12, 16, 22, 26, 27, 28, July 1, 2, 5, 6, 7, 8, 9, 10, 13, 14, 21, 30, Aug 1, 2, 3, 12, 18, 21, 25, 28, 29, Sep 3, 8, 13, 27, Oct 30, Nov 12, 17, Dec 7, 11, 26, 27

THE ONE YEAR WAY

Do-able. Daily. Devotions.

START ANY DAY THE ONE YEAR WAY.

Do-able.
Every One Year book is designed for people who live busy, active lives. Just pick one up and start on today's date.

Daily.
Daily routine doesn't have to be drudgery. One Year devotionals help you form positive habits that connect you to what's most important.

Devotions.
Discover a natural rhythm for drawing near to God in an extremely personal way. One Year devotionals provide daily focus essential to your spiritual growth.

For Women

 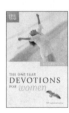   

The One Year Devotions for Women on the Go

The One Year Devotions for Women

The One Year Devotions for Moms

The One Year Women of the Bible

The One Year Daily Grind

For Men

The One Year
Devotions for
Men on the Go

The One Year
Devotions for
Men

For Couples

The One Year
Devotions for
Couples

For Families

The One
Year Family
Devotions

For Teens

The One Year
Devos for Teens

The One Year
Devos for Sports
Fans

For Bible Study

The One Year
Life Lessons
from the Bible

The One Year
Praying through
the Bible

The One Year
through the
Bible

For Personal Growth

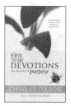

The One Year
Devotions
for People of
Purpose

The One Year
Walk with God
Devotional

The One Year
at His Feet
Devotional

The One Year
Great Songs of
Faith

The One Year
on This Day

The One Year
Life Verse
Devotional

It's convenient and easy to grow with
God the One Year way.

CP0145

THE ONE YEAR WAY

Teach Truth.

MEET JESUS EVERY DAY THE ONE YEAR WAY.

For Kids

The One Year
Devotions for
Girls

The One Year
Devotions for
Boys

The One Year
Devotions for
Preschoolers

The One Year
Devotions for
Kids

The One Year
Make-It-Stick
Devotions

The One Year
Bible for Kids:
Challenge
Edition

The One Year
Children's Bible

The One Year
Book of Josh
McDowell's
Youth Devotions

The Perfect Gift

THOUGHTFUL. PRACTICAL. AFFORDABLE.

The One Year Mini for Women helps women connect with God through several Scripture verses and a devotional thought. Perfect for use anytime and anywhere between regular devotion times. Hardcover.

The One Year Mini for Students offers students from high school through college a quick devotional connection with God anytime and anywhere. Stay grounded through the ups and downs of a busy student lifestyle. Hardcover.

The One Year Mini for Moms provides encouragement and affirmation for those moments during a mom's busy day when she needs to be reminded of the high value of her role. Hardcover.

The One Year Mini for Busy Women is for women who don't have time to get it all done but need to connect with God during the day. Hardcover.

The One Year Mini for Men helps men connect with God anytime, anywhere between their regular devotion times through Scripture quotations and a related devotional thought. Hardcover.

The One Year Mini for Leaders motivates and inspires leaders to maximize their God-given leadership potential using scriptural insights. Hardcover.

CP0161